S0-CHI-726

HOW TO BEAT THE STREET WITH PLAN Z

The New Strategy for Safe and Lucrative Investing in the Money Markets

MORRY MARKOVITZ

WITH MICHAEL LAM

Produced by The Philip Lief Group, Inc.

John Wiley & Sons
New York • Chichester • Brisbane • Toronto • Singapore

This text is printed on acid-free paper.

Copyright © 1993 by Morris J. Markovitz and The Philip Lief Group, Inc.
Published by John Wiley and Sons, Inc.

Published by arrangement with The Philip Lief Group, Inc.,
6 West 20th Street, New York, NY 10011.

All rights reserved. Published simultaneously in Canada.

Reproduction or translation of any part of this work beyond that permitted by Section 107 or 108 of the 1976 United States Copyright Act without the permission of the copyright owner is unlawful. Requests for permission or further information should be addressed to the Permissions Department, John Wiley & Sons, Inc., 605 Third Avenue, New York, NY 10158-0012.

This publication is designed to provide accurate and authoritative information in regard to the subject matter covered. It is sold with the understanding that the publisher is not engaged in rendering legal, accounting, or other professional services. If legal advice or other expert assistance is required, the services of a competent professional person should be sought. *From a Declaration of Principles jointly adopted by a Committee of the American Bar Association and a Committee of Publishers.*

Printed in the United States of America

10 9 8 7 6 5 4 3 2 1

Dedicated to the memory of Samuel Markovitz

Acknowledgments

Morry would like to express his appreciation to family and friends for understanding his unavailability in the course of creating this book. Special gratitude is due Barry Shain for urging Morry to put his ideas on paper and for subsequent technical support (at all hours), to Eva Weiss for inaugurating this work, to Don Farrar, executive vice president at Benham Capital, for historical data, to Jerry and Mark Rubin of Rubin Associates for custom software and invaluable technical support (at all hours), and to Jerry's wife Marilyn Metcalf for her hospitality. Subscribers to Morry's market letter should be getting their next issue soon.

Michael would like to thank Eva, Melissa, The Canaan Group, Diana and Matt, and Lydia and Ted.

The ideas and opinions in this book are the product of innumerable influences. Although, regrettably, only a few of the individuals who contributed can be mentioned by name, our appreciation extends to all the teachers, family, friends, and colleagues who gave unwitting assistance. The errors were the result of a great deal of hard work and are, of course, entirely our own.

Life can only be understood backwards; but it must be lived forwards.

Soren Kierkegaard

I have been asked (by a couple of small boys and a wire-haired fox terrier) to summarize briefly my views on the Business and Financial Outlook for 1931. I would have done this long ago, together with the other financial and business experts, but I wanted first to wait and see if there really was going to *be* a 1931 or not.

Robert Benchley

Contents

Introduction

Life—according to an anonymous sage—is what happens while you're making other plans. Robert Burns put it differently: "The best laid schemes o' mice and men," he wrote, "gang aft a-gley." But without a plan, without a well-defined goal and a strategy for gaining it, some aspirations are pointless. Difficult and desirable ends are rarely met by indirection or luck. (Even luck, Branch Rickey said, is "the residue of design.") Of course, preparation is no guarantor of success. But its absence often accompanies failure. There's a saying: "If you don't know where you're going, you'll probably end up somewhere else."

But how to plan? If we could read the future, we could make our decisions confidently in advance of their consequences—and we would never be wrong. The problem is we must choose our path not knowing what will happen. Many of the decisions we make today will have ramifications years later—and for years to come. How can we choose *now* without being sorry later?

This is the predicament of the long-term investor. Like a traveler with a distant goal, he or she risks prolonged exposure to the vagaries of time and chance. Will gold go up in value? Will stocks? Which stocks? How much? Will interest rates go up or down? Will the value of money rise or fall? Given the necessity of planning to meet specific goals at a far-off time—whether that means planning for retirement, buying or paying off a home, or looking forward to paying a child's college tuition—what's the best course? How do you act prospectively without the wisdom of hindsight?* How can you account for the unknown and unexpected? How do you reasonably commit yourself to a prospect you can barely see?

* Along these lines, Calvin Coolidge is said to have offered the following advice: "The secret of financial success is to buy sound stock, wait until it goes up and then sell it. If it doesn't go up, don't buy it."

Fortunately, the financial markets have a constant, and that constant is change. Bernard Baruch once ventured a timeless forecast: "Gentlemen," he said, "the market will fluctuate." More recently, a publisher asked several prominent financial minds to look back 10 to 15 years and say whether the markets had changed. Only Ed Seykota said they hadn't. His reasoning? They were constantly changing then just as they are constantly changing now.

One of the most reliably changeable features of the financial landscape is interest rates, which gyrate up and down in no foreseeable pattern. A great deal often depends on which way interest rates go, putting a premium on accurate conjectures. But these are hard to come by. Even professionals are generally stymied in their attempts to outguess rates. Imagine then an investment program that didn't rely on the ability to foretell interest rates but depended instead on the mere fact that they change, one that would tend to prosper whether rates went up or down—and whether anyone *knew* they were headed up or down—as long as they fluctuated frequently and vigorously. This investment plan, which would answer every investor's lack of clairvoyance, exists in the form we call Plan Z.

Like many powerful ideas, Plan Z is at root simple. It takes two elements that are fairly well known and combines them to create something unlike either, much in the way a chemist mixes substances that have known properties to form compounds with new and unexpected qualities.* By matching zero coupon bonds (a type of fixed instrument fairly new to the investment scene—known also as *zeros*) with some basic investment techniques (as well as some new ones), Plan Z gives rise to a long-term investment strategy virtually guaranteed to outperform the fixed-instrument market over time.

The theory behind Plan Z can be stated briefly:

1. Some common investment techniques have the power to improve yields, except when the underlying investment falls and never recovers.

* There is nothing *alchemical* about Plan Z, though; it has no power to transform lead into gold.

2. The price of a zero coupon bond cannot, in the long run, collapse.
3. Therefore, zeros solve the practical flaw in these techniques. By combining them, Plan Z offers an investor the potential for speculative gain while retaining maximum safety through the use of U.S. Treasury issues.

We will approach Plan Z gradually, using the first three chapters for preliminaries. Chapter 1 reviews the two conventional types of fixed instruments, bills and bonds. Each of the next two chapters is devoted to one of Plan Z's principal elements: Chapter 2 covers zero coupon bonds, and Chapter 3 discusses dollar-cost averaging and dynamic balancing, a couple of well-known investment techniques. In Part II, we discuss Plan Z itself. First, Chapter 4 explores the difficulties encountered when you combine dollar-cost averaging with zero coupon bonds—a problem few (if any) investment professionals have even begun to suspect. Chapter 5 draws on dynamic balancing to present a prototype of Plan Z. Chapter 6 introduces a more effective variant and chapter 7 presents still another new form with a different twist. Chapter 8 offers Plan Z in its most potent and reliable form. The last part of the book shows the reader how to apply Plan Z by surveying the basic issues, showing different approaches for different personal or market situations as well as some tips and tricks, and makes a few minor additions to the Plan Z canon. The final chapter discusses Plan Z in the context of a portfolio of investments.

We should caution the reader that this is not a get-rich-quick book like the ones that fill bookstore and library shelves. Our aim is to help you get rich *slow.* Our highest concern—and we assume yours—is safety. No one wants to see their life's savings flushed away in an instant on the promise of too-good-to-be-true returns.

As you will see from the computer-generated simulations throughout this book, Plan Z is an investment program with a negligible downside and a potentially huge upside. Actual returns from Plan Z depend on such things as the conditions at start-up, the maturity date of your zeros, and the volatility of interest rates, among others. There are few sure things in this world, and investments are not among them. But, as we shall demonstrate, whatever the particulars might be, Plan Z puts the odds in your favor. If you apply it with understanding, you can be justifiably confident that you will outperform the market*, and—without adding a scintilla of risk—beat the Street.**

* Because the average professional fixed-instrument money manager can be expected to achieve the average return available over a given time, and because Plan Z will in most cases net a return higher than average, the odds are quite good that the investor who sticks with Plan Z will outperform the vast majority of Wall Street's fixed-instrument professionals.

** Vernacular for Wall Street.

Part I

The Elements of Plan Z

1

A Brief Guide to Fixed Instruments

Bills and Bonds

Plan Z is an investment program founded on the novel and judicious use of zero coupon bonds, a special kind of fixed instrument. To understand Plan Z, you must understand zeros and how they are like and unlike other fixed instruments. As we presume you have no prior knowledge of these or other financial matters, we devote Chapter 1 to a brief tour of the grounds.

Alongside stocks, fixed instruments are among the most important and commonplace kinds of investment vehicles—and they are generally regarded as the safest. The most familiar fixed instruments are those issued by the U.S. government: Treasury bills (T-bills) and Treasury bonds (T-bonds). Though you will hear bonds mentioned far less frequently than the stock market on the nightly business broadcasts, the market in fixed instruments (of which bonds are a part) is actually several times larger than the stock market.

Look through the financial pages of any major newspaper and you'll see a sizable listing of several types of fixed instruments.

Stocks and bonds are the primary ways businesses raise money. One represents equity, the other debt. When you own stock in a company, you own a piece of it and have a direct stake in its profit and loss. Bonds, on the other hand, are loans. When you "purchase" a fixed instrument like a bond, you are really lending money. You get a certificate that entitles you to a specific return (interest) in exchange for handing over your money for a predetermined time (or term). As an inducement to forego the use of your funds, you receive interest payments (or, occasionally, a lump sum) at a set rate according to an established schedule. When, at the end of its term, your paper (bond or bill) is retired (or when it *matures*), you get all your original cash back, equal to the amount printed on the certificate's face (its *face value*).

What is distinctive about the way fixed instruments are structured is that the interest rate, face value, and term are *fixed.* Typically, all are established at the outset and do not vary, unlike other investments. When you buy stocks, real estate, or gold, you generally have no certainty about what they are going to do, your period of investment has no set length, and your yield continually varies. With fixed instruments, however, certain characteristics are spelled out and set at the beginning and remain in effect throughout.

Out of the variety of fixed instruments (including CDs and money market funds that behave like fixed instruments but do not ordinarily share the name) emerge three primary types: bonds, bills, and zeros. We will examine each in turn—bonds and bills in this chapter, zeros in the next.

Bonds

Fixed instruments are generally categorized according to whether they (1) are long-term or short-term and (2) pay periodic interest or are discounted up front. Instruments with a life of a year or less are generally deemed short-term, those greater than a year long-term. Long-term instruments are called *bonds.* Bonds pay interest at regular intervals. Today's newspaper, for example, might carry a story of a container company offering $110 million in bonds due in 2001 at an interest rate of 10.75 percent. Buy one of these bonds and you will be entitled to annual payments equivalent to 10.75 percent of the amount you purchased. If you acquired $10,000 worth, you would receive $1,075 every year until 2001, at which time the bond will mature and your original investment will be returned.

Let's look again at how a bond works. Say interest rates are at 8 percent and you buy a 20-year bond with a face value of $1,000. That means the bond issuer* will have your $1,000 for 20 years while you hold a piece of paper that says, in effect: "Pay the bearer $1,000 twenty years from the date of purchase." The certificate also comes with 20 coupons, detachable portions that can be redeemed at predetermined times.** Possession of a coupon identifies you (or the broker holding your bond in your account) as the bond bearer and entitles you to an interest payment. You clip a coupon at the appointed time, bring it to your bank or mail it to the issuer (or have your broker handle matters), and get an interest payment in return. With interest at 8 percent at the time you bought your bond, you would have contracted to receive 20 yearly payments in the fixed amount of $80.

Bills

Bills are short-term fixed instruments that do *not* pay periodic interest. Instead, all interest is paid at maturity at the same time the investor's capital is returned. When the U.S. government borrows

* All kinds of entities and organizations, corporate and governmental, issue bonds. For reasons to be explained later, this book will emphasize federal government instruments over others.

** Nowadays electronic notations in computer records usually take the place of coupons for the individual investor. But the underlying procedure remains the same.

short-term, it does so by means of *Treasury bills** (or T-bills), which mature in a year or less. T-bills do not have coupons. Because of their brief term, they make only one interest payment, at maturity, at the same time the principal is repaid. This procedure is often described as an *up-front discount* because there is a discount in the price the investor pays for the bill right at the start. The size of the discount reflects the current interest rate.** To understand how this works, suppose you had put $91 in a savings account on January 1, 1992. A year later, you withdrew $100. We can say you invested $91 at 10 percent and your money *grew* by $9 to $100, in which case you received $9 in interest. Or we can describe this as the purchase of a piece of paper in 1992 which will have a value of $100 in a year. You paid a current value of $91 for a future value of $100; hence your price was "discounted up front" by $9 (or, your price was discounted at a rate of 10 percent).

Because the price of a T-bill is discounted from its maturity value, it is always less than the maturity value. How much less depends on interest rates at the time of purchase. In the final analysis, the difference between a T-bill's price and its maturity value is the interest that the T-bill pays. The cost of, say, a $10,000 one-year T-bill*** when interest rates are at 10 percent would be a little less than $9,100. That means interest amounting to something more than $900 is deducted from the price of the bill instead of paid out separately ($900 is about 10 percent of a $9,100 investment). Now for a real-life example: Today's paper reports there was "good demand" at the government's recent auction of $13 billion (yes, billion) in one-year Treasury bills sold "at an average discount of 4.34 percent." All this means is that you would pay $958.40 today for a bill that would mature at $1,000 a year from

* Although the private sector offers financial products similar to bills (commercial paper, certificates of deposit, Eurodollars, etc.), and although some special types of commercial paper include the word as part of a longer name, the term "bill" used by itself commonly applies only to Treasury issues.

** This is much simpler than it sounds—in fact, if you have had a savings account, you are already familiar with the concept, if not the terminology.

*** T-bills are available only in minimum denominations of $10,000 and increments of $5,000 thereafter.

Table 1.1 Summary of Bond/Bill Characteristics

	Short-term	Long-term
Regular payouts (or coupons)	Money market funds* Passbook savings accounts*	Bonds
Discounted up front (no payouts or coupons)	Bills	Zeros

*Not normally classified as a fixed instrument. Included for comparison only.

now. Your gain of $41.68 amounts to 4.34 percent interest on your $958.40 investment.

To understand how bills and bonds operate, think of two different savings accounts. With the first account, each time interest is credited, you withdraw it and spend or invest it elsewhere, dropping your balance back to its original total. You start with $1,000 and finish with $1,000 but receive interest (which you deal with separately) in between. That's a bond. Your other savings account functions like a bill. It grows over the course of a year until you withdraw everything at the end. You are capable of taking out $1,000 after a year only because you put $900 in and were credited with $100 interest in the interim.

Different Characteristics of Bonds and Bills

All investments, by definition, promise a return. The flip side of return is risk. The two are directly related: The higher your return, the greater your risk. With fixed instruments, investors are exposed to two kinds of risk—*performance risk* and *market risk*. Performance risk applies to virtually all contractual arrangements. In a discussion of fixed instruments, it means the possibility that the borrower may fail to repay its debt, perhaps because of bankruptcy. The likelihood of default by major bond issuers is rated by agencies such as Moody's

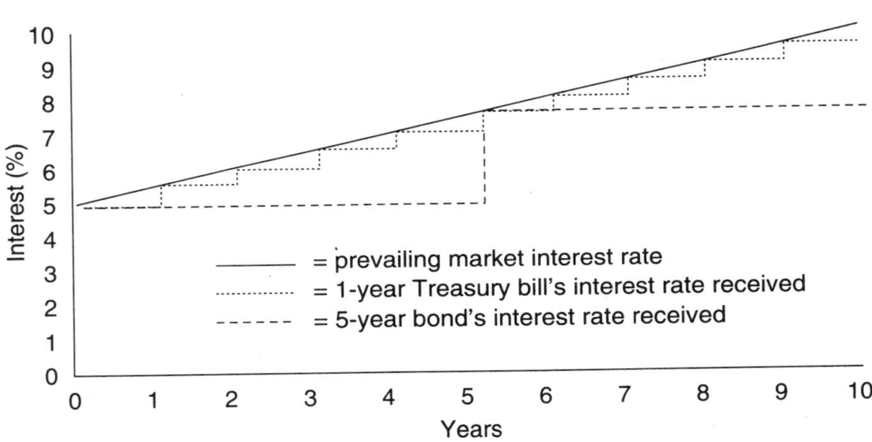

Figure 1.1 Rising rates: The T-bill investor renews his investment every year, keeping his interest rate rising in close step with the current market's. The bond holder must make do with lower rates and wait five years until this bond matures before he has the opportunity to catch up to the prevailing market rate.

and Standard & Poor's. Bonds are usually not formally collateralized; that is, they have no backing beyond the "full faith and credit" of the borrower. So default—when it is a real possibility—is a serious prospect. The safest fixed investments, where the odds of default are next to nil, are those of the U.S. Treasury. Short of a cataclysm, there is little to prevent the U.S. government from fulfilling its obligations. (The same would hold for zero coupon bonds derived from Treasury vehicles. More on these in Chapter 2.) To give you an indication of the government's guaranteed ability to pay, most banks treat government checks as cash and clear them instantly.

Market risk represents the chance that an investor might lose money due to a change in the market value (the current price) of his or her investment. (Because, as we shall see, bond prices vary according to shifts in interest rates, this is also known as interest rate risk.)

T-bills present very little risk of either kind—one reason that they pay a relatively low interest rate. As government issues, they have little or no performance risk, and because they are short-term instruments, market risk is minimized. If interest rates go up dra-

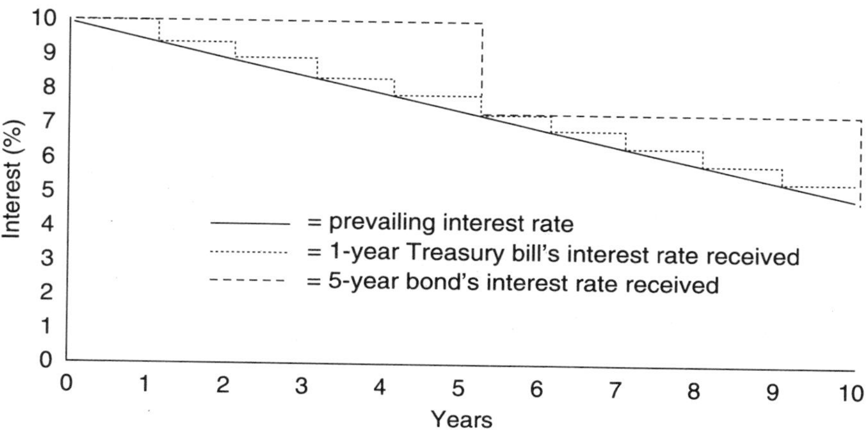

Figure 1.2 Falling rates: The T-bill investor's yield drops lower with every passing year, whereas the bond holder is now insulated from falling rates for the five years he holds his bond.

matically while you hold a T-bill (as in Figure 1.1), your risk is not great because your T-bill will mature soon, enabling you to reinvest promptly at that higher rate. At worst, you'll forego the more-desirable rates for only a year. On the other hand, if interest rates drop (Figure 1.2), you'll regret having failed to lock in a higher rate by buying a longer-term instrument.

With bonds, the situation is reversed. If you buy a bond and then interest rates go up (as in Figure 1.1), you'll deplore missing the rise. After all, your money is now committed to the lower rate for quite a while. You'll be sorry you didn't hold your money in something short-term a bit longer so you could buy your bonds later when the rate was higher. Conversely, if interest rates fall (Figure 1.2), you'll feel fortunate to have secured a higher rate for an extended time.

To sum up: When you invest in bonds, you are locked in for a fairly long time; when you invest in bills, you "float" with the market. When rates are rising, you prefer to let the market carry you upward (you prefer T-bills). When they are falling, you would hope to resist this trend by locking in a higher rate (by owning bonds).

All in all, when interest rates move up, bill investors as a class are delighted while bond owners are distressed. When rates decline, bond investors are pleased and bill investors sad. The only way to stay completely happy and know which way to invest—short-term or long-term, bill or bond—is to have an infallible sense of how interest rates will go, a talent that is notably rare.

Another way in which bills and bonds clearly differ is their liquidity. T-bill investors have fairly ready cash. Their funds aren't committed for long. In fact, the short end of the fixed-instrument spectrum is sometimes called cash* because it is never far from being available in that form. Bond investors, however, do not have easy access to their money. Though they receive interest payments for the duration, their capital can be tied up for as long as 30 years, possibly more.

The Secondary Market

Although the price, term, and interest rate of fixed instruments are initially fixed, prices and yields vary in the secondary market where they may be bought or sold after their original purchase. If you spent $10,000 last year for a 20-year bond and now for some reason need the money, what would you do? You'd probably ask your broker to sell the bond to someone else . . . but how? On the secondary market.** What price will you be able to get for it? That depends on the current interest rate. If you own an 8 percent bond but interest rates have now risen to 10 percent, no one is going to pay you $10,000 for a bond that pays only $800 a year since they can buy a new one and get interest payments of $1,000. To be competitive, to make your bond as attractive as a bond bearing the contemporary yield, you have to give a potential buyer some inducement. So you must offer your bond at a lower price. Remember, bonds always mature at par (the numerical value of par is 100, representing 100 percent of face value). In buying your bond at a

* We will follow this usage as well.

** A secondary market is not an obscure operation run on Sundays in a suburban parking lot. The stock markets—all the various exchanges—provides a secondary market for equities.

price lower than par (less than 100), the purchaser has locked in a capital gain when the bond matures. This is how you compensate him for the lower yield of 8 percent chosen in this example. How much of a concession on the price must you make to compete with a bond yielding 10 percent? You can begin your calculations at $8,000, because $800 income on $8,000 would meet the competition's 10 percent rate. But your bond will still mature at $10,000, not $8,000. So if you let your bond go for $8,000, you'll have given the buyer too good a deal: he'll earn 10 percent on his $8,000 investment *plus* a capital gain of $2,000 when the bond matures. So a more realistic selling price would be closer to $8,200 or $8,300.* The buyer will get a little less than 10 percent in current income, but the capital gain he locks in will make up the difference, producing an effective yield to maturity of 10 percent, in accord with currently available rates.

But what if interest rates had dropped instead, from, let's say, 8 percent to 4 percent since you bought your 20-year bond? At 4 percent, a current $10,000 bond would yield only $400 in income. To match the $800 total annual income that your $10,000 bond produces would require $20,000 in today's market. In this circumstance, people should be willing to pay *more* than face value—a premium over par—for your bond.

The price of a bond in the secondary market is determined in a way that enables it to be competitive with whatever the current interest rate for bonds may be. For instance, someone who buys a $10,000 bond in the secondary market knows that no matter what price he pays *now,* that bond will pay $10,000 at maturity. If he pays less than $10,000, not only will he collect interest over the remainder of the bond's life, but he will also have a capital gain when the bond matures and he collects its $10,000 face value. If, however, he spends more than $10,000 for the bond, he'll collect interest and a capital *loss.* But when the interest and price are combined and the total yield to maturity is calculated—counting both

* When a bond's principal is taken into account in this way to determine its yield, the result is called the yield to maturity. The precise value is obtained through some complex calculations that need not detain us here.

interest *and* the capital gain or loss—the result in each case should be practically the same. In both transactions the yield to maturity should come extremely close to that of a new bond issued at the prevailing interest rate.

The secondary market serves to *equalize the net yield* of all similar fixed instruments, lining up the old and new with the same (current) interest rate through adjustments in *the only variable feature* fixed instruments possess: their current market price. A bond that bears a coupon with interest lower than what is current (and thus pays too little) must compensate the investor with a capital gain. Bonds that carry coupons higher than the current interest command a premium price to induce the seller to relinquish them.

Clearly, the psychology of owners of long-term fixed instruments—glad when interest rates fall and sad when they rise—is firmly based in market realities. When rates fall, they are rewarded by a rise in the price of their investments on the secondary market, and when rates increase, their investments decline in value. Although in both instances the effective total interest payment they will earn remains the same, the current market value of their bond holdings changes daily.

Price Fluctuations

The price of a bond is fixed at both issuance and maturity, but, as we have seen, it oscillates in the interim according to changes in the prevailing interest rate. (It is important to stress that regardless of such changes, bonds ultimately expire at the price contracted for when they were originally issued. Whether interest rates fall from 6 percent to 4 percent, or rise to 12 percent, a $10,000 bond always matures at $10,000.)

A bill's price fluctuates minutely (Figure 1.3). As a short-term instrument, it acts like a passbook savings account. Its value rises over the course of a year by accruing interest, but it doesn't rise much, certainly not more than the interest rate at the time. By contrast, bond prices can fluctuate much more widely (Figure 1.4).

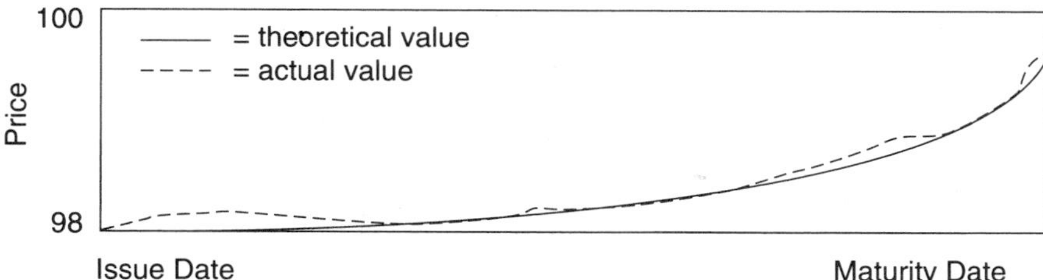

Figure 1.3 The price of a bill: The theoretical value shows the market price the investment would have throughout its life if the interest rate did not fluctuate at all but held at the same level from purchase date until maturity. The actual value is intended to illustrate how its price might fluctuate if interest rates did change—something they can be counted on to do in the real world. For a bill, these fluctuations are barely noticeable.

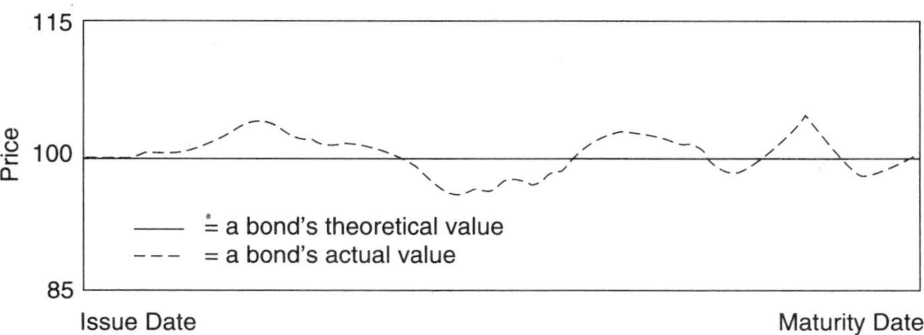

Figure 1.4 The price of a bond.

The effect of interest payouts is multiplied because they compound over a long period.* A bond begins with a *par value* of 100 and ends with a par value of 100, but it can fluctuate well above or below that mark during its long life, if interest rates shift back and forth significantly.

As we shall see in the next chapter, zeros are just like bills and bonds, but different.

* Compounding is explained in the next chapter.

2

Zero Coupon Bonds and the Power of Compounding

Some of the impetus behind the invention of zeros in the early 1980s came from brokerage firms looking for a way to handle the influx of funds earmarked for individual retirement accounts (IRAs). It seemed appropriate to offer ultrasafe investments despite their relatively low yields, because the tax-exempt status of IRAs would boost the net after-tax yield. Bonds were an obvious choice, but (among other difficulties) they were available only in denominations too steep for most individual retirement accounts. So brokers created a new kind of bond—one without coupons—that they called a zero coupon bond.

Initially, a zero was a government bond that had been "stripped." In other words, the principal (or "body") had been disassociated from the coupons and each part sold separately as *zero coupon bonds.** Nowadays (and possibly even then), bonds are

* Or, more accurately in many cases, they escrowed the coupons and sold certificates of ownership.

stripped electronically, not with scissors. The certificates themselves are not physically altered, but computer entries recording their existence are changed. A fiduciary institution (brokerage house, bank, insurance company, or investment banking firm) will purchase a T-bond and deposit it in its own account with the Federal Reserve Bank (FRB) where it will be held. The institution will then "strip" the bond by selling all its pieces, coupons and body, individually. When people or institutions buy these zeros, they are assigned the right to the future income the bond's various components can claim—all guaranteed by the U.S. Treasury (which borrowed the money in the first place and hence is obligated to pay it back). The assignation of rights is formalized by a certificate that says something like, "Upon maturity, we assign the *x* dollars of proceeds of our bond, #123456789, stored at the FRB, to be paid to Mr. Smith" or "We assign the coupon maturing in 2005 . . . "

This is the way virtually all zeros are created. The trustee, the owner of record, the assignor of rights, the signer of the IOU certificate, and the guarantor of the signature may vary, but the procedure remains the same.

There is another way to create a zero coupon bond: produce one directly rather than derive it from another bond. This is something a number of corporations have more recently decided to do.*

To get a better grasp of how a zero functions, suppose you buy a regular $1,000 bond that pays 8 percent in interest and matures in the year 2010. It comes with coupons labeled 1993, 1994, all the way to 2010. You clip these coupons and present them to the issuer, who "cashes" them and pays you $80 in interest for each year's coupon. Now what if you want that income but need some cash today? It might occur to you to first strip the coupons from the bond and set them aside to assure your $80 in annual income and then sell the body to fulfill your need for immediate cash. This last piece, a bond without a coupon, would become a zero coupon bond with a face value of $1,000. Should you decide to sell one (or more) of the coupons you stripped, it too would become a zero, with a face value of $80 "maturing" in the year it is scheduled to be redeemed.

* Corporate zeros are touched on in Chapter 9.

Zeros are ideal for anyone of even modest means with a specific and sizable long-range investment target. As already mentioned, you can purchase them in amounts well below the minimum of many bonds. And, because of the way they are constructed, a small sum put into a zero today can yield a large payoff in the future without the need for additional investment. For the new or part-time investor, zeros are attractive because they are easy to administer, in most cases demanding little or no monitoring—the very reason many people continue to commit their IRAs to zero coupon bonds. Zeros also provide a way—in fact, the only easy way—to lock in a compound, fully reinvested yield that guarantees a particular rate of return for a lengthy period *and extends that guarantee to all reinvested income automatically.* With conventional bonds, an investor must continually make decisions regarding the interest income they generate, if it is reinvested at all. Finally, like other fixed instruments, zero coupon bonds offer a specific return with certainty. Because their rate of return is locked in at inception, an investor knows from the start the precise dollar value at maturity—a level of predictability not found in most other common investment vehicles.

Zero coupon bonds are hybrids, a unique mix of bill and bond. Like T-bills, their price is discounted up front. But their time horizon is long-term like a bond. Initially called zero coupon *bonds* partly because they were derived from government bonds and partly because people were influenced by their bondlike time to maturity, they would be more accurately described as *long-term T-bills.* This seemingly contradictory expression—T-bills are by definition short-term—does perfect justice to how a zero behaves. Despite its greater time duration and volatility, a zero is more like a bill than a bond because, like the former, its price rises inexorably over the course of its life. (Compare Figure 2.1 with Figures 1.3 and 1.4 and note that the curve which a zero's price follows is similar to a T-bill's, not a bond's.) Perhaps because zeros are relatively new instruments, until now the full implications of this fact have not been exploited, but they are fundamental to Plan Z.

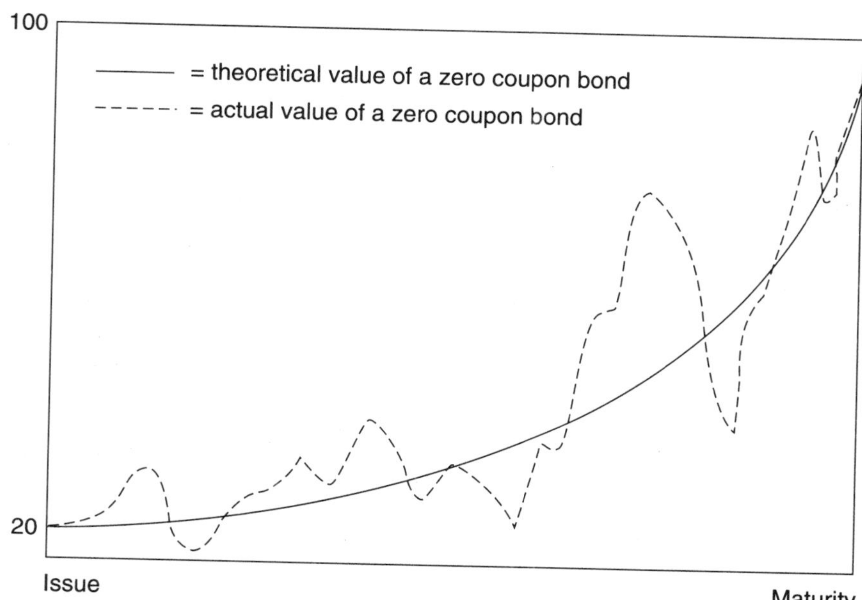

Figure 2.1 The price of a zero coupon bond.

Compared to a T-bill, a zero's initial price is dramatically discounted. Accordingly, the rise in its price over its term is striking. Where a T-bill may move from 95 to 100, a zero's value can increase many times over, from the single digits or low teens all the way to its ultimate par of 100. Because of the difference in their maturity lengths—zeros can last 20 or more times longer than T-bills—zeros afford greater opportunities for gains, not just by fractions or multiples but by *orders of magnitude,* even over comparable periods of time. The cause of this price differential is compound interest, a critical notion for investments of all kinds and one particularly important for understanding zero coupon bonds.

The Power of Compounding

It is said that the game of chess so delighted the maharajah to whom it was presented that he promised its inventor his heart's desire.

Table 2.1 How $100 Will Compound at Various Rates from 10 to 100 Years

		Number of years invested				
		10	**20**	**30**	**40**	**100**
Rate of return	4%	148	219	324	480	5,050
	5%	163	265	432	704	13,150
	6%	179	321	574	1,029	33,930
	7%	197	387	761	1,497	86,772
	8%	216	466	1,006	2,172	219,976
	9%	237	560	1,327	3,141	552,904
	10%	259	673	1,745	4,526	1,378,060
	12%	311	965	2,996	9,305	8,352,220
	15%	405	1,637	6,621	26,786	117,431,000

A clever man, the inventor asked that one grain of wheat be placed on the board's first square, two on the second, four on the next, and so on, doubling the amount from square to square until all 64 had been covered. The maharajah was pleased with this modest request and ordered it done. It was not long, however, before its impossibility became clear. The number of grains started small but mounted swiftly: 1, 2, 4, 8, 16, 32, 64, 128, 256, 512, 1,024, 2,048, 4,096, 8,192, 16,384, 32,768, 65,536, 131,072, 262,144, 524,288, 1,048,576, 2,097,152, 4,194,304, 8,388,608, 16,777,216, 33,554,432, 67,108,864, and so on, until they reached a sum greater than all the wheat ever produced by man, even to this day. Unable to satisfy the inventor's wish, the maharajah had his head cut off instead.

That's compounding.

Compound interest occurs when you collect interest *on your interest.* Over time, you earn not only interest on your interest, but interest on the interest *from* your interest, and interest on that interest, and so on. In this way an investment can build and build and build, adding up after many years to a great deal of money. Table 2.1 shows how much an initial investment of $100 amounts to if left to compound for 10, 20, 30, 40, and 100 years, assuming a constant rate of interest.

The first lesson of compounding is this: time, as it passes, becomes increasingly valuable. After 10 years at 4 percent, $100 becomes $148. After 20 years at 4 percent, it grows to $219, gaining $71 interest in its second decade compared with $48 in its first. It amasses $105 in interest in its third decade, and $156 in its fourth. After a century—if you can imagine that—it would accumulate interest of $4,570 during the last 60 years. Each decade gathers more interest than the one before. As the years wear on, not only does the rate of growth increase, but so does the rate of the rate of growth (that's what acceleration means). So, although interest rates remain constant, the sums they operate on get greater and greater as the interest earned in previous years is added to interest from each succeeding one. On a graph, constant growth is represented by a straight line. Compound growth—growth at an exponential or ever-increasing rate—is described by a sharply rising curve (as in Figure 2.2).

The only guaranteed way to get rich is to put your money away and let it compound for a very long time. If you can wait a hundred years, $100 can turn into more than a million. But even if you have a more immediate goal, you can raise a considerable sum, if you start as early as possible and commit for as long as you can. Every year counts. Look again at the 4 percent row in Table 2.1. If you put away $100, you would earn $4 in interest the first year. Hardly worth mentioning. But by the 30th year, your balance would be up to $324. By then you would be earning an annual interest payment equivalent to nearly 13 percent of your initial $100 investment, even with rates still at 4 percent.

If we travel up and down Table 2.1 instead of across, you can see how small differences in interest rates can make huge differences in the size of the ultimate return. For example, if you could get 9 percent instead of 7 percent on your $100, after 30 years you would have $1,327 instead of $761, almost twice as much. The longer the time period, the more dramatic the contrast. After 10 years, the difference between 7 percent and 9 percent is only $40; after 20 years it's $173; and after 100 years, it's $466,132. If you have a long-term investment, you should be extremely careful about your interest rate, because even *an extra 1 or 2 percent can multiply your final return several times over.* Indeed, this is what Plan Z is

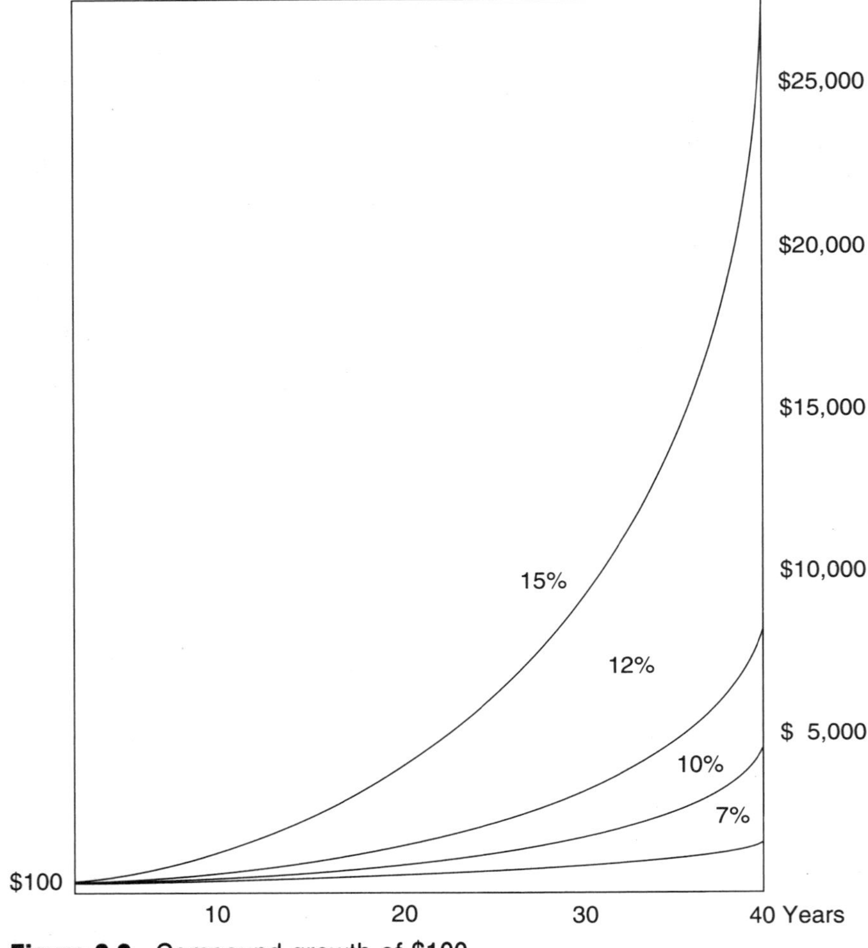

Figure 2.2 Compound growth of $100.

designed to do: get you the best possible yield without conceding safety. Ordinarily, if you want a higher return you have to shoulder additional risk. Plan Z will help you boost your results while maintaining a high level of security.

The importance of investing early is driven home by the following contrast: What if we invest $10 every year (Table 2.2) instead of depositing $100 at the start (Table 2.1)? A hundred dollars down wins every time. Investing $10 every year for 40 years at 15

Table 2.2 Compounding of $10 Annual Investment

		Number of years invested			
		10	20	30	40
Rate of return	4%	125	310	583	988
	5%	132	347	698	1,268
	6%	140	390	838	1,641
	7%	148	439	1,011	2,136
	8%	157	494	1,224	2,798
	9%	166	558	1,486	3,683
	10%	175	630	1,809	4,869
	12%	197	807	2,703	8,591
	15%	234	1,178	5,000	20,460

Table 2.3 Compounding of $2,000 Annual Contribution

		Number of years invested			
		10	20	30	40
Rate of return	4%	24,973	61,938	116,657	197,653
	5%	26,414	69,439	139,522	253,680
	6%	27,943	77,985	167,603	328,095
	7%	29,567	87,730	202,146	427,219
	8%	31,291	98,846	244,692	559,562
	9%	33,121	111,529	297,150	736,584
	10%	35,062	126,005	361,887	973,704
	12%	39,309	161,397	540,585	1,718,285
	15%	46,699	235,620	999,914	4,091,908

percent earns you $20,460 (Table 2.2). Someone who plunks down $100 and never adds a dollar (Table 2.1) would net $26,786, over 30 percent more. You invested four times as much—why did you do less well? Because you did not enjoy the benefits of compounding to the same extent. The other investor's $100 compounded for the full 40 years. The only part of your investment that compounded that long was the $10 you deposited in year 1. Your last $100 in contributions, spread out over the last 10 years, hardly compounded at all.

Let's see compounding at work in a real-life example. If you made a $2,000 contribution every year into an IRA account that had no starting balance, you would obtain the results shown in Table 2.3.

The effect of annual contributions (as in Table 2.3) can be augmented by a sizable initial deposit (much as you might find in an IRA rollover account). Say you start with $10,000 from a pension fund to which you continue to add $2,000 every year. After 20 years at 8 percent interest, you'd obtain a total of $145,455 (compared to $98,846 for an IRA with no starting balance as in Table 2.3). Your initial $10,000 deposit could compound for the whole period, whereas the $40,000 (contributed in $2,000 annual increments) would be spread out over 20 years. The difference becomes even more exaggerated if you assume a higher interest rate for a longer period. Invested for 40 years at 10 percent, a $10,000 initial deposit would make a difference of $452,592 in your favor. You'd earn $1,426,296 on a total investment of $90,000, compared with $973,704 for an IRA with no initial deposit (total investment: $80,000). A mere 12 percent increase in the total dollar investment would have yielded a 46 percent greater final return.

The moral is: Long-term investing works. You can make a lot of money out of a little—if you have a lot of time. You won't get rich quick but you *will* get rich. Start early. Invest your money up front if you can. Get the best possible interest rate. Make the power of compounding work for you.

The Nature of Zeros: Price and Volatility

The reason compound interest is so important to zero coupon bonds is that, except for their initial cost, *zeros consist entirely of compound interest.* The money that is repaid when a zero matures is the accumulated (or accreted) interest resulting when its initial price is permitted to compound at its stated rate over its term. A $1,000 30-year zero will cost you around $100 now (if interest rates are 8 percent), because that's how much you would need to invest for 30 years at 8 percent compound interest to get $1,000 (look at Table 2.1 again—it's right there). Another way of putting it: The price of a zero is the present (discounted) value of its price at maturity. In the world of finance, a *present value* is the cash value

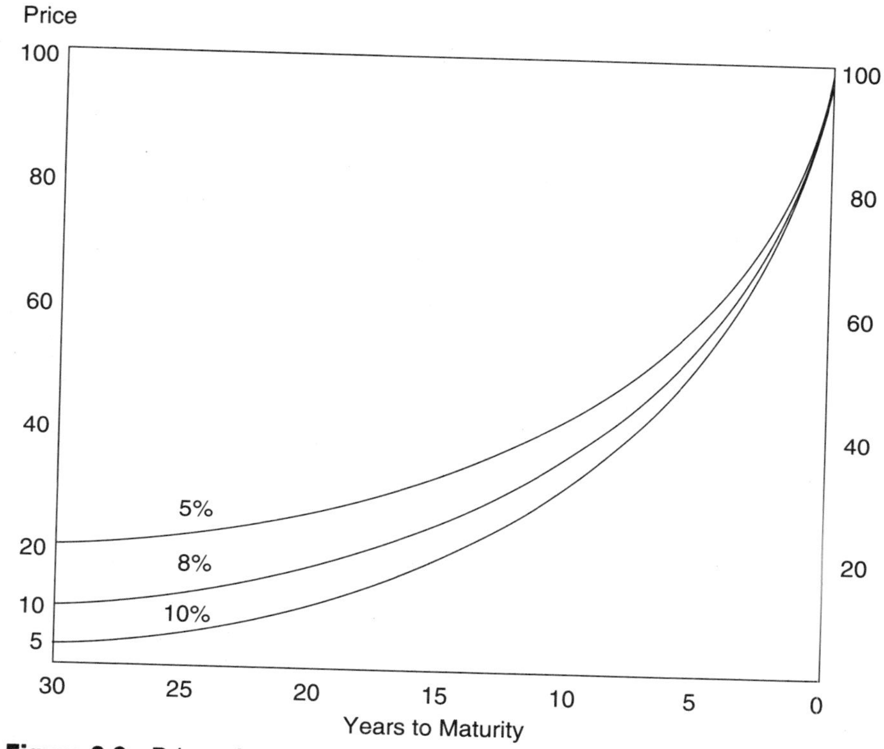

Figure 2.3 Price of a zero at constant rates of 5, 8, or 10 percent.

today of some future return. It is the current price, after the up-front discount. If you know you are going to receive $1,000 in so many years, you can precisely calculate this present value—what its cost to you would be today—by plugging in the interest you expect to earn.

The three curves in Figure 2.3 depict a zero's price at constant rates of 5, 8, and 10 percent. If they greatly resemble the compound interest curves in Figure 2.2, it's because both illustrate the same phenomenon from different perspectives. Figure 2.2 asks: "If I invest a fixed amount now, how will interest rates affect the value to which it ultimately grows?" Figure 2.3 turns this around: "If I want a particular ultimate value, how much do I need to invest now, at various interest rates?" In the first question, the beginning value is fixed and the final value is determined by the interest rate. In

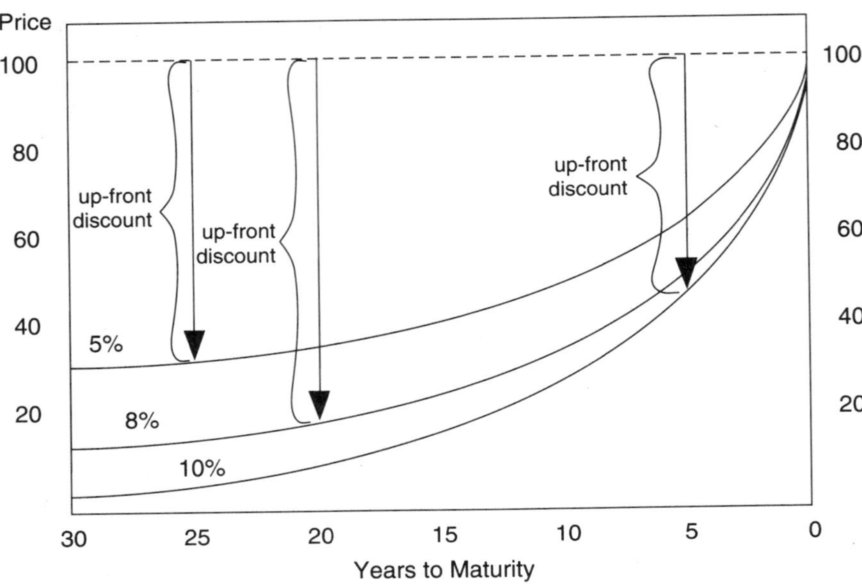

Figure 2.4 The up-front discount of a zero is the difference between its price and par.

the second question, the final amount is given and the first is determined by the rate. Figure 2.2 shows how a certain sum invested today will have different *future values* at various rates of interest. Figure 2.3 shows how interest rates affect the amount you would need to invest today to reach the same future value of 100.

Another difference between Figures 2.2 and 2.3: The former shows the relationship between interest and final return, the latter between interest and initial price. The curves marking the highest interest rates are on top in Figure 2.2 but on the bottom in Figure 2.3. Why? Zeros are priced at a discount from par. Return and price are *inversely related*—when one goes up, the other comes down. The higher the interest rate, the higher the yield and the lower the price—and the *less* you need to invest now in order to reach a particular final goal.

If we alter Figure 2.3 slightly (see Figure 2.4), we can get a visual explanation of up-front discount. By adding a dotted line across the top at 100, the known future value, we can see the distance between par and price at any point. That difference is the up-front discount. The three arrows in Figure 2.4 cover three specific instances, but with enough curves and arrows we could illustrate the extent to which any zero of any term and rate is discounted up-front. We see, for example, that when rates hit 5 percent, a 25-year zero has a price of about 30. Thus, the up-front discount, measured by the arrow, is around 70. When rates are at 8 percent, a 20-year zero is priced at 15 and thus discounted by 85. At 10 percent, a five-year zero has a price of approximately 60, which entails an up-front discount of 40.

Compound interest accounts for a zero's starting price, but what about interim pricing? Like other fixed instruments, zeros are traded in the secondary market. Prices change when interest rates change. Zeros, in fact, are far more sensitive to interest rate variations than bills or bonds because they are made up almost entirely of accreted interest. As we saw when we examined the compound interest tables earlier, a small change in interest rates can have a tremendous influence on compound returns years later. Because zeros *are* primarily compound interest, the same is true for them. A matter of a point or two can easily double or halve a long-term zero's value. Look again at Figure 2.4. Suppose a small change in rates makes a small difference in the up-front discount—say, from 90 to 80. This modest alteration would cause the zero's price to go from 10 to 20, a 100 percent increase.

The close connection between zeros and interest rates, and the severe effect that small changes in those rates can have, means that zeros are extremely volatile* in price. Figure 2.1 contrasted a picture of an imaginary zero's smooth (theoretical) curve and actual interim prices. As you can see, the actual price zigzags back and forth across the ascending curve.

There are limits to a zero's volatility. Every zero—whether it is one year or 100 years long—will mature at a par of 100. Given that fact, zeros tend to get less volatile as the years pass. The closer they get to maturity, the less interest rate changes matter (because

* Volatility refers to the degree of fluctuation away from an average value or series of values. As volatility increases, so ordinarily does risk.

the up-front discount is smaller—changes in it don't affect zeros that much). We saw the same phenomenon at work earlier when the final decade's worth of $10 annual contributions made little difference to a long-term account. There was just not enough time for the money to compound to magnify results much. A similar thing occurs in the latter years of a zero's life. There is not as much time for the effects of changing interest rates to matter.

You can clearly see this decrease in volatility by looking at the two outermost curves in Figure 2.3, the ones illustrating the 5 and 10 percent zeros. If interest rates were to stay between 5 and 10 percent* over the 30 years shown, these curves would describe the price range—the highest and lowest possible prices—of any zero during that time. You can tell that the distance between these curves narrows as time moves it toward par. With 30 years to maturity, a jump in rates from 5 to 10 percent would mean a price drop from 23.14 to 5.73 (−75.2 percent). By the same token, a fall from 10 to 5 percent would make prices move in the other direction, from 5.73 to 23.14, a rise of 304 percent. Twenty years later, this price range contracts considerably. A similar move from 5 to 10 percent would result in a loss of only 37 percent (from 61.39 to 38.55), whereas a drop from 10 to 5 percent would translate into a price gain of only 59 percent (from 38.55 to 61.39). By the time this zero is within one year of maturity, a five-point shift in interest rates makes a mere five-point difference in price (90.91 to 95.24 going down and 95.24 to 90.91 going up).

If we mapped the price consequences of interest rate swings from 5 to 10 percent and 10 to 5 percent at any point over the life of a 30-year zero, the result would be the two curves shown in Figure 2.5. The topmost curve defines the percentage gain to be enjoyed when interest rates drop from 10 percent to 5 percent. The bottom curve shows the percentage decrease in a zero's price when rates rise from 5 percent to 10 percent. Figure 2.5 illustrates the volatility exposure over time for this particular pair of interest rates. In other words, it shows how much you would stand to benefit

* These are reasonable interest rate assumptions. Other equally sound choices would have resulted in only slightly different curves.

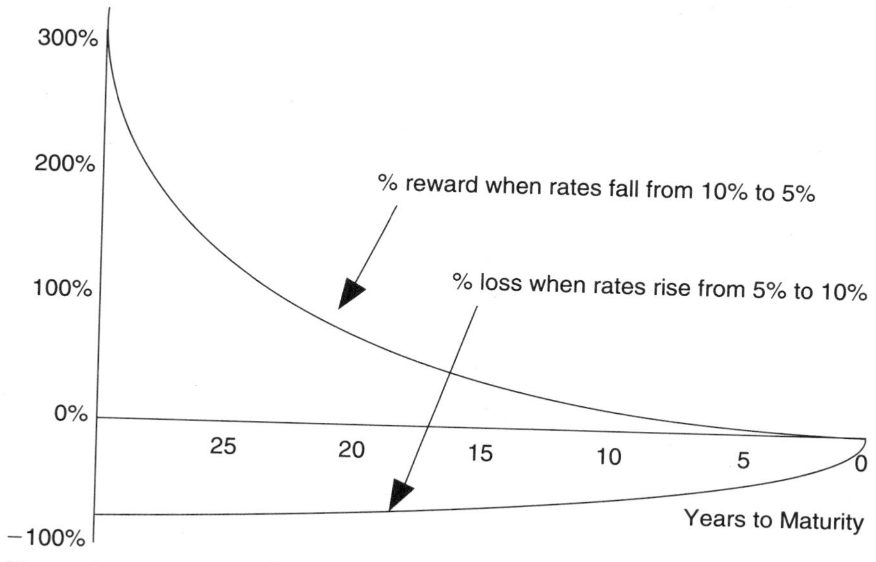

Figure 2.5 Speculative risk and reward diminish as a zero nears maturity.

or suffer, as a percentage profit or loss, from owning a zero coupon bond as interest rates vary between 5 and 10 percent—the outline of your potential risk and reward. It is apparent from looking at Figure 2.5 that interest rates have a much greater effect in the early years of a zero's life—another way of saying that as a zero approaches maturity, its volatility diminishes significantly.

Figure 2.5 also illustrates why it is important for Plan Z investors to follow through on their initial commitments. The volatility of a zero in its early years means there's a greater chance your price will be off course—far from its theoretical price. If you wait, the odds of its being on track improve. In fact, if you wait until your zero matures, a point at which its volatility falls to nothing, you're guaranteed no better or worse than precisely par.

If we copied the path of the zero drawn in Figure 2.1 so it moves about the curves described in Figure 2.3, we would get Figure 2.6. If you follow this (imaginary) zero as it wanders up and down on its way toward par, you will notice it crossing and recrossing the three constant growth curves shown there. If we were somehow able to draw an infinite number of such curves in Figure

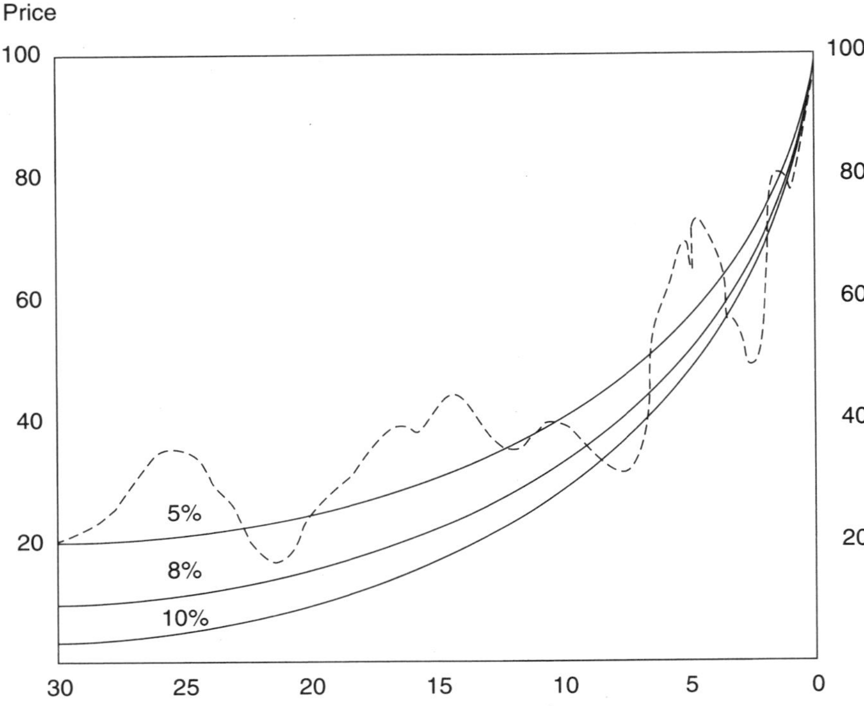

Figure 2.6 Actual zero price compared to several theoretical price curves.

2.6, one for each possible interest rate, then the conclusion we are about to draw might be more obvious—namely, zeros don't meander around a single constant growth curve; they are always on *some* particular idealized exponential growth curve, depending on the current interest rate. When interest rates change, a zero's price will rise or drop instantly to the appropriate interest rate growth curve and immediately resume its path along *that* upward curve toward par. The point is this: Zeros may be thought of as *always* moving relentlessly forward and upward along one or another of the various growth curves (see Figure 2.7). Whatever curve-hopping they do, however near or far they rise or fall, they instantly resume their upward movement toward par.

We can adjust Figure 2.3 in a new way to make yet another point. Figure 2.8 is identical to Figure 2.3 except the vertical axis

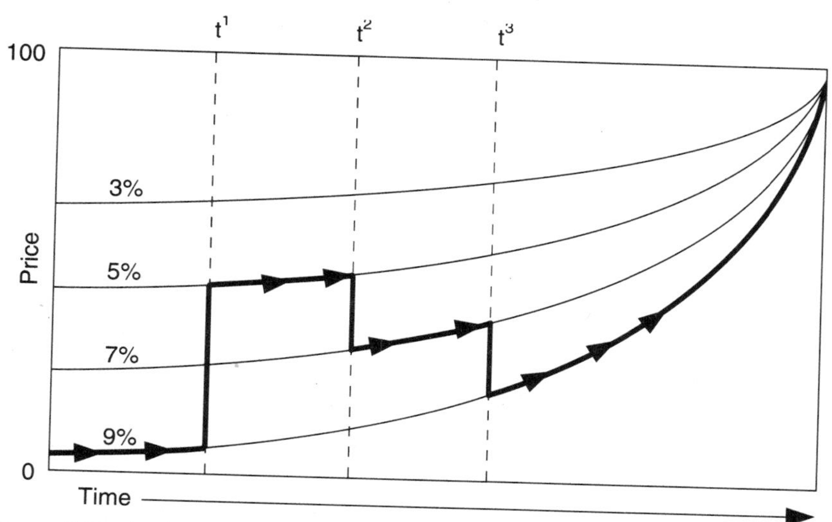

Figure 2.7 At time t^1, rates dropped from 9 to 5%. At time t^2, they rose to 7%. Then, at t^3, they rose again, to 9%. But at *all* times, a zero is rising on *some* growth curve, determined by the current interest rate.

has been changed to a logarithmic scale. All this means is that instead of the regular *arithmetic* spacing in which equal numerical differences are the same distance apart (whether it's the 40 units between 100 and 60 or the 40 between 28 and 68), we've used a log chart where equal *percentage* changes are represented by equal distances on the chart. So 10 is halfway between 1 and 100 because 1 is to 10 as 10 is to 100. The main reason for shifting to a semi-logarithmic chart (*semi* because only one axis is logarithmic) is that you can immediately *see* the difference a percentage change makes, at whatever price it occurs. As investors we're chiefly interested in percentages (relative differences), not numbers (absolute differences). After all, would you prefer a stock that moved from 1 to 10 or one that improved from 71 to 80? Both gained nine points, but the first is obviously the better investment.

You can directly see the volatility—the percentage difference between prices at various interest rates—in Figure 2.8 by measuring the vertical distance between price points with your eye (or a ruler). Volatility at a particular time in a zero's life is proportional to the

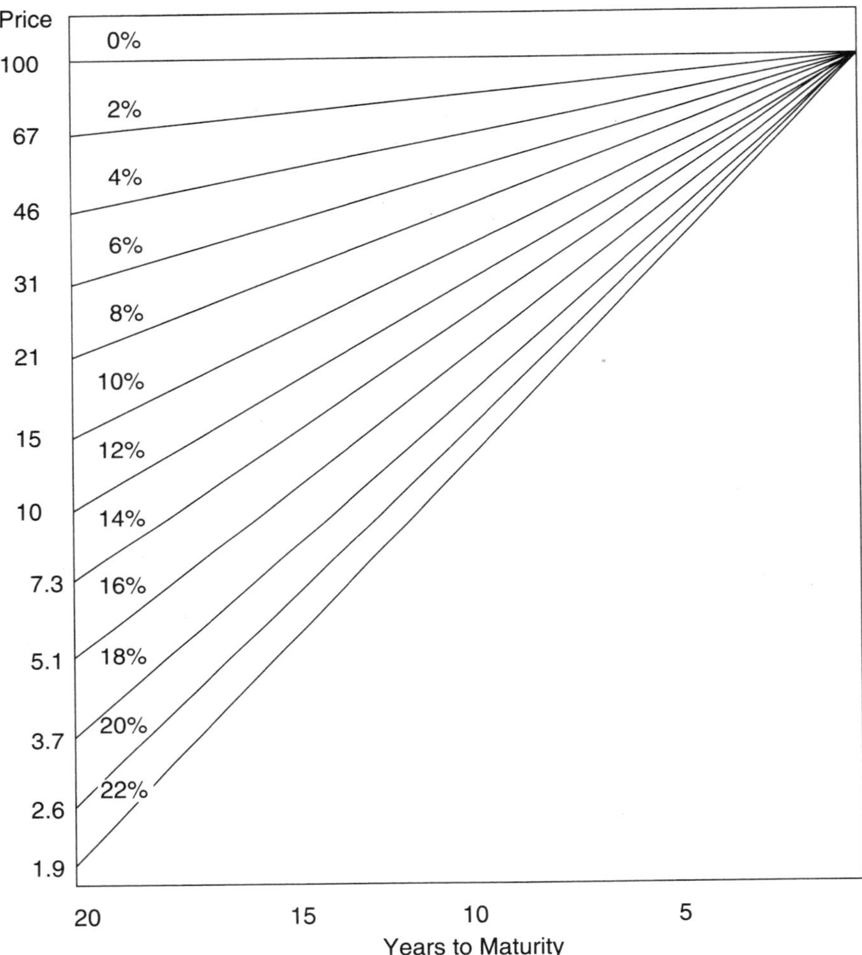

Figure 2.8 Universal zero map.

vertical distance between possible growth curves (although they become straight lines in a semilog chart, they are still curves). These are the same growth curves we saw in Figure 2.7, just stretched or straightened by changing the price scale somewhat.

If we could draw enough lines to represent every possible interest rate, Figure 2.8 could serve as a universal zero map that would visually demonstrate the relationship between price, interest,

Table 2.4 Risk/Reward Quick Reference Chart

Years to maturity	Current interest rate 4%	6%	8%	10%
30	34 (25)	33 (25)	32 (24)	32 (24)
25	27 (21)	27 (21)	26 (21)	26 (20)
20	21 (17)	21 (17)	20 (17)	20 (17)
15	16 (13)	15 (13)	15 (13)	15 (13)
10	11 (9)	10 (9)	10 (9)	10 (9)
5	5 (5)	5 (5)	5 (5)	5 (4)

and maturity length for every imaginable zero. If you knew any two of these elements, you could readily determine the other by moving along the chart to the intersection of the known values and reading off the third. And if you knew only one, you could visualize the exact relationship between the other two. For example, if you want to find the price of a zero 15 years to maturity when interest rates are at 6 percent, all you have to do is locate the 6 percent line and move along its slope until you reach 15 years. The answer is that point's corresponding value on the vertical axis. You might use this method to check how prices quoted by your broker compare with the correct value for the current interest rate, or to deduce the effective interest rate a zero currently offers, from knowledge of its price and maturity length.

The very fact that we can in theory create a universal zero map by condensing all possible price paths on a single sheet testifies to how much simpler zeros are (conceptually) compared to bonds. The zero map needs only three dimensions: price, time, and interest rate. A universal bond map would require yet another dimension to account for the interest payments (or coupons) that zeros do without. Such a map would require an infinite number of charts like Figure 2.8 (one for bonds with an 8 percent coupon, another for those with an 8.1 percent coupon, and one for every other possible rate) because we need to know time, price, and *two* interest rates to describe each bond. (In addition to the current market rate, we need to know what rate the bond's fixed coupon pays.) With zeros, there are no coupons to complicate matters.

Placing each bond bearing a different-sized coupon on a separate page makes comparison among them more than a practical difficulty. It points out that such bonds are *essentially* different from one another. Each has its own life, its own course, its own particular features. By comparison, zeros are much more homogeneous. All are moving toward 100 on one of the lines (drawn or undrawn) in Figure 2.8. In fact, at any given time, *all zeros are on the same line*—the one representing the current interest rate. Their relative position on that line differs only according to their time to maturity.

Zeros have an egalitarian cast because their individual histories are irrelevant. Nothing about their past prevents them from (possibly) becoming identical at some point (whereas a 30-year bond "born" with a 9 percent coupon is indelibly marked and could never be mistaken for a 30-year bond with a 10 percent coupon). With zeros, the only pertinent consideration at all times is *time to maturity.* A 20-year zero issued in 1980 and a 10-year zero issued in 1990 are equivalent and indeed indistinguishable. Both say, "Pay the bearer *x* number of dollars in the year 2000."

Another table of practical interest for zero strategy is Table 2.4. You can use it to get some idea of how much each 1 percent drop in interest rates will increase your zero's price and how much each 1 percent rise will decrease it (number in parentheses). But if all you need is a rough measure, you can dispense with this table by using the following risk/reward rule of thumb: Take the number of years to maturity, treat it as so many percent, then add 10 percent of that number to get the approximate reward if rates fall 1 percent—or subtract 10 percent to estimate the price risk if rates rise 1 percent. Thus, if rates fall 1 percent:

	Rule of thumb	**Estimated price change**	**Actual price change***
a 30-year zero =>	30% + (10% of 30)	≈ 33% (reward)	32% to 34%
a 20-year zero =>	20% + (10% of 20)	≈ 22% (reward)	20% to 21%
a 10-year zero =>	10% + (10% of 10)	≈ 11% (reward)	10% to 11%

* From Table 2.4. A range is given because price changes vary slightly depending on the absolute level of interest rates.

And if rates rise 1 percent:

	Rule of thumb	Estimated price change	Actual price change
a 30-year zero =>	30% − (10% of 30)	≈ 27% (risk)	24% to 25%
a 20-year zero =>	20% − (10% of 20)	≈ 18% (risk)	17%
a 10-year zero =>	10% − (10% of 10)	≈ 9% (risk)	9%

Zeros and Capital Gains

Thus far we have talked of investing as though it were a uniform activity, but there are really two kinds: genuine investing (in its precise meaning) and speculating. Investors get *returns* and speculators *gains.* Investors seek income through involvement in an economically productive activity (for example, making shoes or building generators) and expect to make a profit from the use of their capital. They forego consumption and instead put their wealth to use for productive purposes capable of creating more wealth in the future. Speculating, on the other hand, entails *anticipating market trends.* With reference to fixed instruments, it means predicting their market prices. Speculation performs different economic functions than investing; namely, liquidity and price discovery (among others). Speculating is riskier than investing. The speculator may not be the engine of the economy—the investor is—but he or she plays a valuable role.

Investment and speculation are rarely found in pure form. Fixed instruments, with their guaranteed income (in the case of bonds) and guaranteed maturity value, are more amenable to investment than to speculation. Commodities, by comparison, are almost entirely objects of speculation. You cannot invest in a side of bacon, but you can speculate on its price. (You may, however, invest in a *business* that processes the bacon.)

Fixed instruments, though, are not entirely devoid of speculative features. As we have seen, they do fluctuate in price. When you purchase a fixed instrument for its income and safety, you are also implicitly speculating on its future price. In the case of a long bond, you are speculating on the course of interest rates, because that is what most affects the price of a bond (if you expected its price to be significantly lower tomorrow, you would not have bought today). However, almost no one thinks of a T-bill as a speculative investment, because its total price growth ranges over no more than a few percentage points before it matures—and virtually all of that can be accounted for as accumulated interest, not as a capital gain. Thus, T-bills are close to being pure investments whereas bonds possess an inherent element of speculation.

What about zeros? Although a zero's price is almost entirely made up of interest, it doesn't fit the standard definitions. Because of its structure, a zero has some of the safety that makes fixed instruments attractive, yet it retains the potential for speculation as wild as one would care to make it.

Viewed in these terms—as vehicles for capital gains—the extraordinary thing about zeros is that they are *guaranteed to rise in price by a substantial amount.* The market will ultimately "buy back" your zero at a price significantly higher than you paid. Bought at a steep discount, its value *must rise sharply* to par by maturity. From the perspective of a long-term investor, *zero coupon bonds are always in a bull market.*

By virtue of the unique character of zero coupon bonds, Plan Z is able to incorporate the safety of bills and bonds while providing benefits from a rise *or* fall in interest rates, thus offering performance potential well beyond that of most other fixed instruments. Plan Z will automatically give the average investor a significant edge at a minimum of additional effort and without any significant increase in ultimate risk. Its superior performance is built in, independent of genius or luck. It accomplishes this by using a "mechanical" trading rule to "force" investors to automatically, repeatedly, and consistently buy zeros low and sell them high, never doing the reverse.

Next, we'll explore two of the mechanical rules important to Plan Z.

3

Understanding the Rules

If you're a knowledgeable investor, some of what follows will be familiar to you, and you may wish to turn to the final section of this chapter. A word to beginners as well: Understanding this topic—indeed, this entire book—is easier than it may appear. On the one hand, the Wall Street terminology, which we cannot entirely avoid, tends to sound complex because it is designed to overawe and impress, but not because the concepts themselves are difficult. Financial marketeers occasionally use mathematics to obscure the actual simplicity of their ideas. On the other hand, much of the math and neologisms we use here are entirely justified, both in this chapter and throughout the rest of the book. We do venture into new territory that requires fresh signposts and markings. The ideas and arguments throughout are cumulative, and we give you ample preparation for each notion and symbol. Some unfamiliar terms are nothing more than shorthand descriptions of oft-used concepts that are not difficult in themselves. These will become clear through explication, context, and repetition. As for the math, it's not as difficult as it seems either—it's mainly addition and subtraction with some division and multiplication (and a little algebra if you do things the hard way in Appendix A). If you can handle that, then you are more than prepared for this chapter and what follows.

What Are Rules—and Why?

This chapter presents two so-called "mechanical" trading rules or procedures some investors regularly use to enhance their investment performance. What *is* a mechanical rule? One you can follow more or less automatically, step by step, without any need for judgment about market conditions. In fact, a mechanical rule is something a computer (even a fancy hand calculator) might easily be programmed to accomplish. So it is something people can manage easily as well.

You may have noticed that people are always eager to find a simple method that will make them a million dollars instantly. Let's be clear—there is no such animal. But there are investment techniques—derived directly from common sense—that tend to improve performance. Common sense, it turns out, is fairly uncommon, particularly in the markets where greed, fear, and all manner of passion tend to prevail. Hence, the advantage of mechanical rules is that they can immunize you from the unsteadying influence of your emotions and enforce the consistent application of reasoned decision making instead.

The first rule-based technique we will examine is dollar-cost averaging.

Dollar-Cost Averaging

Despite the impressive name, *dollar-cost averaging* means nothing more than investing equal dollar amounts at regular intervals—buying, for example, a fixed dollar amount (say, $1,000) of the same stock every quarter instead of (say) a fixed number of shares. Put this way, it sounds almost trivial. What's the point?

Dollar-cost averaging can be a powerful instrument when the item you are investing in fluctuates in price. Over time, buying a fixed dollar amount will cause you to buy fewer units when the price is high and more when the price is low. You've heard the classic advice, buy low and sell high? Dollar-cost averaging *forces* you to buy in quantity when prices are low and prevents you from buying much at high prices. If you follow its simple decree, your unit price will be lower than the market's average. You don't need extraordinary discipline or market savvy. Dollar-cost averaging does it for you.

How does it work? First of all, it doesn't depend on psychology—yours or the market's. According to one view of how the market works (called *contrary opinion theory*), the time to buy a particular investment is when everyone else is selling it, and the time to sell is when everyone else is buying. When the outlook is blackest, most people will have already sold, and the price will be depressed—the best time to get it cheap. On the other hand, when the news is wonderful and excitement is high, it's time to sell. Everyone has put his or her money in, pushing the price up, so there's no one left to buy. Demand is drained, and the price *has to* come down. Now, all this is straightforward in theory but difficult to put into practice. It isn't easy to swim against the tide. Dollar-cost averaging prevents you from riding your emotions and joining the herd by denying you the option of acting on impulse. It therefore insulates you from the fear that otherwise prevents you from buying at the bottom and guards against the greed that impels you to buy at the top.

To understand the dispassionate alternative that dollar-cost averaging offers, let's look at it in action. For the sake of illustration, suppose we have three stocks (though they could as easily be almost any other investment), one called Uptown Industries (which does nothing but go up), another called Nowhereland (which goes nowhere), and a third called Downtown Industries (which goes down

Table 3.1 Price History of Three Stocks

	1	2	3	4	Return
Uptown	$10	$15	$25	$30	+200%
Nowhereland	$10	$ 5	$15	$10	0%
Downtown	$10	$ 6	$ 1	$ 2	−80%

Table 3.2 Results for the Fixed-Share Investor

	Amount spent for 10 shares							
Investor A	**Year 1**	**Year 2**	**Year 3**	**Year 4**	**Total**	**Number of shares**	**Average cost per share**	**Average market price**
Uptown	$100	$150	$250	$300	$800	40	$20	$20
Nowhereland	$100	$ 50	$150	$100	$400	40	$10	$10
Downtown	$100	$ 60	$ 10	$ 20	$190	40	$ 4.75	$ 4.75

dramatically). Their share prices over a four-year period are shown in Table 3.1. The net return for an investor who bought these stocks in Year 1 and held them through Year 4 is given, too.

Now, let's consider how two investors with different strategies would fare in this situation. Investor A buys a fixed number of shares (say, 10) every year. Whatever the stock's price—$15, $25, or $5—he buys 10 shares. At the end of four years, he has 40 shares of each. But not all of the stocks cost the same. In fact, he paid $800 for Uptown Industries—10 shares at $10 ($100) the first year, then 10 shares at $15 ($150), 10 shares at $25 ($250), and finally 10 shares at $30 ($300). This means his average price per share is $20 ($800 divided by the 40 shares owned). Similarly, he spent $400 for Nowhereland (average share price $10) and $190 for Downtown Industries (average share price $4.75). Table 3.2 summarizes.

Investor B tries dollar-cost averaging. He buys the same fixed *dollar amount* of each stock ($150) every year, and thus will be spending exactly $600 on Uptown Industries, $600 on Nowhereland, and $600 on Downtown Industries over the four years. The question is: How many shares can he buy with that amount? In the case of Uptown Industries, Investor B buys 15 shares the first year. When it rises to $15 per share in the second year, he can afford only 10

Table 3.3 Results for the Dollar-Cost Averaging Investor

Investor B	Fixed dollar amount spent Year 1	Year 2	Year 3	Year 4	Total	Number of shares	Average cost per share	Average market price
Uptown	$150	$150	$150	$150	$600	36	$16.67	$20
Nowhereland	$150	$150	$150	$150	$600	70	$ 8.57	$10
Downtown	$150	$150	$150	$150	$600	265	$ 2.26	$ 4.75

Table 3.4 Comparison of the Two Strategies' Results

	Investor A			Investor B		
	Total investment	Current value	Net return	Total investment	Current value	Net return
Uptown	$ 800	$1,200	+50%	$ 600	$1,080	+80%
Nowhereland	$ 400	$ 400	0%	$ 600	$ 700	+17%
Downtown	$ 190	$ 80	−58%	$ 600	$ 530	−12%
TOTAL	$1,390	$1,680	+20.9%	$1,800	$2,310	+28.3%

shares. When it goes up to $25, his fixed $150 buys just 6 shares, and when it climbs to $30, he can buy no more than 5. So he winds up buying 36 shares for $600—an average cost of $16.67. We apply the same analysis to the other stocks with the results summarized in Table 3.3.

As you can see by comparing the average price per share columns in Tables 3.2 and 3.3, dollar-cost averaging enabled Investor B to pay less for his shares than Investor A in every case. For this reason alone, his net return is higher for all three stocks (see Table 3.4). You can also see from Tables 3.2 and 3.3 that Investor B wound up with 10 percent fewer shares of Uptown than Investor A. But he has more of each of the other stocks than Investor A, including a whopping 265 shares of Downtown Industries. If Downtown were to continue to decline, Investor B would not be helped by dollar-cost averaging. On the other hand, even a modest upturn would pay off because of his large holding of these low-cost shares. For example, if Downtown fell to $1 in Year 5, Investor B would buy 150 shares (in keeping with his program of spending $150 every year on each stock), giving him 415 shares all told. Their value would be $415 while their cost to him would be $750, a net loss of $335 (or −44.7 percent on his investment). However, if Downtown went up a dollar instead (to $3), Investor B would buy only 50 new shares, bringing his total shares to 315. But at $3, they would be worth $945. He would have *made* $195 on this stock, a positive net return of 26 percent—on a stock that declined in price by 70 percent!

All in all, Investor A paid $1,390 for stock now worth $1,680, giving him a net return of 20.9 percent. Investor B has $2,310 worth of stock for which he paid $1,800, a net return of 28.3 percent.

A pretty impressive result from such a modest action. A word of caution, however, about what dollar-cost averaging can and cannot do. It does not promise better results than *any* other method. Someone who put all his or her money into Uptown in Year 1 and sold it four years later would have outdistanced Investor A and B by far. Nothing beats a perfect job of picking the best investment, buying it low, and selling it high. But finding an investment's absolute bottom and absolute peak isn't easily done—if it can be done at all. That's where dollar-cost averaging comes in. It may not give you the best performance every time—someone somewhere might do better through brains, luck, or determination—but it does give you a leg up and, hence, a high probability of doing better than average.

The Practical Flaw in Dollar-Cost Averaging

Let's look again at the preceding example. Investor B lost money on Downtown Industries, but not as much as Investor A, because the large number of shares he purchased when the price dropped to $1 drastically reduced his average cost per share. On the flip side, Investor B wound up with only 36 shares of Uptown Industries, because dollar-cost averaging restricted him to purchasing fewer and fewer shares as its price soared. This alone does not necessarily constitute a major drawback. Investor B still obtained a favorable rate of return—better than Investor A's. He just spent less money on fewer shares, leaving him with more cash to invest elsewhere. On occasion, dollar-cost averaging's built-in penury may hurt, especially when an investment zooms ever skyward. This in itself is not a fatal flaw. There is, however, another more serious problem with dollar-cost averaging that demonstrates how its theoretical strengths can be negated in practice.

Suppose that in the next year, Year 5, every one of the stocks we just tracked fell to zero due to bankruptcy or some other calamity. In consequence, the stocks would be worthless. Investors A and B would lose their money—however many shares they had or whatever price they had paid. The moral of the story: If an investment's value continually falls and never recovers, no strategy in the world—nothing—can save it. Dollar-cost averaging can remain useful if a declining investment shows even the slightest degree of resilience, as when Downtown Industries moved from $1 to $2 in Year 4, enabling Investor B to recoup some of his losses. The value of his Downtown holdings jumped from $190 to $530, and his return improved from −67 percent to −12 percent.

Put another way, the practical flaw in dollar-cost averaging is this: It won't wring gains from a losing proposition. Dollar-cost averaging can improve the health of a temporarily ailing investment, but it cannot revive a lifeless one.

Dynamic Balancing

Imagine that you manage a multibillion-dollar pension fund. Bound by fiduciary duty to prudent investments like stocks and bonds, you take pains to avoid circumstances that might violate your conservative mandate (or lead to criticism). What if you resolve to keep half your fund in the bond market and half in the stock market, not risking too many eggs in either basket? Suppose that after 10 years the bonds have not moved but stocks have tripled. For each 2 dollars in the fund at the start, there are now four dollars ($1 in bonds, $3 in stocks), altogether a 100 percent gain. Great, right? Wrong.

Because now three-quarters of your fund is in stocks. Most of your eggs are in *one* basket. What if stock prices fall from $3 to a dollar and a half? With bonds still sitting at a dollar, your 100 percent gain just fell to 25 percent. You're fired!

Portfolio managers originally adopted dynamic balancing to help them avoid just such portfolio imbalances. But it has additional virtues that emerge under further investigation. Dollar-cost averaging, as you recall, showed us how to buy low but said nothing about selling. Dynamic balancing fills that role. Briefly, dynamic balancing means redistributing your holdings periodically according to some set proportion. The benefits of this simple rule can be considerable.

To take a real-life example: In 1987, the stock market zoomed to an all-time high early in the year before crashing in October. Interest rates rose for the first nine months of that year, which meant bond prices were declining. Meanwhile, the bull market in stocks was rising toward a peak. Over this period, anyone maintaining a dynamically balanced portfolio evenly split between stocks and bonds—with every dollar of stock matched by a dollar in bonds—would have been forced by his or her own rules into selling stocks to buy bonds. With stocks rising in value and bonds falling, a 50–50 apportionment at the start of 1987 would quickly become lopsided, just as in the example above. Repeated redistribution of funds would be required to restrain the stock market holdings at 50 percent.

After the crash, the Federal Reserve Board lowered interest rates to stimulate the economy. This caused the bond market to rally. At this point, a dynamic balancer would have taken a profit by selling some bonds to buy crash-depressed stocks. Whereas most people sold during or after the crash trying to salvage what they could, the dynamic balancer would have sold some of his or her stock holdings *before* the crash and bought afterwards. He or she would have been buying bonds before they rallied (cheap) and sold them after (dear). Thus, merely by maintaining a simple, prudent balance between sectors in his or her portfolio, the dynamic bal-

Table 3.5 Two Stocks Going Nowhere Slowly

	Year 1	Year 2	Year 3	Year 4	Return
Stock A	$12	$24	$ 6	$12	0%
Stock B	$12	$ 6	$24	$12	0%

ancer would have automatically made some well-timed buy-and-sell decisions.

Let's look at a simple example of dynamic balancing to see how dramatic the results can be. Consider two stocks, A and B. Although each starts at $12 and ends at $12 after four years, their prices gyrate wildly in the interim. Still, anyone who put his or her money in each and let it alone would have wound up with a net value that was static (see Table 3.5).

Given this scenario, how would you expect dynamic balancing to do? Let's take $24,000 and split our portfolio 50–50 between A and B. We buy 1,000 shares of each. By Year 2, prices change considerably. Stock A doubles in value while B falls by half. Thus, the total value of A and B is now $30,000. Following the dictates of dynamic balancing, we *rebalance* these accounts so that we again have half our total investment in each, just as we had at the start. That means keeping $15,000 (half of $30,000) in each stock. To do this, we sell $9,000 worth of A and use it to buy $9,000 of B. By the end of Year 3, prices have changed again. Stock A has dropped all the way to $6 while B has soared to $24. Our holdings in A are now valued at $3,750, one-quarter of their value the year before. But our equity in stock B has quadrupled to $60,000. Once again, we reapportion our investment so we have the same dollar amount in each stock by selling $28,125 worth of B and buying that much more of A. In Year 4, both stocks return to $12. This time A has doubled in value while B is worth half as much. Stock A is valued at $63,750 and B at $15,937.50. The final tally is $79,687.50, an astonishing net return of 232 percent for two stocks that essentially went nowhere. Table 3.6 summarizes this exercise.

You could say this example is unrealistic. Stocks don't triple that often, nor do they frequently fall by half. However, there are

Table 3.6 From Nowhere to Somewhere with Dynamic Balancing

	Year 1	**Year 2**	**Year 3**	**Year 4**
Price of A	$ 12	$ 24	$ 6	$ 12
Current value of A	$12,000	$24,000	$ 3,750	$63,750
Price of B	$ 12	$ 6	$ 24	$ 12
Current value of B	$12,000	$ 6,000	$60,000	$15,938
Total portfolio value	$24,000	$30,000	$63,750	$79,688
% change in portfolio value	—	+25%	+112.5%	+25%
Amount to be invested in each, to start the next period	$12,000	$15,000	$31,875	$39,844

Table 3.7 Price History of Stocks A and B

	Year 1	**Year 2**	**Year 3**	**Year 4**	**Year 5**	**Year 6**	**Year 7**	**Year 8**
A	$12	$24	$36	$24	$36	$45	$36	$24
B	$12	$12	$ 6	$ 9	$ 6	$ 3	$ 4	$ 6

investment vehicles (not necessarily stocks) that routinely exhibit precisely the behavior shown above in that they generally move inversely and yet, over the long haul, never get too far apart. For instance, a gold mining stock might soar in an inflationary period whereas a bond would collapse. And the reverse would be true in a deflationary era. There are even more volatile vehicles (such as puts and calls on commodity futures) that lie outside the scope of this book.

Nonetheless, let's look at a more indisputably realistic scenario involving two couples planning for retirement: Dynah and Mike, and Dynah's parents. Dynah and Mike have brought two stocks to her folks' attention. All expect the stocks to rise over the long run (see Table 3.7 for the price history of each). But both are looking for a fairly easy way to manage their accounts. Dynah's parents are content to buy and hold, splitting their funds equally between the two stocks. Their kids want to do something more aggressive. So they undertake a program of dynamic balancing.

Dynah's parents have put half their funds in A and half in B. For every dollar they put in, they get back $1.25, a 25 percent return. If they had put $12,000 in each stock, stock A would have returned $24,000 and stock B $6,000 for a total of $30,000.

Table 3.8 Value of the Dynamically Balanced Account Over Time

	Year 1	Year 2	Year 3	Year 4	Year 5	Year 6	Year 7	Year 8
Year-end value of A	$12,000	$24,000	$27,000	$12,000	$29,250	$26,406	$14,787	$13,144
Year-end value of B	$12,000	$12,000	$ 9,000	$27,000	$13,000	$10,563	$24,646	$29,575
Total	$24,000	$36,000	$36,000	$39,000	$42,250	$36,969	$39,433	$42,719
Amount to invest in A and B	$12,000	$18,000	$13,000	$19,500	$21,125	$18,485	$19,716	$21,360

Table 3.9 Shares Held in Dynamically Balanced Account Through Time

	Year 1	Year 2	Year 3	Year 4	Year 5	Year 6	Year 7	Year 8
A	1,000	750	500	812.5	586.8	410.8	547.7	547.7
B	1,000	1,500	3,000	2,166.7	3,520.8	6,161.4	4,929.1	4,929.1

Dynah and Mike, in contrast, rebalance their accounts each year to reestablish a 50–50 distribution. At the beginning, they buy $12,000 of each stock. At the end of Year 1, their investment in stock A doubled to $24,000 while their investment in stock B stood still at $12,000, so their portfolio is worth $36,000. To regain their original 50–50 balance, they must have $18,000 in each. To do this, they sell off some of stock A (in this case $6,000 worth) and buy more of B with the proceeds. They perform a similar rebalancing in succeeding years, always selling some of the stock that went up most (or down least) and buying the stock that went down most (or up least). Table 3.8 shows the value of their portfolio year by year. The number of shares owned after rebalancing is represented in Table 3.9.

In the end, Dynah and Mike have a net return of 77.9 percent, over three times better than Dynah's parents' conservative buy-and-hold strategy.

On the face of it, it doesn't seem possible to wring a better than 50 percent performance out of two stocks, one of which doubles in price while the other halves. But through dynamic balancing, you can. Dynamic balancing compels you to consistently sell (relatively) dear and buy (relatively) cheap.*

* For simplicity, we have ignored taxes in this and other examples. In tax-exempt retirement accounts, this omission would have no effect on the outcome.

Table 3.10 One of Two Investments Rises Temporarily

	Year 1	Year 2	Year 3	Year 4
Stock E	$12	$12	$12	$12
Stock F	$12	$12	$24	$12

Table 3.11 Two Investments Rise at Different Rates

	Year 1	Year 2	Year 3	Year 4
Stock G	$12	$15	$30	$30
Stock H	$12	$15	$15	$18

Table 3.12 Two Investments Fall at Different Rates

	Year 1	Year 2	Year 3	Year 4
Stock I	$12	$6	$2	$2
Stock J	$12	$4	$4	$2

For almost any pattern of prices we might choose,* dynamic balancing outperforms buying and holding. Even if just one of two investments rises temporarily, as in the example shown in Table 3.10, then a 50–50 dynamic balancing act will yield a return of 12.5 percent, compared to zero for someone who held both stocks for all four years (calculations omitted). Similarly, if both investments rise at different rates, as in Table 3.11, dynamic balancing noses out buying and holding 106.25 percent to 100 percent. If both investments fall at different rates, as in Table 3.12, the net return from buying and holding is −83.3 percent whereas the dynamic balancer loses slightly less, −79.2 percent.

The key to dynamic balancing's success is volatility. The more prices zig and zag, the better. Dynamic balancing does not require an investment to continually rise—in fact, as we have seen, it doesn't have to go anywhere, as long as it moves up and down. (If an investment just goes up and up, you don't have to be particularly

* An exception: If your various investments move up or down in lockstep, they never present an opportunity for rebalancing, and dynamic balancing does no better or worse than buying and holding.

Table 3.13 Two Diverging Investments

	Year 1	Year 2	Year 3
Stock C	$12	$24	$36
Stock D	$12	$ 6	$ 0

clever to make money. There's a saying on the Street: "Don't confuse genius with a bull market.")

Three final points about dynamic balancing: (a) Whereas dollar-cost averaging applies to a single investment, dynamic balancing operates in the context of a portfolio of two *or more* investments. It need not be limited to two. (b) In our original example, Dynah and Mike rebalanced every year, but the period within which rebalancing occurs can be any length—years, months, or days. (c) You can also divide funds in any proportion. A 50–50 split was chosen merely for simplicity. You might decide, for example, to dynamically balance a portfolio this way: 50 percent stocks, 30 percent bonds, and 20 percent precious metals.

The Problem with Dynamic Balancing

What happens if you select two investments—any at all—and one shoots straight up and the other straight down, no fluctuations? Dynamic balancing would force you repeatedly and perpetually to sell the one that was rising and buy the one that was sinking. You would wind up worse off than someone who just bought and held because you would be taking profits too soon on the rising investment and then plowing it back into the one that was diving.

Let's look at a specific scenario of this sort. Suppose Dynah's parents bought two other stocks and decided to hold them. The net return for a buy-and-hold portfolio holding equal measures of stocks C and D (Table 3.13) would be 50 percent, $1.50 for every dollar invested (no thanks to D).

What if they used dynamic balancing to maintain a 50–50 split? The value of their holdings would be as in Table 3.14.

Table 3.14 Value of Two Diverging Investments Over Time

	Period 1	Period 2	Period 3	Return
Stock C	$12,000	$24,000	$22,500	87.5%
Stock D	$12,000	$6,000	$0	−100%

The result is a net *loss* of 6.25 percent. In this case and others like it, dynamic balancing won't work. In its defense, certain types of investments, like a blue chip mutual fund, are not going to hit zero. Neither is a bond mutual fund. For a government bond to fall to nothing is virtually impossible. They all may head down for a time, even a long time, but they are unlikely to become completely worthless. The problem remains, however, that dynamic balancing (like dollar-cost averaging) cannot vouch for the character of the investment to which it is applied. If that investment is destined for zero, it doesn't matter whether you buy it every Tuesday, at its lowest price each month, or when the moon is full. Under those circumstances, no strategy will make you money or, for that matter, leave you a cent. But there is a safe way to avoid such deadbeat investments and employ dynamic balancing without hindrances. As we shall see in Part II, the answer is Plan Z.

Part II

The Varieties of Plan Z

4

The Problem with Dollar-Cost Averaging

Using dollar-cost averaging with zeros appears to be a good idea. Why not boost your yield by lowering the average cost of your zeros? Because they are destined to rise in price, zeros appear to eliminate what we have identified as the practical flaw in dollar-cost averaging. Indeed, in the last year or so, a handful of new zero coupon bond mutual funds has emerged, advertising their use of dollar-cost averaging, and a recent book on zero coupon investments offers the following advice: "Over long periods, dollar-cost averaging can work powerfully for IRA contributions to zero funds. You can have the growth of zeros plus the purchase advantages associated with dollar-cost averaging."*

As attractive as the idea may look, though, *it won't work.* As we shall see, a subtle but serious problem arises when dollar-cost

* Donald R. Nichols, *The New Dow Jones-Irwin Guide to Zero Coupon Investments* (Homewood, Ill.: Dow Jones-Irwin, 1989), p. 117.

averaging is applied to zeros. In finding out *why* this is so, we shall gain considerably in our understanding of the distinctive nature of zero coupon bonds—and what *will* work.

Dollar-Cost Averaging with Zero Coupon Bonds: Computer Simulations

Let's start by seeing what happens when we buy zeros using dollar-cost averaging.* The first series of simulations matches two investors: One puts his money in cash (or T-bills, a money market fund, or CDs), and the other purchases zeros using dollar-cost averaging (a strategy we will call ZA for *Z*eros with dollar-cost *A*veraging). Results will be computed for periods of 15 and 25 years. Each investor makes an initial deposit of $2,000 and contributes $2,000 annually (following the dictates of dollar-cost averaging). The ZA investor buys zeros of progressively shorter maturity lengths (25, 24, and 23 years, and so on, and 15, 14, and 13 years, and so on). He does this because, like many long-term investors, he has a specific goal in mind and wants all his bonds to mature at the time he will need the funds. So he keeps only zeros with the same maturity date.

Table 4.1 compresses 13 possible future scenarios exploring the consequences of constantly falling interest rates. The beginning rates are set at 4, 6, 8, and 10 percent. These are set to drop at various speeds—by .05, .1, and .15 percent annually. We make a concession to reality and grant the zero investor a 1 percent premium in interest rates. Normally, long-term rates are higher than short-term ones and zero investors get a better rate of return—at least 1 percent (and in the past couple of years, 3 or 4) higher than cash.

As you can see, zeros outperform cash in every single instance, most dramatically where interest rates are highest and fall fastest.

* The examples in this chapter (and the rest) are hypothetical rather than historical. Zero coupon bonds have not been around long enough to compile a conclusive record and Plan Z is an even more recent invention.

Table 4.1 Dollar-Cost Averaging with Zeros when Interest Rates Are Falling

				$ Results					
		To this rate, after:		15 years			25 years		
Initial interest rate	Drops each year by	15 years	25 years	Cash	Zeros	Difference	Cash	Zeros	Difference
4%	0.05%	3.25%	2.75%	43,515	48,701	11.92%	82,178	102,397	24.60%
	0.10%	2.50%	1.50%	41,845	47,942	14.57%	73,478	98,036	33.42%
6%	0.05%	5.25%	4.75%	52,046	58,411	12.23%	111,329	140,291	26.01%
	0.10%	4.50%	3.50%	50,033	57,543	15.01%	99,265	134,677	35.67%
	0.15%	3.75%	2.25%	48,097	56,690	17.87%	88,540	129,350	46.09%
8%	0.05%	7.25%	6.75%	62,469	70,279	12.50%	152,671	194,245	27.23%
	0.10%	6.50%	5.50%	60,039	69,284	15.40%	135,838	186,987	37.65%
	0.15%	5.75%	4.25%	57,702	68,307	18.38%	120,879	180,072	48.97%
10%	0.05%	9.25%	8.75%	75,205	84,788	12.74%	211,494	271,233	28.25%
	0.10%	8.50%	7.50%	72,270	83,646	15.74%	187,897	261,780	39.32%
	0.15%	7.75%	6.25%	69,446	82,524	18.83%	166,925	252,784	51.44%
	0.20%	7.00%	5.00%	66,729	81,421	22.02%	148,296	244,224	64.69%
	0.25%	6.25%	3.75%	64,114	80,337	25.30%	131,755	236,078	79.18%

One reason is that zeros, as long-term instruments, lock in a rate of return. The higher rates secured in the early years raised ZA's overall yield. On the other hand, CDs or T-bills, because they are short-term, periodically force *all* funds to the current interest rate. When rates are falling, there is no recourse but to accept an ever-diminishing yield.

What if interest rates move steadily upward instead? Table 4.2 provides the answer. All aspects of the scenario are otherwise identical to the ones described in Table 4.1.

In the case of steadily rising rates, zeros occasionally underperform cash—particularly when rates rise most steeply. The same property that benefited ZA when rates fell every year (that zeros can lock in rates for a long time) becomes a detriment when rates perpetually rise. One thing that we should point out: This scenario is as unlikely as the one that preceded it. Interest rates usually fluctuate and rarely, if ever, rise or fall uninterrupted—certainly not for as long as 15 or 25 years.

Next, we'll inject some more variability into our interest rate assumptions. In Table 4.3, interest rates will be the same at the beginning and end of the period but fluctuate in between. Rates move in a uniform curve resembling a sine wave (Figure 4.1), but the frequency of peaks and valleys differs from example to example. We have specified an upper and lower limit for rates and allowed for a varying number of cycles. Rates essentially move sideways in a smoothly flowing manner but with different degrees of volatility, depending on the number of oscillations in each period.

Once again, ZA beats cash handily (Table 4.3). In fact, this has been the case in all but a few instances in all three tables thus far—and those few embodied fairly unrealistic assumptions about interest rates. But to what can we attribute ZA's success? Is dollar-cost averaging lowering Plan Z's average price and thereby raising its yield (as we saw in Chapter 3)? Or can ZA's advantage be traced to the higher rate of return that accompanies all long-term instruments? To be absolutely sure, let's recompute the previous scenarios, this time removing the 1 percent premium zeros have (rightfully) been allowed to enjoy (Table 4.4).

Table 4.2 Dollar-Cost Averaging with Zeros when Interest Rates Are Rising

Initial interest rate	Rises each year by	To this rate, after:		Results					
				15 years			25 years		
		15 years	25 years	Cash	Zeros	Difference	Cash	Zeros	Difference
4%	0.05%	4.75%	5.25%	47,055	50,259	6.81%	102,942	111,856	8.66%
	0.10%	5.50%	6.50%	48,930	51,060	4.35%	115,285	116,981	1.47%
6%	0.05%	6.75%	7.25%	56,312	60,194	6.89%	140,150	152,444	8.77%
	0.10%	7.50%	8.50%	58,571	61,109	4.33%	157,292	159,015	1.10%
	0.15%	8.25%	9.75%	60,919	62,041	1.84%	176,551	165,940	−6.01%
8%	0.05%	8.75%	9.25%	67,616	72,322	6.96%	192,895	209,944	8.84%
	0.10%	9.50%	10.50%	70,341	73,371	4.31%	216,822	218,416	0.74%
	0.15%	10.25%	11.75%	73,172	74,438	1.73%	243,702	227,332	−6.72%
10%	0.05%	10.75%	11.25%	81,422	87,131	7.01%	267,866	291,609	8.86%
	0.10%	11.50%	12.50%	84,712	88,332	4.27%	301,386	302,582	0.40%
	0.15%	12.25%	13.75%	88,130	89,555	1.62%	339,028	314,113	−7.35%
	0.20%	13.00%	15.00%	91,679	90,799	−0.96%	381,278	326,232	−14.44%
	0.25%	13.75%	16.25%	95,365	92,064	−3.46%	428,675	338,967	−20.93%

Table 4.3 Dollar-Cost Averaging with Zeros when Interest Rates Are Oscillating

Initial/Final interest rate	High/Low	Number of oscillations	Results					
			15 years			25 years		
			Cash	Zeros	Difference	Cash	Zeros	Difference
4%	3% ↔ 5%	1	44,358	50,902	14.75%	88,914	113,438	27.58%
		2	44,813	50,215	12.05%	90,393	110,653	22.41%
		5	45,130	49,724	10.18%	91,374	108,683	18.94%
6%	5% ↔ 7%	1	53,130	61,101	15.00%	121,069	155,706	28.61%
		2	53,640	60,246	12.32%	122,889	151,780	23.51%
		5	54,000	59,613	10.39%	124,143	148,754	19.82%
6%	4% ↔ 8%	1	52,131	63,101	21.04%	117,355	166,853	42.18%
		2	53,125	61,398	15.57%	120,844	159,078	31.64%
		5	53,839	60,127	11.68%	123,304	152,987	24.07%
8%	6% ↔ 10%	1	62,722	76,052	21.25%	162,065	231,801	43.03%
		2	63,835	73,963	15.87%	166,338	221,171	32.96%
		5	64,648	72,333	11.89%	169,511	211,940	25.03%
10%	7% ↔ 13%	1	74,409	95,241	28.00%	220,067	350,556	59.30%
		2	76,227	91,460	19.98%	227,552	329,661	44.87%
		5	77,606	88,324	13.81%	233,612	308,686	32.14%

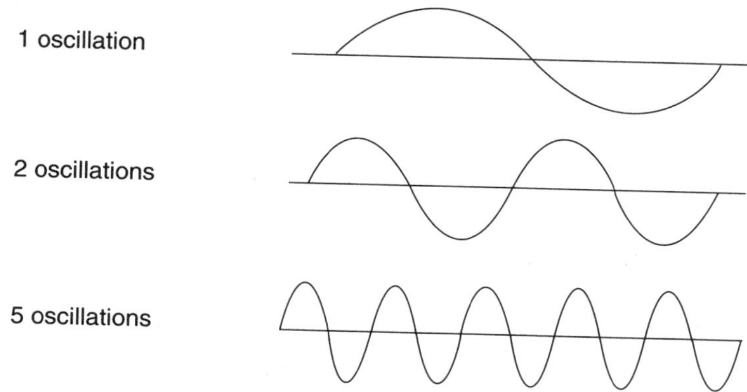

Figure 4.1 Idealized interest rate fluctuations.

As before, ZA bests cash—but not by nearly as much. With a long-term rate advantage of 1 percent, ZA had outdone cash by 16.35 percent after 15 years and by 41.73 percent after 25 years (when we averaged the results of all Table 4.1's entries). Stripped of this edge, ZA's lead in Table 4.4 slips to only 6.02 percent after 15 years and 20.2 percent after 25.*

When we turn to constantly rising rates, ZA, now shorn of its premium, no longer outperforms cash at all (Table 4.5). In fact, where it once led by an average of 3.52 percent after 15 years (Table 4.2), it is now *behind* by 5.52 percent. When it had its higher long-term rate working for it, Plan ZA was behind cash by 1.28 percent after 25 years. Without that edge, it lags by 15.72 percent on average (Table 4.5).

Similarly, removing the interest rate premium from the oscillating rate scenario also reduces the uniform advantage of zeros over cash by nearly 10 percentage points (on average) after 15 years and almost 20 percentage points after 25 years (Tables 4.6 and 4.3).

What have we learned? Any enhancements of performance by the ZA strategy appear to be of roughly the same magnitude that

* Percentages of this kind, here and throughout the book, are the average lead or lag, and are not based on the average *dollar* difference. This method affords some protection from skewing by extreme results and gives every individual scenario equal weight.

Table 4.4 Falling Rates Revisited, with Zeros Denied Their Normal Premium

Initial interest rate	Drops each year by	To this rate after:		Results					
				15 years			25 years		
		15 years	25 years	Cash	Zeros	Difference	Cash	Zeros	Difference
4%	0.05%	3.25%	2.75%	43,515	44,529	2.33%	82,178	87,887	6.95%
	0.10%	2.50%	1.50%	41,845	43,820	4.72%	73,478	84,034	14.37%
6%	0.05%	5.25%	4.75%	52,046	53,312	2.43%	111,329	119,682	7.50%
	0.10%	4.50%	3.50%	50.033	52,501	4.93%	99,265	114,737	15.59%
	0.15%	3.75%	2.25%	48,097	51,705	7.50%	88,540	110,049	24.29%
8%	0.05%	7.25%	6.75%	62,469	64,047	2.53%	152,671	164,883	8.00%
	0.10%	6.50%	5.50%	60,039	63,118	5.13%	135,838	158,499	16.68%
	0.15%	5.75%	4.25%	57,702	62,205	7.80%	120,879	152,439	26.11%
10%	0.05%	9.25%	8.75%	75,205	77,170	2.61%	211,494	229,320	8.43%
	0.10%	8.50%	7.50%	72,270	76,104	5.31%	187,897	221,036	17.64%
	0.15%	7.75%	6.25%	69,446	75,057	8.08%	166,925	213,159	27.70%
	0.20%	7.00%	5.00%	66,729	74,028	10.94%	148,296	205,669	38.69%
	0.25%	6.25%	3.75%	64,114	73,016	13.88%	131,755	198,547	50.69%

Table 4.5 Rising Rates Revisited, with Zeros Denied Their Normal Premium

Initial interest rate	Rises each year by	To this rate after:		Results					
				15 years			25 years		
		15 years	25 years	Cash	Zeros	Difference	Cash	Zeros	Difference
4%	0.05%	4.75%	5.25%	47,055	45,986	−2.27%	102,942	96,251	−6.50%
	0.10%	5.50%	6.50%	48,930	46,735	−4.49%	115,285	100,787	−12.58%
6%	0.05%	6.75%	7.25%	56,312	54,979	−2.37%	140,150	130,396	−6.96%
	0.10%	7.50%	8.50%	58,571	55,835	−4.67%	157,292	136,195	−13.41%
	0.15%	8.25%	9.75%	60,919	56,707	−6.91%	176,551	142,310	−19.39%
8%	0.05%	8.75%	9.25%	67,616	65,955	−2.46%	192,895	178,686	−7.37%
	0.10%	9.50%	10.50%	70,341	66,935	−4.84%	216,822	186,143	−14.15%
	0.15%	10.25%	11.75%	73,172	67,932	−7.16%	243,702	193,996	−20.40%
10%	0.05%	10.75%	11.25%	81,422	79,357	−2.54%	267,866	247,196	−7.72%
	0.10%	11.50%	12.50%	84,712	80,480	−5.00%	301,386	256,832	−14.78%
	0.15%	12.25%	13.75%	88,130	81,622	−7.38%	339,028	266,966	−21.26%
	0.20%	13.00%	15.00%	91,679	82,783	−9.70%	381,278	277,624	−27.19%
	0.25%	13.75%	16.25%	95,365	83,966	−11.95%	428,675	288,832	−32.62%

Table 4.6 Oscillating Rates Revisited, with Zeros Denied Their Normal Premium

			Results					
			15 years			25 years		
Initial/Final interest rate	High/Low	Number of oscillations	Cash	Zeros	Difference	Cash	Zeros	Difference
4%	3% ↔ 5%	1	44,358	46,517	4.87%	88,914	97,223	9.34%
		2	44,813	45,905	2.44%	90,393	94,904	4.99%
		5	45,130	45,474	0.76%	91,374	93,323	2.13%
6%	5% ↔ 7%	1	53,130	55,747	4.93%	121,069	132,732	9.63%
		2	53,640	54,979	2.50%	122,889	129,413	5.31%
		5	54,000	54,421	0.78%	124,143	126,968	2.28%
6%	4% ↔ 8%	1	52,131	57,533	10.36%	117,355	141,972	20.98%
		2	53,125	56,003	5.42%	120,844	135,387	12.03%
		5	53,839	54,883	1.94%	123,304	130,461	5.80%
8%	6% ↔ 10%	1	62,722	69,254	10.41%	162,065	196,488	21.24%
		2	63,835	67,365	5.53%	166,338	187,370	12.64%
		5	64,648	65,924	1.97%	169,511	179,861	6.11%
10%	7% ↔ 13%	1	74,409	86,609	16.40%	220,067	296,144	34.57%
		2	76,227	83,169	9.11%	227,552	227,958	22.15%
		5	77,606	80,389	3.59%	233,612	260,787	11.63%

would result simply from the compounding of its 1 percent premium. Denied this, ZA's dominance over cash is so slight as to be, in some cases, nonexistent. In Chapter 3 Dynah and Mike were able to capitalize on just a few broad fluctuations to almost triple their stake. Here, after *25 years* of the interest rate volatility that dollar-cost averaging supposedly thrives on (though without a premium), ZA could not at any time advance much more than 50 percent beyond the mere passive holding of cash. In fact, ZA's average increase in performance was closer to 10 percent, a slim superiority indeed after 25 long years. This is clearly *not* what we were led to expect from dollar-cost averaging. Accordingly, we must conclude that the superior performance of ZA presented in Tables 4.1 to 4.3 was due primarily to the rate premium allotted it and that dollar-cost averaging—*in contradiction to everything we know so far*—contributed little or nothing. How can this be?

Constant Duration versus Constant Maturity

Let's make one final attempt to revive dollar-cost averaging. To this point, all our examples have employed zeros of a constant maturity. Constant maturities are what you have when all the zeros in your investment plan mature at a single date. However, if you continually adjust your portfolio so your zeros' *time to maturity* remains the same—selling your old ones and buying new ones so you always have zeros with, for instance, 20 years left until they expire—then you are invested in zeros of a *constant duration.* For example, if you buy a few zeros every year, all designed to mature in the year you expect to retire (say, 2025), then regardless of when they were purchased or issued, your portfolio consists of zeros of a *constant maturity.* If, on the other hand, you buy two 30-year zeros, sell them a year later (after they've become 29-year zeros), and buy two new ones that are (again) 30 years from maturity, then your portfolio would contain zeros of a constant duration. In one case, the maturity date is fixed, so the time to maturity gradually decreases; in the other, the time to maturity is fixed, pushing the maturity date one year forward with every year that passes.

The characteristics of a zero of constant maturity change over time; specifically, its volatility diminishes and its price tends to rise. When you buy a zero in 1995 that matures in 2025, you're buying a 30-year zero. Ten years later, when you buy a zero of the same maturity date—one that also matures in 2025—you're buying a 20-year zero, an essentially different investment with different characteristics. You're comparing apples to oranges when you try to "average" them. No average is possible because they're not commensurate. (As Branch Rickey once said, take a man with one leg in a bucket of ice and the other on fire—on average, that man is comfortable.) When you attempt to average zeros of a constant maturity on the basis of their prices at different times—what dollar-cost averaging was doing in Tables 4.1 through 4.6—then you are doing something nearly as meaningless. When you dollar-cost average with zeros of a constant maturity, you are not necessarily buying something cheaper just because its price is lower—because as time goes on, you are not buying the same thing.

In Chapter 3, when we used dollar-cost averaging with stocks, the characteristics of each investment remained identical through time. Stock A was always Stock A and Stock B was always Stock B. Only their prices changed, and dollar-cost averaging made its decisions by comparing those prices at different times. The characteristics of a zero, however, do change through time (it gets closer to maturity; its volatility decreases; it moves further along its hypothetical growth curve). True, all zeros change their characteristics in the same way, which permits us to regard them as being equal in an important sense. Nevertheless, the mere fact that their characteristics change—equally or not—means that a dollar-cost averager is not really buying the identical item from one year to the next. *This is the reason that the use of dollar-cost averaging couldn't help ZA's performance,* why dollar-cost averaging will not work its magic with zeros despite the claims for its effectiveness made by several recent public investment offerings. There is a difference between being equal and being identical. It just doesn't make sense—in fact it's an error—to compare prices at different times (exactly what dollar-cost averaging does) unless those prices refer to the *identical* item.

So let us now try to compare apples to apples by using zeros of constant duration instead. These *do* have the same time to maturity and hence the identical inherent characteristics. Remember that to maintain zeros of constant *duration* in an account, each year we sell out our old zeros (which have changed—they've matured by one year), and we replace them with new zeros having the identical characteristics the old ones had at the time we'd bought *them.* This means we are always buying the same apples, and prices paid in different years should be validly comparable and properly susceptible to dollar-cost averaging.

Three scenarios have been extracted from Table 4.6 to create Table 4.7, to examine what happens when zeros of a constant duration are purchased. Otherwise, the same assumptions hold: The cash and zero investors have each made an initial deposit of $2,000 to which they add another $2,000 every year. The interest rate premium for long-term rates has been suppressed to better focus on the isolated effect of dollar-cost averaging.

As you can tell by comparing the results of Table 4.7 with those of Table 4.6, the constant duration zeros do not perform appreciably better than the constant maturities. It seems that, whether we use zeros of either kind, dollar-cost averaging just won't work.

The Price of Time

Where have the vaunted benefits of dollar-cost averaging gone? Does this mean Chapter 3 was wrong about dollar-cost averaging? Definitely not . . . when it comes to equities. We clearly saw dollar-cost averaging help investors buy wisely by leading them to purchase stocks at lower than average prices. But something has been lost in the translation to zeros. Why is dollar-cost averaging—a poten-

Table 4.7 Dollar-Cost Averaging with Constant-*Duration* Zeros

Initial/Final interest rate	High/Low	Number of oscillations	Duration	15 years			25 years		
				Cash	Zeros	Difference	Cash	Zeros	Difference
4%	3% ↔ 5%	1	10	44,358	44,751	0.89%	88,914	90,149	1.39%
		2	20	44,813	45,477	1.48%	90,393	92,253	2.06%
		5	30	45,130	46,053	2.05%	91,374	93,661	2.50%
6%	4% ↔ 8%	1	10	52,131	53,519	2.66%	117,355	122,075	4.02%
		2	20	53,125	55,753	4.95%	120,844	128,806	6.59%
		5	30	53,839	57,901	7.54%	123,304	134,304	8.92%
10%	7% ↔ 13%	1	10	74,409	78,671	5.73%	220,067	238,244	8.26%
		2	20	76,227	84,257	10.53%	227,552	259,536	14.06%
		5	30	77,606	89,751	15.65%	233,612	277,479	18.78%

tially powerful technique for equity investors—so feeble in combination with zero coupon bonds?

First of all, buying stocks "wisely" *always* means buying them cheap—that is, getting them at a relatively low price. But among zeros, the best buy is the one with the highest *yield*—something to which price is (at best) a fitful guide. The proof of this is that zeros with different prices can have identical yields, and identically priced zeros can have different yields. Look at points A and B in Figure 4.2 (the universal zero map introduced in Chapter 2), which represent two zeros. Although identically priced at 50, these two investments could not be more different. One is a 4 percent zero with 17 years to maturity and the other a 19 percent zero 4 years to maturity. Consider now a single zero, one that matures in 2025. Has a person who pays a price of 49 for it in the year 2000 bought it "cheaper" than someone who pays 51 in the year 2024? No. The former will slightly more than double his money over 25 years, whereas the latter will slightly less than double his—but he'll do it only *one* year. So, although he paid a slightly higher price (perhaps he bought the zero from the first investor), he made a far, far better purchase than the earlier investor. The moral to the story is that *the "cheapest" zero is not the one with the lowest price, but the one that climbs at the steepest angle to par—that is, the one with the highest yield.* Which, for example, of the two prices shown in Figure 4.3 is more desirable, 20 or 60? Because of the different timing of the purchases, 60 is actually a better deal, because its angle of ascent to 100 is greater from that point. In effect, the zero purchased at 20 is not the same vehicle as the one bought at 60—so much so that *it makes no sense to compare their absolute prices.*

Remember, to identify a zero you need to state at least two of the three characteristics that define it. Only when the times to maturity are exactly the same can price alone be a useful means of comparing yields. Dollar-cost averaging is unidimensional. Its sole focus is price. When you try to apply dollar-cost averaging to zeros, a critical dimension is entirely overlooked: the dimension of time.

The most essential characteristic of any zero is its time to maturity. After all, what *is* a zero? Accreted interest. And what is

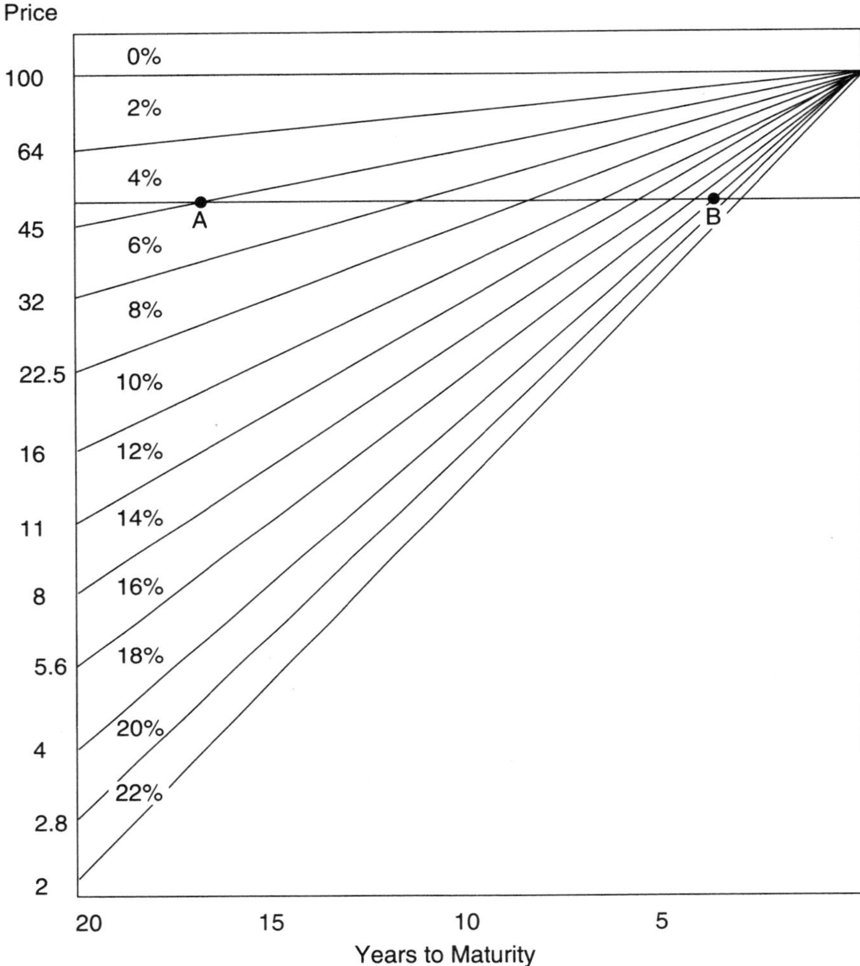

Figure 4.2 How two prices can be the same—but very different.

interest? The price of time. Time is what creates interest. In the world of fixed instruments, "price" is shorthand for the passage of time. When you lend money, you sell time, and when you borrow money, you buy it. Knowing this, you cannot evaluate a zero without asking in some form or other the question: When?

The money value of time is something with which we are all familiar. If you had $105 in a passbook savings account after a year

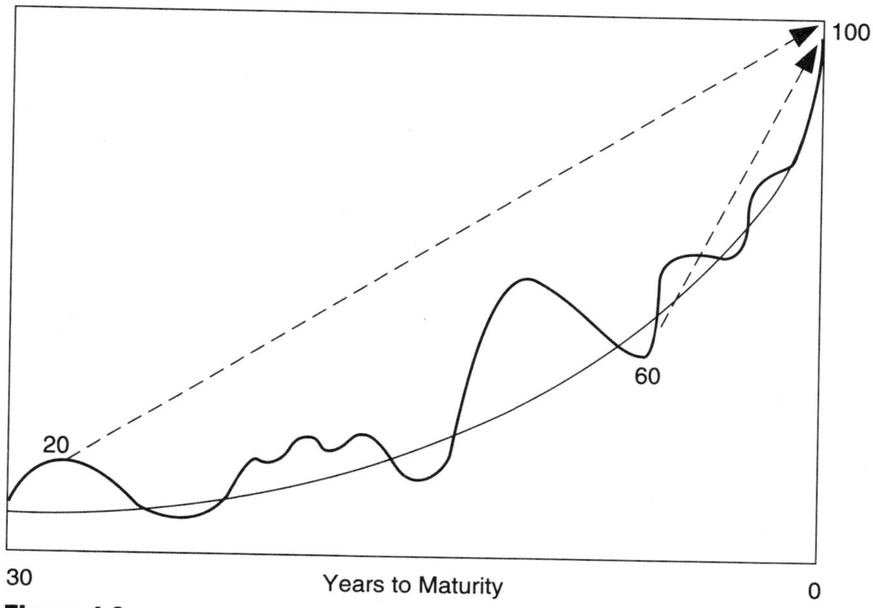

Figure 4.3

of earning 5 percent interest, you would probably not be tempted to think, "What a genius I was to have bought this passbook for only $100 last year," because you know that $105 today is equivalent to, and not more than, $100 a year ago. All you were getting was the current interest rate (an average deal). To compare two zeros from different periods by merely looking at their relative price would be just as misguided.

From Here to Maturity

It would be helpful at this point to track the equity of one of our simulations year by year. Let's lift the lid on the final scenarios recorded on the bottom lines of both Tables 4.6 and 4.7—the ones that played out the consequences of an initial 10 percent rate that had five oscillations ranging between 7 percent and 13 percent—and look at what was actually happening rather than rely on a summary of the whole or glimpses at a few isolated points. Figure 4.4 plots the current worth at year's end for the cash and ZA investments from both tables.

Whereas Tables 4.6 and 4.7 provided us with a snapshot of the 25th year of these investments, Figure 4.4 allows us to see what was going on all along. You can see that although all three investments finished in close order, they arrived there by markedly different routes. In fact, if all had been abandoned in the 24th year, then the constant duration zeros would have been worth more than twice as much as either of the other two. It is clear too that both forms of ZA do in fact repeatedly bestow a return superior to cash, *only to reclaim it again and again.* The investment that used constant maturities always remained closely bound to the level of cash point by point, whereas the zeros of constant duration did succeed in pulling much further away from cash at regular intervals—at one point dramatically. But no matter how high they soared, they were always yanked back again when interest rates next turned up.

What we learn from Figure 4.4 is that dollar-cost averaging, in the case of zeros of a constant duration, *does* come somewhat closer to making good on its promise—but only temporarily.* In order for the investor to reap the rewards it continually dangles before him, he must be lucky enough to close his account before they are snatched away.

Why does dollar-cost averaging not help the investor preserve his gains? For one thing, it's a one-sided activity. It helps him only to buy better, but says nothing about selling. In every scenario in this chapter, zeros have been bought and held. None were sold.** Each account remained fully invested in zeros at all times, so profits piled up when interest rates fell (because zero prices climbed) but remained perpetually exposed to loss when interest rates rose (and zero prices fell back). Dollar-cost averaging did indeed help our

* Note that using zeros of a constant duration gains something, but not without some cost. You sacrifice your immunity from market risk to some degree because of the increased volatility.

** Technically, to maintain a constant maturity, zeros are sold—but only to be replaced via the immediate reinvestment in other zeros. They were not, however, sold *out* in the sense of reducing the amount of the investor's commitment in dollar terms.

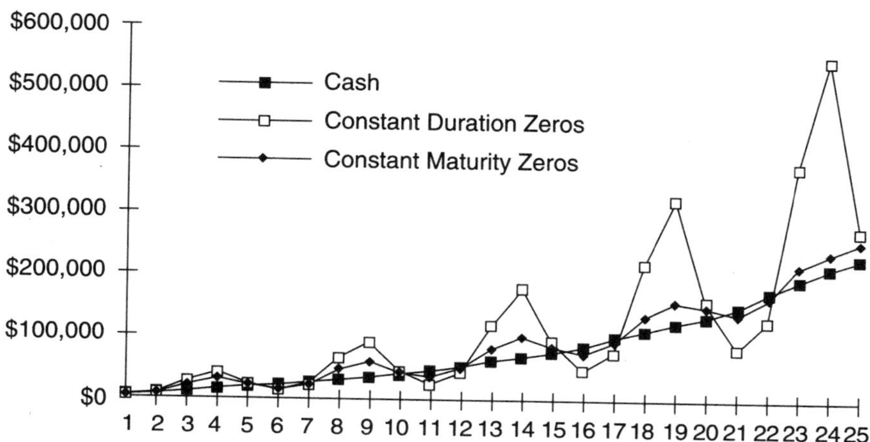

Figure 4.4 Growth paths of three investment strategies in an environment of interest rates oscillating between 7% and 13%.

several investors buy more zeros when rates were low, but the zeros were not disposed of at a particularly opportune time, if at all. Dollar-cost averaging makes no provision for cashing out. You can't "dollar-cost *sell.*"

But why should this matter? Wasn't this the case for dollar-cost averaging when we saw it work in Chapter 3? Yes, but zeros are different. True, dollar-cost averaging enables us to buy more zeros at low prices—all it ever promised to do. But not only is price alone not a relevant consideration in evaluating zero coupon bonds; *how many you buy* is not important either. What *is* critical is the *dollar amount* of money you invest in a zero *at a given yield.*

Zeros are fixed instruments, not stocks. *They are debt, not equity.* When you buy additional shares of stock, you are acquiring more units of something, whether a factory or the legal fiction (the corporation) that comprises it. When you buy a zero, you're not really *buying* anything; you're lending money. You don't own something—someone else owes *you* something. One more zero will not give you another piece of anything. It is merely an opportunity to lend more. The zero investor's goal is not to pile up more zeros at relatively low prices but *to lend more money at higher rates.* If you bought $1,000 worth of zeros and rates dropped so prices doubled,

Table 4.8 Zeros and Stocks Are Affected in Different Ways by the Same Investment Strategies

	Fixed quantity	**Dollar-cost averaging**	**Plan Z**
Zeros	Below-average yield	Average yield	Above-average yield
Stocks	Average yield	Above-average yield	—

would it matter if you held 20 zeros at $50 each or 50 zeros at $20? No, it wouldn't. In either form your money would double. The main thing is the amount of money you invest, not the number of zeros it buys.

Technically, zeros of different maturities are not "fungible" as stocks, dollars, and commodities are—that is, they are not indistinguishable units readily exchanged one for another. The form of the transaction we undertake when we "purchase" zeros fools us into thinking we are buying some "thing" with a "price" when all we are doing is lending money.

The purchase of a zero at a low price is desirable, for only one reason: if it offers a chance to lend your dollars at a high rate. A zero is merely a container for your dollars, and its price tells you how many of them it will hold. Sure, you can "buy" more zeros for your money at lower prices. But the important fact is the number of dollars you can place in high-rate containers, *not* the number of containers themselves. If you had two savings accounts of $55 each versus one with $110, which would give you more? Clearly, neither. Two accounts or one account, their value would be identical and your net worth would be the same. The number of accounts, like the number of zeros, is beside the point. What matters is how many dollars they hold at what rate of interest.

With dollar-cost averaging, the number of dollars you invest in any period is (by definition) fixed. You *can't* lend more money at higher rates. In fact, you're always lending the same amount of money at *every* rate, which is why dollar-cost averaging with zeros (of whatever kind) has results that approximate the average yield. What works with equities does not work in the same way with zeros (Table 4.8). If you buy a fixed number of shares of stock each period, you get an average return. But that same method garners a *below-average* return with zeros. Dollar-cost averaging with equities generally grants a return that is above average. With zeros, dollar-cost averaging is necessary *simply to lift your return to average.*

Let's look at the fallacy of dollar-cost averaging with zero coupon bonds from one final perspective. Because dollar-cost averaging is by definition *fixed-dollar investing,* it forces you to lend the same number of dollars at each interest rate. What if you were to use dollar-cost averaging with zeros, investing $2,000 every year? You buy $2,000 worth the first year when rates are at 8 percent. The next year, rates rise to 10 percent, and you scoop up "cheap" zeros by the bucketful. In accordance with the dictates of dollar-cost averaging, your constant $2,000 has bought you more zeros at cheap prices and fewer zeros at high prices. But the relevant fact is that you have locked in a 10 percent return on $2,000 and an 8 percent return on another $2,000, regardless of the *number* of zeros it took to accomplish this. Because your $4,000 is riding 50–50 at 8 percent and 10 percent, your average yield will be 9 percent—exactly the average rate for the two periods and no better, despite your having bought many cheap zeros and few dear ones. Dollar-cost averaging with zeros cannot give you what Plan Z can: better-than-average returns. When you combine dollar-cost averaging with zero coupon bonds, all you succeed in doing is getting the average interest rate. (You may have a lower-than-average *purchase* price, but that may mean only that you bought more zeros early and fewer late, obtaining a low "average" price as your zeros moved along the *same* growth curve, getting the *same* yield.) This explains why the performance of the zeros in Figure 4.4 flutters about, but remains closely tied to, the yield offered by cash.

What motivates investors to use dollar-cost averaging is the notion that it is possible to improve their investment return by systematic speculation. But speculation in fixed instruments, if they are held to maturity, actually *ends* at the moment of purchase—the very point at which speculation in stocks begins! The ultimate selling price of a fixed instrument is *fixed.* You know it will mature at face value, that it will be "sold" at a price of 100. The only question is what price you are going to pay for it at the beginning. Speculation *precedes* the actual purchase. You will not buy a fixed instrument (that is, lend your money) if you think rates will be higher tomorrow. You will buy, if you speculate that rates will be lower. When, finally, the current rate is acceptable to you and you do buy, you have thereupon simultaneously contracted to sell at par at maturity. Thus, at the moment of purchase, both your buy *and* sell prices have been determined. The transaction is complete and only awaits time to be actualized. In a sense, your check is in the mail the day you buy, but it will take 10 or 20 or more years to arrive. Should you hold your investment until maturity, there is absolutely no suspense about the ultimate result.

Dollar-cost averaging is built around the kind of speculation possible with equities. Speculation begins at the moment you buy a stock and continues thereafter. Your ultimate selling price is not fixed. Every day you hold it entails speculation on its future course. When you buy more shares at a "low" price through dollar-cost averaging, you are speculating that this price is in fact low. If prices fall lower, you're wrong. If they rise instead, you can sell and get a capital gain. But when you "sell" a zero at maturity, you are not really "selling high." You're just reaping your previously contracted-for interest. No speculative profit is possible with that kind of "sale."

Finally, let's examine a realistic example. If your fixed investment amount were used to purchase an item that fell in price from \$20 to \$10, you would buy twice as many at the lower price, and your average cost would turn out to be \$13.33 (well below the average market price of \$15). If you were buying a stock, fine, you did better than the average. But if we're talking about a 20-year zero, the story's a little different. From Appendix B, we extract the following:

a) At a price of \$10, a 20-year zero is yielding *12.3%*
b) At a price of \$20, a 20-year zero is yielding *8.4%*
c) At a price of \$13.33, a 20-year zero is yielding *10.6%*

The average of your two *yields* is 10.35 percent (12.3 percent plus 8.4 percent divided by 2)—*not appreciably different from the 10.6 percent yield which dollar-cost averaging provided.* (In fact, the two would have been *identical* if we'd assumed a steady rise in yields over the period instead of a steady drop in prices—a mathematical fine point.) If we instead were to buy equal *amounts* of the investment, then our average price would be $15 and, for the stock investor, that means he's achieved the average price. But the zero investor, whose average *price* is $15, has achieved a *yield* of slightly under 10 percent—*less* than the average yield during the period (see Appendix B)!! That's because he invested *fewer dollars* at high rates—it took fewer of them to buy the same amount of zeros at their lower price.

He spent $20 to buy a zero, then he spent $10 to buy another one—he invested twice as much money at *low* rates as he did at *high* rates. This explains why, in Table 4.8, fixed-quantity buying of zeros will actually produce a yield *below* average, and why dollar-cost averaging serves merely to bring the effective yield back up to average.

As we shall see in Chapter 5, there is a way to systematically speculate with zero coupon bonds. But dollar-cost averaging is not it.

In summary, dollar-cost averaging with zeros that are held to maturity sounds like a good idea but it is conceptually confused and, finally, ineffectual. Dollar-cost averaging will exaggerate the upswings in your equity if you use zeros of a constant duration (as in Figure 4.4), but these, like other zeros, remain fettered to an average yield. There are those who will claim, in good conscience, that dollar-cost averaging has advantages—and they may even point to good results. But, as we have shown, these won't last. They depend entirely on luck, on the moment the financial snapshot was taken. Ask what is behind the performance of a zero fund recommended on the basis of dollar-cost averaging. Is it (1) the higher yield almost always available to anyone investing in a long-term instrument, (2) a temporary foray above the average, a level that we now know cannot be sustained, or (3) the benefits conferred on all fixed investments by a period of falling rates (of the kind we have seen in the U.S. for the past few years)?

Beyond Dollar-Cost Averaging

It is possible that an investor might still find ZA attractive once we reinstate the long-term interest rate premium zeros are entitled to (removed only for experimental purposes). Although dollar-cost averaging (the A of ZA) has been proven to contribute no reliable benefit, the long-term interest rate premium alone (the Z of ZA) gives it an edge. A bold investor might regard that as the worst he could do and chance something better: namely, the possibility of getting out of his account when it was at or near one of its temporary peaks. If he were to buy zeros of a constant duration under the conditions detailed in Figure 4.4, the long-term premium would give him $327,695 after 25 years, an increase of 40.3 percent over cash instead of the 18.8 percent margin exhibited by ZA at that time without such a premium. If he were even luckier, he might cash out in Year 24 and garner $642,796, 197 percent better than cash. On the other hand, he might choose or be forced to close out in Year 21 when his account is worth only $99,379, fully 35 percent below cash at that time.

Such an investor, awakened to the risks as well as the rewards, might temper his daring with a dash of prudence and decide to keep 10 percent of his money in reserve so that an emergency need for cash will not force him to "sell" at an inopportune time, like Year 21 above. Let's say he adopts a simple rule: to reassess his portfolio every year to ensure that Plan ZA never absorbs more than 90 percent of his funds. How would he do? As a result of this modest precaution, his return would jump to $453,817 after 25 years, 94.5 percent ahead of cash. He has seemingly cut the leash that has tethered ZA to cash. But how? Merely by maintaining 10 percent in cash, he has forced himself to engage in systematic *selling*. In order to adhere to his self-imposed rule, he had to convert some zeros to cash whenever they rose in price. He has unwittingly broken the buy-only constraint of dollar-cost averaging and stumbled onto the welcome prospect of dynamic balancing.

In Chapter 5, we liberate zeros and explore in depth dynamic balancing within the scope of Plan Z.

5

Plan Z Unleashed

Zeros and Dynamic Balancing

You may recall that a number of examples in Chapter 3 involved imaginary stocks that doubled, tripled, or halved repeatedly, a fact that moved us to ponder their plausibility. No such questions arise here. Stocks may not typically exhibit price movements of that kind, but zeros do. Zeros are ideal for dynamic balancing. In general, dynamic balancing requires three conditions for success: a minimum of two investments whose values fluctuate but do not move in lockstep, and at least one of which retains value. Zeros fulfill all three.

Dynamic balancing with zero coupon bonds is Plan Z in its primitive form. At its simplest, ZB (for *Z*eros plus dynamic *B*alancing) involves holding two accounts—one cash, one zeros—and maintaining some preset proportion of funds in both by rebalancing them periodically. We shall spend most of this chapter inspecting a variety of computer simulations to convey how—and how well—ZB works. But before we examine specific cases, let's get a clearer picture of the mechanism that underlies dynamic balancing with zeros by playing a game.

Imagine you're given a suitcase with $100 and ushered before two elevators serving a skyscraper with 100 floors. Every time you pass a floor going up, you win a dollar. For every floor you go by on the way down, you lose one. Both elevators always move in the same direction at any given time, but one is an express that zips past several floors at once without stopping—its speed changes, so the exact number of floors can't be determined—whereas the other opens its doors at almost every floor. Its speed is variable too, but it's far, far slower. You have no control over what direction the elevators take or for how long—in fact, it seems fairly random. For a while they go up, then down, then up. All you know is you have a limited time (say, 30 minutes) to ride whichever elevator you wish—when you step off one, the other is somehow always there—and that both will wind up at the 100th floor at game's end, no matter how many ups and downs in between. What would you do?

When the elevators are rising together, you would probably want to be on the express, collecting dollars as you fly past floor after floor. When the elevators are jointly falling, you would prefer the local so you'd be forced to give back as few dollars as possible. When you step on the express elevator at the 20th floor and it shoots up to the 35th, you make $15. When it starts to move down, you want to switch, lest you lose all your gains. Fortunately, it stops at the 29th floor and you take the slow elevator to the 27th. You're still ahead $7. Now the slow elevator goes up: 27, 28, 29. Maybe it's time to switch elevators again?

In the world of ZB, the fast elevator is a highly volatile (long-term) zero; the slower car, a shorter-term zero (or cash)* that is much less volatile. You have no influence over, or foreknowledge of, which way the elevators move, just as you have no control over the direction of interest rates, the factors that determine whether zeros go up in value or down. But you know that when prices rise, your zeros will gain value, and when prices fall, they will lose some.

* In this analogy, the slow elevator is a shorter-term zero. Cash would be represented by a special vehicle, perhaps a service elevator, that rises very slowly and never goes down.

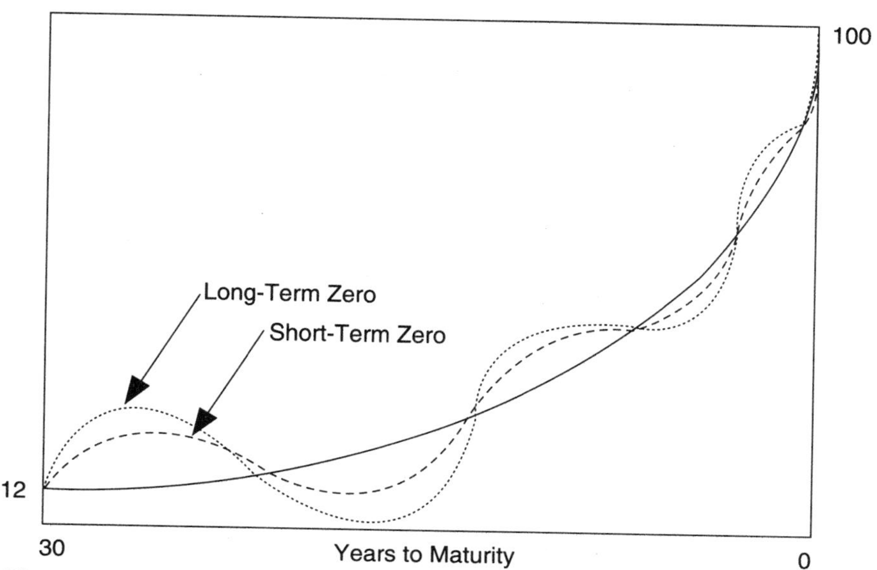

Figure 5.1 As interest rates fluctuate, a longer-term zero's price will respond more than a shorter-term zero's.

You also know higher volatility means more sensitivity to interest rate changes. A more volatile zero reacts more strongly, losing or gaining more value than a less volatile one. When prices are on the way up, you want your money in a more volatile zero that will take greater advantage of the direction they are heading—just as you preferred the express when both elevators were going up. When rates reverse and prices start falling, you will be better off selling your zero and buying one whose price falls more gently. You have no fear of switching your funds into a zero that is going down because you know it will eventually turn back up (all zeros mature at 100). So you welcome lower prices as an opportunity to buy new zeros cheaply. But you also wish to sidestep the effects of that decline on your existing portfolio by switching to the "local" in the form of cash or a zero that is closer to maturity.

We can represent the relationship of the "fast" and "slow" zeros graphically in Figures 5.1, 5.2, and 5.3. Each shows how a long-term zero runs away from its (hypothetical) constant growth curve when rates stray up or down whereas a short-term zero clings

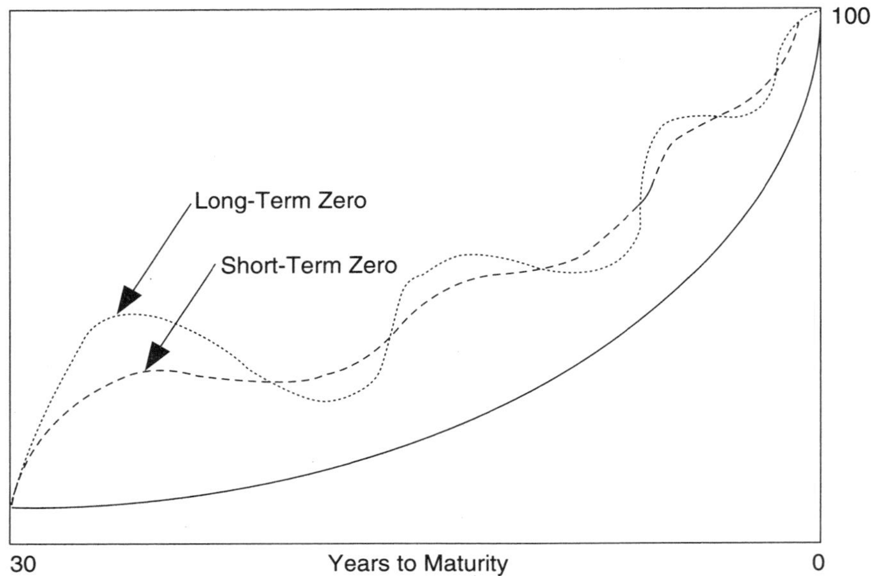

Figure 5.2 Interest rate fluctuations take place entirely at levels below their starting point.

to it more closely.* The important thing to understand is that when you dynamically balance accounts, funds *automatically* shift from the long-term account to the short-term one when rates are relatively low and prices high, forcing you to sell high. And your money moves in the other direction when rates are high and prices low, thus ensuring that you buy low almost programmatically.

Anticipating the Future: Interest Rate Scenarios

The strongest claim that can be made for Plan Z is that it is the best investment bet whatever the future brings. To test this, we will run a number of computer simulations examining it in a variety

* If rates should fall and never return to their original level, prices would move above the curve and stay there (as in Figure 5.2). If rates continually rose, prices would come in contact with the theoretical growth curve only at the last moment (Figure 5.3).

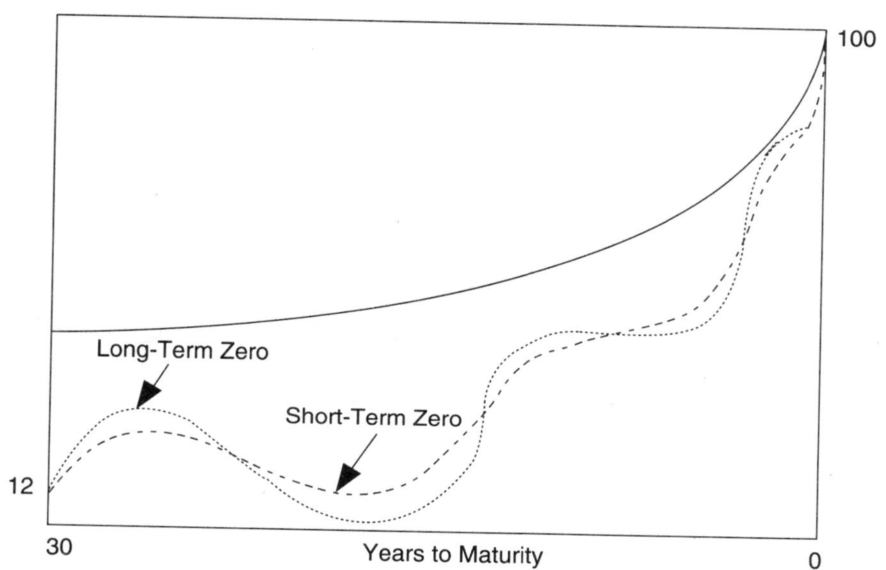

Figure 5.3 Interest rate fluctuations take place entirely at levels above their starting point.

of circumstances. The first problem is to fairly represent the kinds of conditions that we might encounter. Fortunately, as fixed-instrument investors, we can safely reduce the welter of reality to a single factor: interest rates. But which way will interest rates go? No one knows. As you can see from the zigzag lines that describe actual rates from 1968 through 1991 (Figure 5.4), the past is no clear guide. The best we can do is to create a broad sample of potential outcomes that express certain trends. To do this, we can vary the direction rates take, the frequency with which they fluctuate, and the magnitude of those fluctuations. We can also dictate whether the overall tendency of rates is up or down (or neither) and whether the pattern they display is entirely regular or not. The number of scenarios that could be generated by combining these elements in every conceivable way is limitless. So we are forced to restrict our production to a representative few and use simplifying assumptions. For example, instead of testing every possible degree of ascent or descent, we will designate some rates as rising or falling "gently" and others as "rapidly."

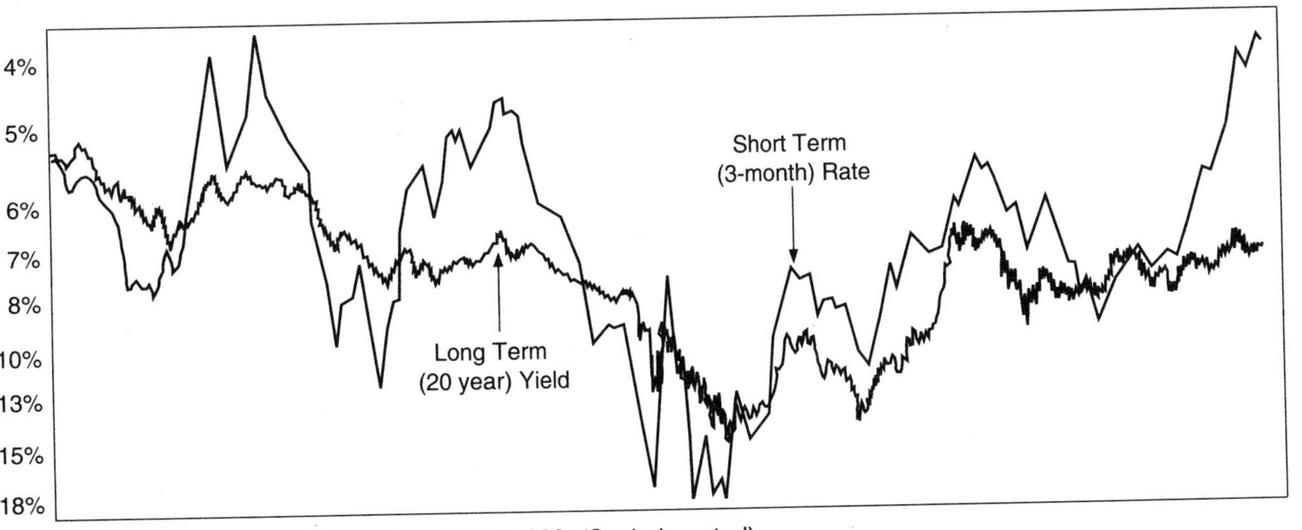

Figure 5.4 Actual U.S. interest rates, 1968–1992. (Scale inverted)

Seventeen different interest rate scenarios will serve as our model of economic reality—a stand-in for the crucial factors outside any investor's control. In the next section we will throw Plan Z against each of these scenarios and see how well it does compared to cash and bonds.

We start with scenarios that are conceptually simple and gradually add complexities so they approach the real world. Although all are *logically* possible and some are more probable than others, none is entirely likely—especially over a period as long as 25 years. It might be fair to say that the more an individual scenario approximates the gyrations of Figure 5.4, the more realistic it is. But that by no means guarantees it will actually occur.

Though each scenario can be defined mathematically (see Table 5.1), the pictures that follow (Figures 5.5 through 5.21) convey them more than adequately.

As you can see, most of the scenarios are highly schematic—almost cartoonish. They represent variations on a handful of simple notions readily described by the phrases we have chosen for them. The latter three (Figures 5.19 through 5.21) are not quite so easily defined. One feature that moves them closer to a still-stylized "reality" is the eruption of one or more *spikes.* These jagged peaks (up or down) sometimes accompany a startling world event—a president's death, a moon landing, or the outbreak of war—causing interest rates to temporarily climb or plunge. Another is a temporary *yield inversion,* the technical term for those infrequent occasions, typically at the end of an extended period of rising rates, when the short-term rate briefly rises above the long-term rate. You may have noticed that on all charts except these three, a careful distance is maintained between the long-term and the short-term rates. They move in concert but never touch or cross. The three "realistic" scenarios, however, incorporate the yield inversion phenomenon.

Given that each chart is intended to portray the course of rates over 25 years, few of our idealized scenarios seesaw back and forth with quite the energy of actual interest rates (Figure 5.4). To this extent, all 17 scenarios are schematic. The future is unlikely to look like any one of them but will probably resemble some unknown (and

Table 5.1 Interest Rate Scenarios

Number	Name	Description	Start %	Big band	Number oscillations	Small band	Number oscillations	Spike 1 period	Spike 1	Spike 2 period	Spike 2	Long-term yield premium	Yield inversion
1	GR	Gently rising	5%	4%	0.25	–	–	–	–	–	–	1.0%	–
2	RR	Rapidly rising	4%	16%	0.25	–	–	–	–	–	–	1.0%	–
3	GF	Gently falling	7%	4%	−0.25	–	–	–	–	–	–	1.0%	–
4	RF	Rapidly falling	12%	16%	−0.25	–	–	–	–	–	–	1.0%	–
5	GU	Gently undulating	6%	2%	−2.00	–	–	–	–	–	–	1.0%	–
6	RU	Rapidly undulating	8%	8%	4.25	–	–	–	–	–	–	1.0%	–
7	GRU	Gently rising/undulating	5%	4%	0.25	2.0	9.0	–	–	–	–	1.0%	–
8	RRU	Rapidly rising/undulating	4%	16%	0.25	3.0	14.0	–	–	–	–	1.0%	–
9	GFU	Gently falling/undulating	8%	4%	−0.25	2.0	9.0	–	–	–	–	1.0%	–
10	RFU	Rapidly falling/ undulating	13%	16%	−0.25	3.0	14.0	–	–	–	–	1.0%	–
11	GR/F	Gently rising/falling	5%	6%	0.50	1.5	14.0	–	–	–	–	1.0%	–
12	RR/F	Rapidly rising/falling	4%	16%	0.50	2.5	19.0	–	–	–	–	1.0%	–
13	GF/R	Gently falling/rising	8%	6%	−0.50	1.5	14.0	–	–	–	–	1.0%	–
14	RF/R	Rapidly falling/rising	12%	16%	−0.50	2.5	19.0	–	–	–	–	1.0%	–
15	Real-R/F	Realistic rising	8%	8%	0.95	3.0	13.0	10	5%	15	−2.5%	1.5%	0.9
16	Real-F/R	Realistic falling	8%	7%	−0.90	3.0	8.0	16	4%	20	−2.5%	1.5%	0.9
17	Real-U	Realistic undulating	7%	4%	3.00	4.0	2.5	16	4%	20	−2.5%	1.5%	0.9

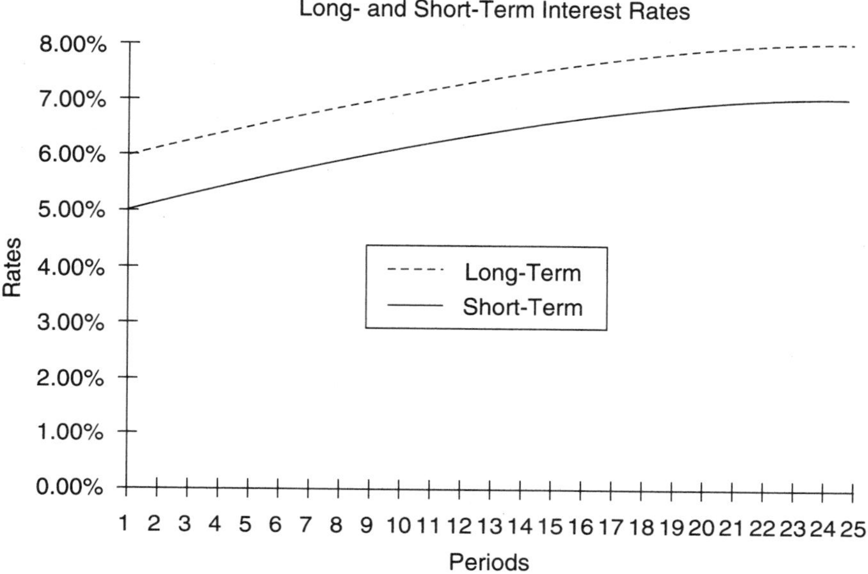

Figure 5.5 Gently rising rates (GR).

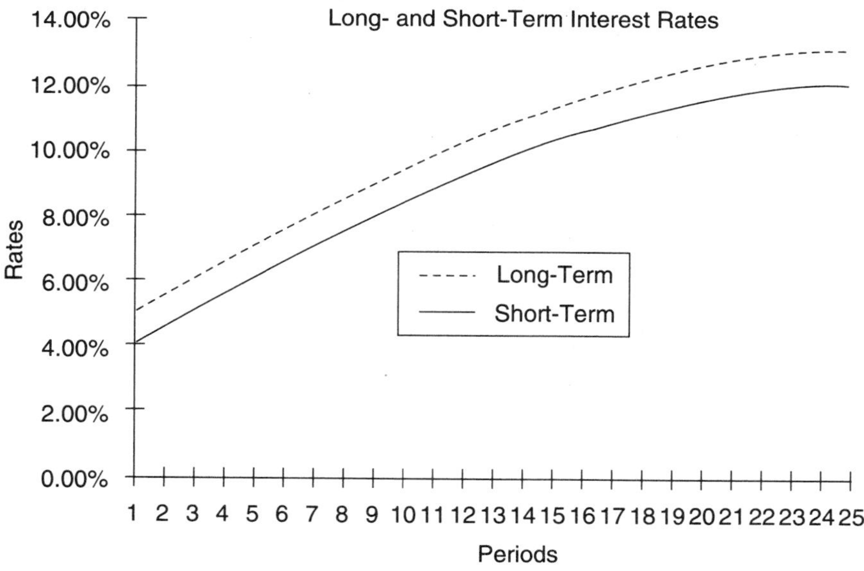

Figure 5.6 Rapidly rising rates (RR).

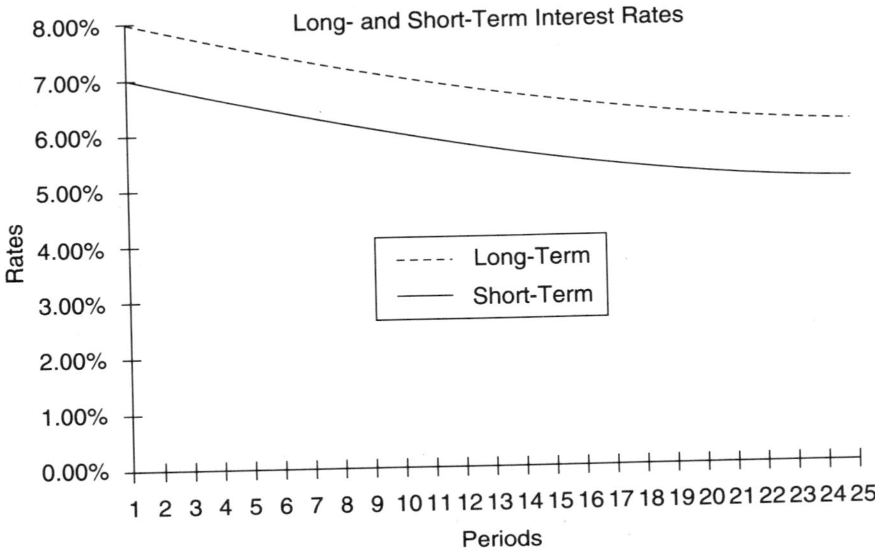

Figure 5.7 Gently falling rates (GF).

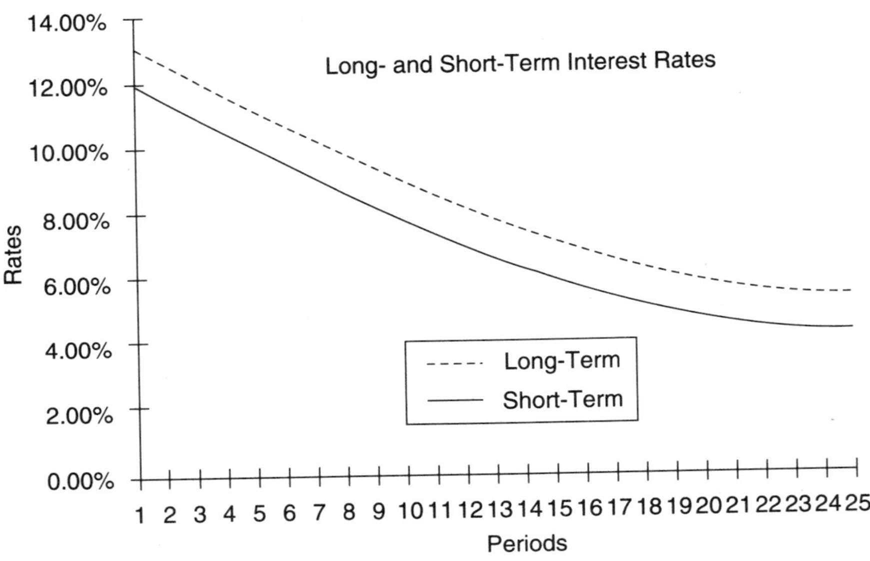

Figure 5.8 Rapidly falling rates (RF).

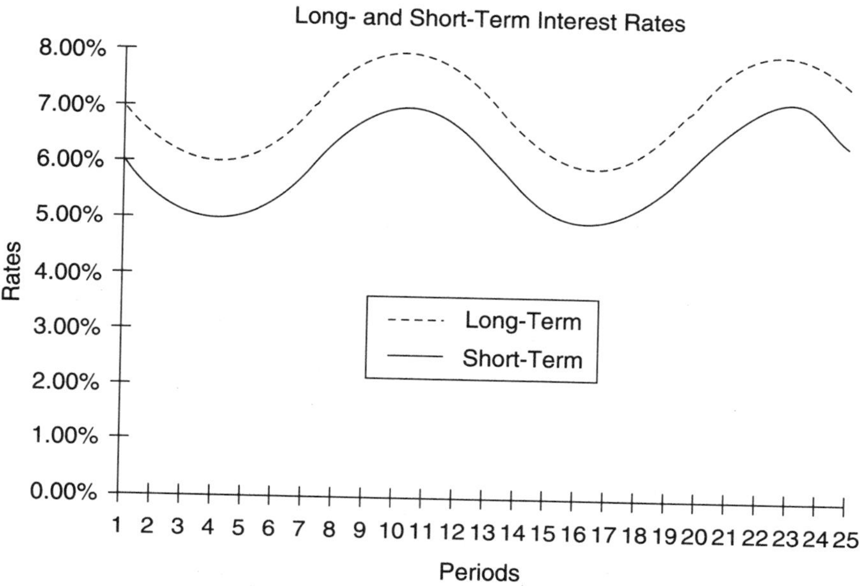

Figure 5.9 Gently undulating rates (GU).

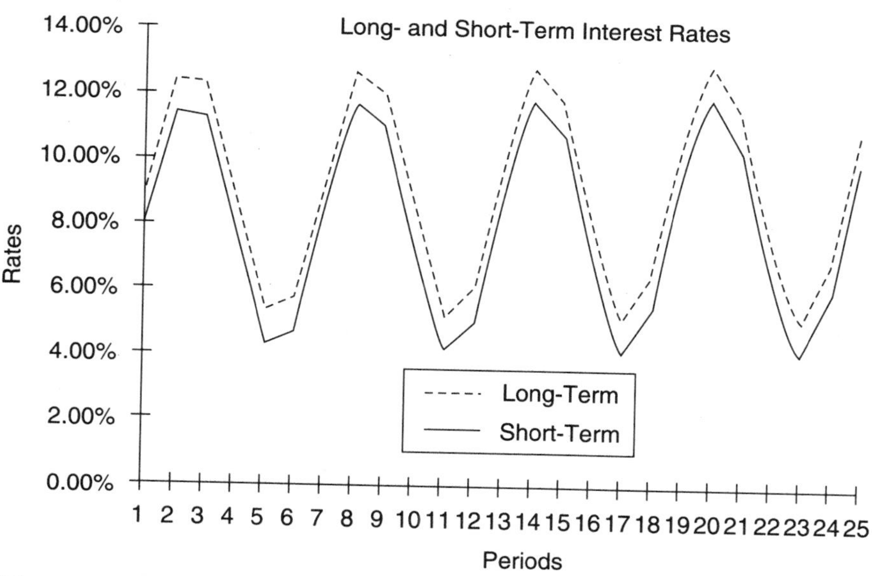

Figure 5.10 Rapidly undulating rates (RU).

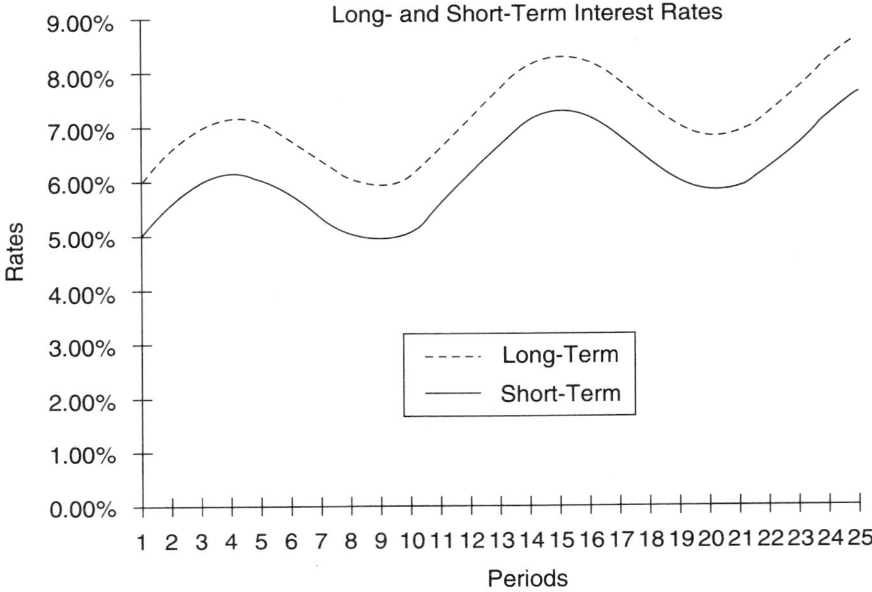

Figure 5.11 Gently rising and undulating rates (GRU).

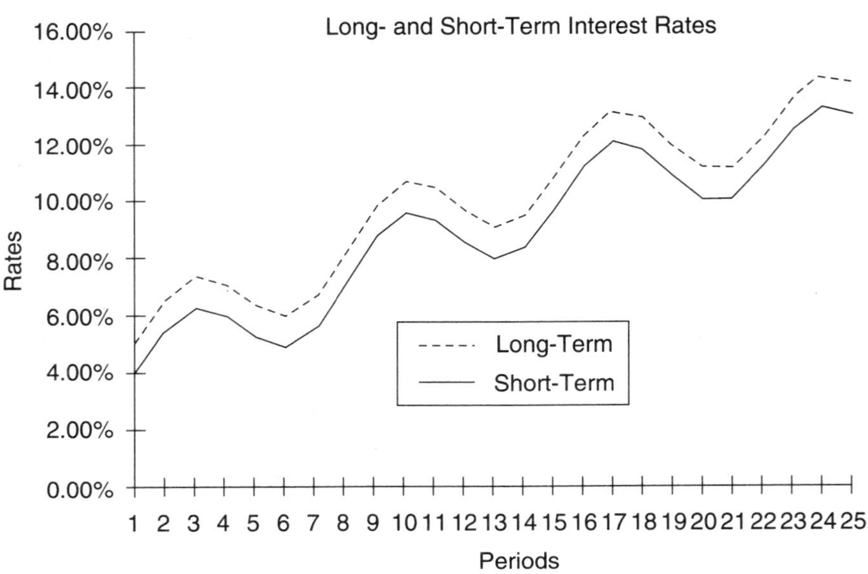

Figure 5.12 Rapidly rising and undulating rates (RRU).

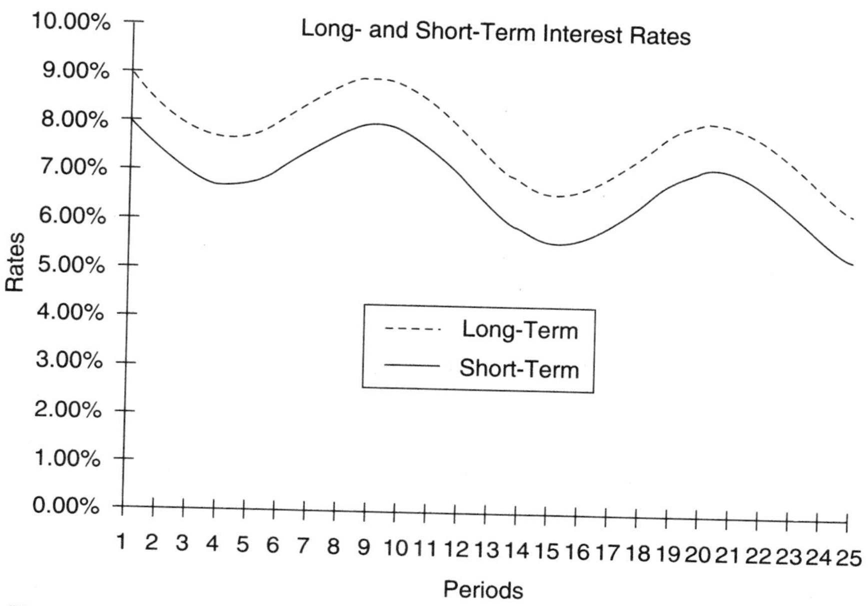

Figure 5.13 Gently falling and undulating rates (GFU).

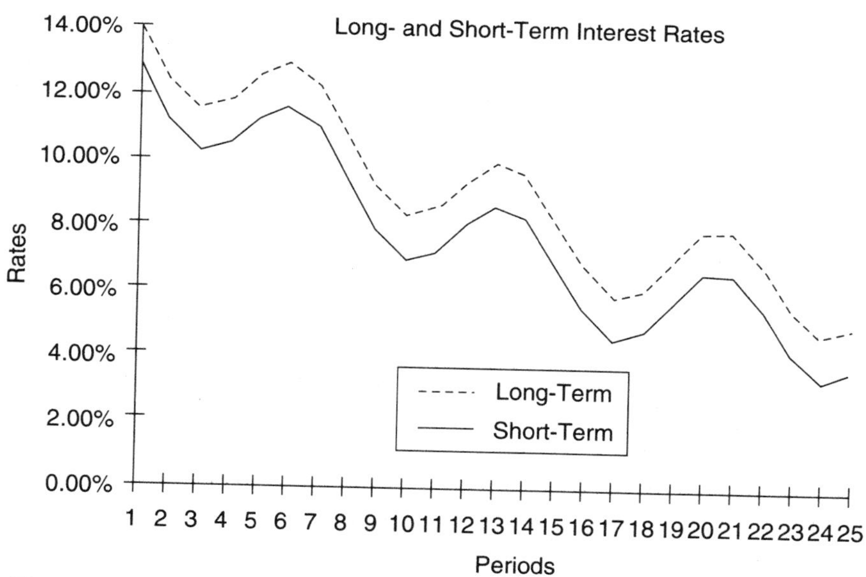

Figure 5.14 Rapidly falling and undulating rates (RFU).

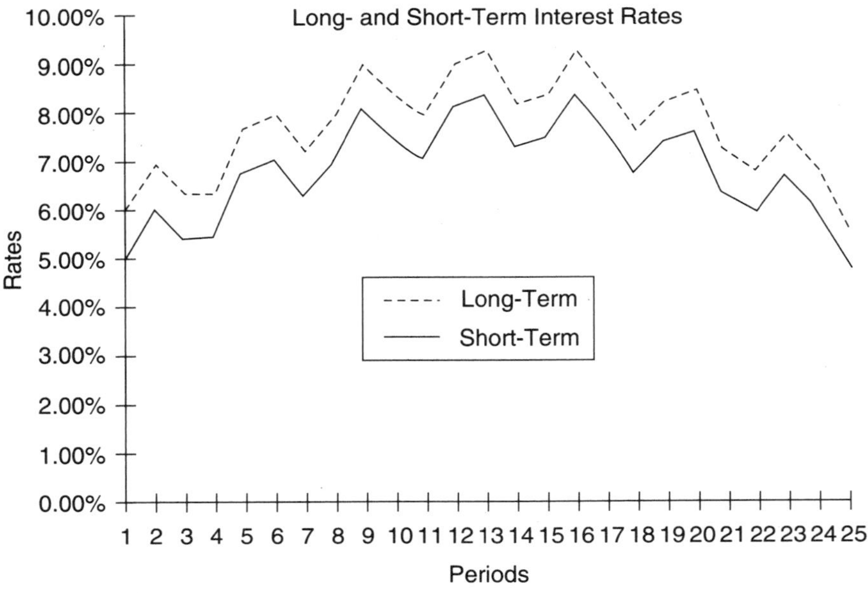

Figure 5.15 Gently rising, then falling rates (GR/F).

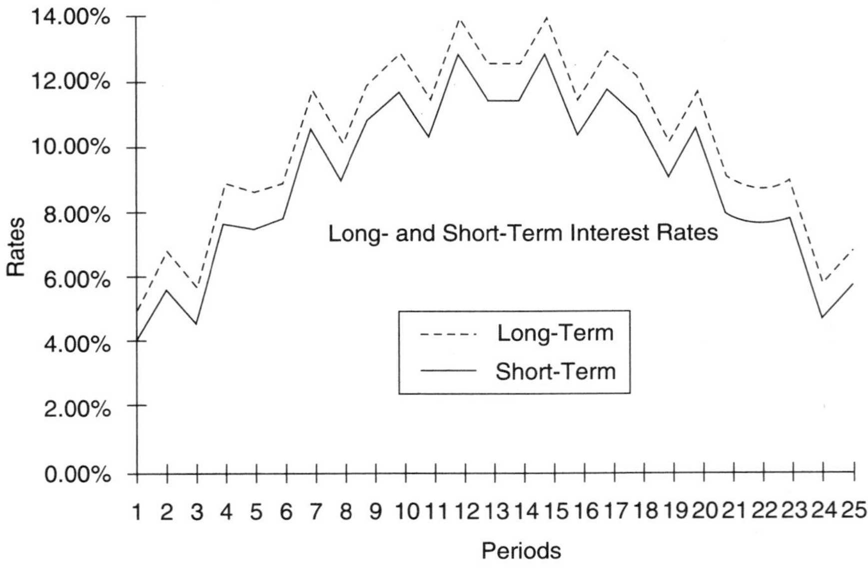

Figure 5.16 Rapidly rising, then falling rates (RR/F).

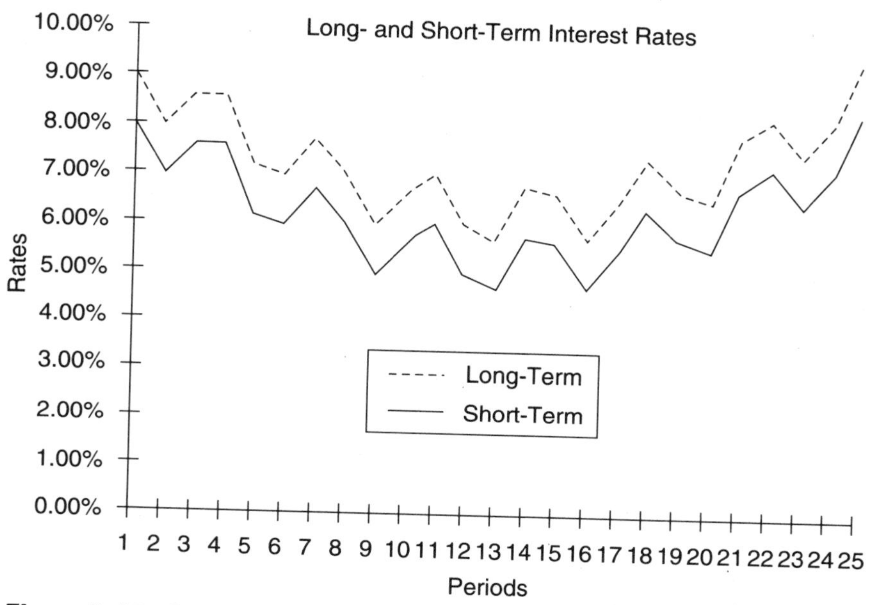

Figure 5.17 Gently falling, then rising rates (GF/R).

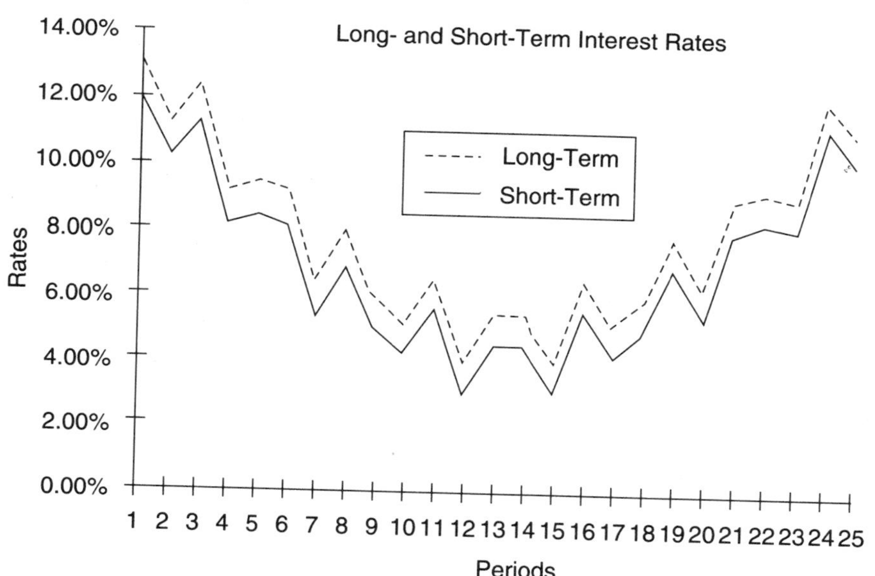

Figure 5.18 Rapidly falling, then rising rates (RF/R).

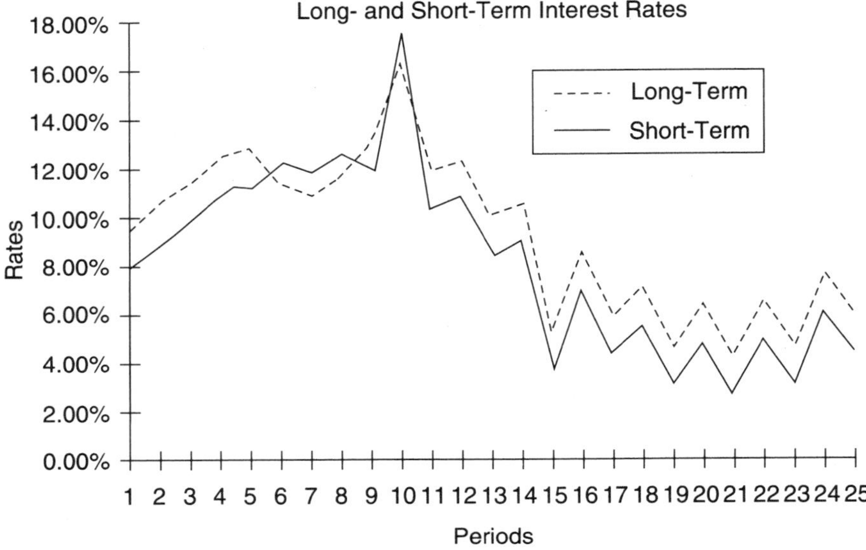

Figure 5.19 Real—rising then falling rates (Real-R/F).

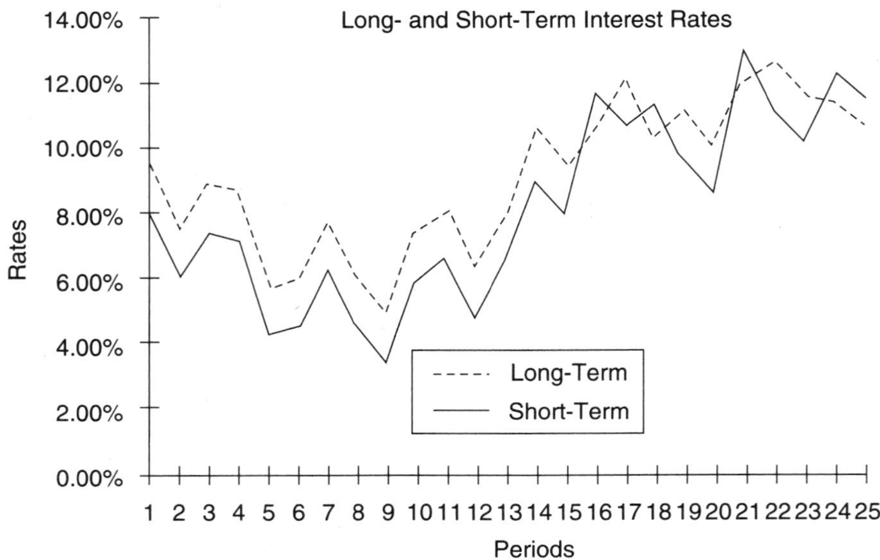

Figure 5.20 Real—falling then rising rates (Real-F/R).

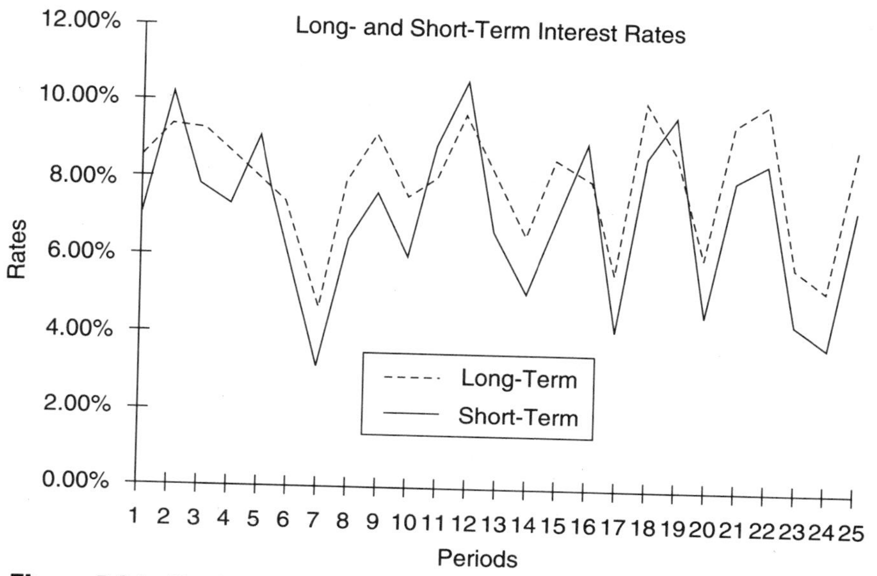

Figure 5.21 Real—undulating rates (Real-U).

unknowable) combination. Thus, no scenario by itself is likely to foretell the course of interest rates, but together in their variety and simplicity they constitute a formidable test, a gauntlet through which we will now make Plan Z run.

ZB in Action: Computer Simulations

In the simulations that follow, we consider two investment alternatives: (1) $2,000 annual contributions with no initial deposit, and (2) a $25,000 initial deposit with no additional investments. We match ZB against cash (an investor who keeps his money exclusively in short-term instruments like CDs, T-bills, or a money market fund) and bonds* (an investor who purchases a long-term bond but reinvests his coupon interest in short-term instruments), running them through the 17 interest rate scenarios just reviewed. (The investor who rolls over an initial deposit into Plan Z and continues to make

* The bonds comparison is made only in the case of the second investment alternative.

regular contributions can simply add the results of the two.) Although dynamic balancing permits you to parcel out your funds in any proportion among any number of investments, for the moment we will uncomplicate matters by holding just two, zeros and cash. We will test a range of balances, from 90/10 in favor of zeros (what we call a Z percent of 90, or Z-90 for short) all the way to a Z percent of 10 (10 percent in zeros, 90 percent in cash). The length of each investment is 25 years, and rebalancing in all cases occurs yearly.*

The consequences of investing $2,000 annually is arrayed in two tables. Table 5.2 displays the final disposition of each account in dollar amounts. Table 5.3 shows the relationship of ZB to cash in percentage form. Next, we calculate how an initial deposit of $25,000 would fare (Tables 5.4 through 5.6). Again, Table 5.4 presents dollar figures, Table 5.5 ZB versus cash, and Table 5.6 pits ZB against bonds.

How does Plan Z do? That depends, in part, on how you look at these tables. If you take each scenario singly, it's a mixed bag. Plan Z does brilliantly in some (as high as +120 percent), well in most, and poorly in others (negative in 14 out of 51 cases). Analysis of the scenarios where Plan Z fares poorly shows that virtually every such instance falls into one of two categories: either (1) predominantly rising rates, a circumstance where "cash is king" and all long-term instruments falter—a principle we first saw at work in Table 4.2; or (2) a few special cases of mostly falling rates, where "cash is trash" and the Z percentage was so low Plan Z functioned almost like cash.

When its Z percentage is robust, Plan Z tends to perform superlatively when rates fall continually (again, a phenomenon first seen in Chapter 4). Thus, every consistently negative scenario with rising rates (RR, RRU, Real-R) was offset by a positive counterpart featuring falling ones (RF, RFU, Real-F).

* Z-50 recapitulates the 50-50 balance used throughout Chapter 3. We omit a Z percentage of 0 because that would be equivalent to cash, holding no zeros at all. Similarly, we overlook Z-100 because it is equivalent to dollar-cost averaging, holding only zeros so no selling or rebalancing is possible.

Table 5.2 Results of Investing $2,000 Annually for 25 Years

Annual contribution	Yield premium	Rate scenario	Cash	Z-90	Z-80	Z-70	Z-60	Z-50	Z-40	Z-30	Z-20	Z-10
$2,000	1.0%	GR	$125,483	$128,940	$128,547	$128,157	$127,769	$127,383	$126,999	$126,617	$126,237	$125,859
		RR	$213,042	$160,297	$164,961	$169,885	$175,084	$180,575	$186,385	$192,502	$198,975	$205,815
		GF	$107,787	$138,826	$134,872	$131,056	$127,372	$123,815	$120,382	$117,066	$113,864	$110,773
		RF	$116,472	$231,306	$213,148	$196,657	$181,678	$168,069	$155,702	$144,459	$134,236	$124,936
		GU	$118,286	$130,044	$128,738	$127,431	$126,123	$124,815	$123,508	$122,201	$120,895	$119,590
		RU	$154,681	$224,408	$228,120	$228,415	$225,308	$218,986	$209,788	$198,180	$184,720	$170,015
		GRU	$125,084	$132,733	$131,949	$131,147	$130,328	$129,493	$128,642	$127,775	$126,892	$125,995
		RRU	$216,248	$165,529	$170,836	$176,253	$181,770	$187,375	$193,056	$198,799	$204,589	$210,410
		GFU	$125,764	$158,237	$154,304	$150,454	$146,685	$142,999	$139,393	$135,867	$132,421	$129,054
		RFU	$133,961	$266,471	$247,333	$229,408	$212,649	$197,012	$182,449	$168,911	$156,350	$144,716
		GR/F	$135,771	$148,987	$148,019	$146,923	$145,700	$144,350	$142,875	$141,277	$139,558	$137,722
		RR/F	$198,866	$203,324	$205,246	$206,680	$207,564	$207,843	$207,470	$206,407	$204,628	$202,116
		GF/R	$115,973	$143,892	$140,918	$137,887	$134,810	$131,697	$128,561	$125,410	$122,256	$119,107
	↓	RF/R	$126,139	$200,697	$193,380	$185,499	$177,198	$168,622	$159,907	$151,186	$142,580	$134,200
	1.5%	Real-R/F	$140,788	$254,345	$245,513	$235,294	$223,853	$211,375	$198,062	$184,126	$169,787	$155,268
		Real-F/R	$174,717	$161,738	$166,023	$169,660	$172,602	$174,816	$176,280	$176,989	$176,948	$176,180
	↓	Real-U	$134,230	$168,850	$168,774	$167,554	$165,255	$161,960	$157,765	$152,778	$147,113	$140,890

Table 5.3 Plan Z's Performance as a Percentage Better (or Worse) than Holding Cash ($2,000/Year, 25-Year Plan)

Annual contribution	Yield premium	Rate scenario	Z-90	Z-80	Z-70	Z-60	Z-50	Z-40	Z-30	Z-20	Z-10	Average
$2,000	1.0%	GR	2.8%	2.4%	2.1%	1.8%	1.5%	1.2%	0.9%	0.6%	0.3%	1.5%
	↓	RR	−24.8%	−22.6%	−20.3%	−17.8%	−15.2%	−12.5%	−9.6%	−6.6%	−3.4%	−14.8%
		GF	28.8%	25.1%	21.6%	18.2%	14.9%	11.7%	8.6%	5.6%	2.8%	15.3%
		RF	98.6%	83.0%	68.8%	56.0%	44.3%	33.7%	24.0%	15.3%	7.3%	47.9%
		GU	9.9%	8.8%	7.7%	6.6%	5.5%	4.4%	3.3%	2.2%	1.1%	5.5%
		RU	45.1%	47.5%	47.7%	45.7%	41.6%	35.6%	28.1%	19.4%	9.9%	35.6%
		GRU	6.1%	5.5%	4.8%	4.2%	3.5%	2.8%	2.2%	1.4%	0.7%	3.5%
		RRU	−23.5%	−21.0%	−18.5%	−15.9%	−13.4%	−10.7%	−8.1%	−5.4%	−2.7%	−13.2%
		GFU	25.8%	22.7%	19.6%	16.6%	13.7%	10.8%	8.0%	5.3%	2.6%	13.9%
		RFU	98.9%	84.6%	71.2%	58.7%	47.1%	36.2%	26.1%	16.7%	8.0%	49.7%
		GR/F	9.7%	9.0%	8.2%	7.3%	6.3%	5.2%	4.1%	2.8%	1.4%	6.0%
		RR/F	2.2%	3.2%	3.9%	4.4%	4.5%	4.3%	3.8%	2.9%	1.6%	3.4%
		GF/R	24.1%	21.5%	18.9%	16.2%	13.6%	10.9%	8.1%	5.4%	2.7%	13.5%
		RF/R	59.1%	53.3%	47.1%	40.5%	33.7%	26.8%	19.9%	13.0%	6.4%	33.3%
	1.5%	Real-R/F	80.7%	74.4%	67.1%	59.0%	50.1%	40.7%	30.8%	20.6%	10.3%	48.2%
	↓	Real-F/R	−7.4%	−5.0%	−2.9%	−1.2%	0.1%	0.9%	1.3%	1.3%	0.8%	−1.3%
		Real-U	25.8%	25.7%	24.8%	23.1%	20.7%	17.5%	13.8%	9.6%	5.0%	18.4%
Average all			27.2%	24.6%	21.9%	19.0%	16.0%	12.9%	9.7%	6.5%	3.2%	15.7%
Average "real"			33.0%	31.7%	29.7%	27.0%	23.6%	19.7%	15.3%	10.5%	5.4%	21.8%

Table 5.4 Results of a $25,000 Initial Investment with No Further Contributions

Initial deposit	Yield premium	Rate scenario	Cash	Bonds	Z-90	Z-80	Z-70	Z-60	Z-50	Z-40	Z-30	Z-20	Z-10
$25,000	1.0%	GR	$113,296	$113,814	$107,893	$108,490	$109,089	$109,687	$110,287	$110,887	$111,489	$112,090	$112,693
		RR	$210,767	$148,863	$ 93,034	$102,164	$112,110	$122,937	$134,718	$147,527	$161,446	$176,563	$192,970
		GF	$101,512	$126,666	$162,587	$154,376	$146,562	$139,125	$132,049	$125,316	$118,910	$112,818	$107,023
		RF	$136,929	$199,716	$465,646	$408,119	$357,346	$312,574	$273,131	$238,416	$207,893	$181,081	$157,553
		GU	$107,237	$122,744	$132,860	$130,023	$127,177	$124,325	$121,470	$118,614	$115,760	$112,911	$110,069
		RU	$171,995	$185,786	$246,080	$270,505	$287,117	$294,763	$292,968	$281,971	$262,688	$236,609	$205,657
		GRU	$114,571	$113,439	$108,354	$109,340	$110,255	$111,098	$111,866	$112,559	$113,177	$113,719	$114,183
		RRU	$216,832	$150,563	$ 94,876	$105,800	$117,428	$129,747	$142,742	$156,390	$170,662	$185,521	$200,928
		GFU	$126,938	$157,310	$205,183	$195,142	$185,451	$176,105	$167,097	$158,422	$150,075	$142,050	$134,340
		RFU	$167,586	$239,469	$587,418	$519,685	$458,016	$402,070	$351,506	$305,983	$265,160	$228,703	$196,285
		GR/F	$132,612	$120,372	$111,189	$114,829	$118,192	$121,261	$124,015	$126,440	$128,522	$130,250	$131,616
		RR/F	$219,321	$139,575	$ 99,395	$114,658	$130,160	$145,594	$160,640	$174,977	$188,294	$200,295	$210,715
		GF/R	$109,527	$147,862	$204,361	$193,158	$182,021	$170,995	$160,127	$149,458	$139,029	$128,876	$119,033
	↓	RF/R	$131,401	$216,144	$488,754	$445,199	$400,947	$356,815	$313,567	$271,891	$232,390	$195,565	$161,809
	1.5%	Real-R/F	$174,356	$177,997	$264,914	$249,390	$249,037	$245,829	$239,813	$231,113	$219,924	$206,510	$191,194
		Real-F/R	$166,388	$219,044	$246,187	$247,854	$246,629	$242,508	$235,566	$225,958	$225,958	$199,723	$183,747
	↓	Real-U	$138,834	$157,943	$195,904	$197,259	$196,288	$193,105	$187,867	$180,775	$172,062	$161,985	$150,816

Table 5.5 Plan Z's Performance as a Percentage Better (or Worse) than Holding Cash ($25,000 Initial Investment; No Additions)

Initial deposit	Yield premium	Rate scenario	Z-90	Z-80	Z-70	Z-60	Z-50	Z-40	Z-30	Z-20	Z-10	Average
$25,000	1.0%	GR	−4.8%	−4.2%	−3.7%	−3.2%	−2.7%	−2.1%	−1.6%	−1.1%	−0.5%	−2.7%
		RR	−55.9%	−51.5%	−46.8%	−41.7%	−36.1%	−30.0%	−23.4%	−16.2%	−8.4%	−34.4%
		GF	60.2%	52.1%	44.4%	37.1%	30.1%	23.4%	17.1%	11.1%	5.4%	31.2%
		RF	240.1%	198.1%	161.0%	128.3%	99.5%	74.1%	51.8%	32.2%	15.1%	111.1%
		GU	23.9%	21.2%	18.6%	15.9%	13.3%	10.6%	7.9%	5.3%	2.6%	13.3%
		RU	43.1%	57.3%	66.9%	71.4%	70.3%	63.9%	52.7%	37.6%	19.6%	53.6%
		GRU	−5.4%	−4.6%	−3.8%	−3.0%	−2.4%	−1.8%	−1.2%	−0.7%	−0.3%	−2.6%
		RRU	−56.2%	−51.2%	−45.8%	−40.2%	−34.2%	−27.9%	−21.3%	−14.4%	−7.3%	−33.2%
		GFU	61.6%	53.7%	46.1%	38.7%	31.6%	24.8%	18.2%	11.9%	5.8%	32.5%
		RFU	250.5%	210.1%	173.3%	139.9%	109.7%	82.6%	58.2%	36.5%	17.1%	119.8%
		GR/F	−16.2%	−13.4%	−10.9%	−8.6%	−6.5%	−4.7%	−3.1%	−1.8%	−0.8%	−7.3%
		RR/F	−54.7%	−47.7%	−40.7%	−33.6%	−26.8%	−20.2%	−14.1%	−8.7%	−3.9%	−27.8%
		GF/R	86.6%	76.4%	66.2%	56.1%	46.2%	36.5%	26.9%	17.7%	8.7%	46.8%
	↓	RF/R	272.0%	238.8%	205.1%	171.5%	138.6%	106.9%	76.9%	48.8%	23.1%	142.4%
	1.5%	Real-R/F	51.9%	43.0%	42.8%	41.0%	37.5%	32.6%	26.1%	18.4%	9.7%	33.7%
		Real-F/R	48.0%	49.0%	48.2%	45.7%	41.6%	35.8%	35.8%	20.0%	10.4%	37.2%
		Real-U	41.1%	42.1%	41.4%	39.1%	35.3%	30.2%	23.9%	16.7%	8.6%	30.9%
Average all			58.0%	51.1%	44.8%	38.5%	32.1%	25.6%	19.5%	12.5%	6.2%	32.0%
Average "real"	↓		47.0%	44.7%	44.1%	41.9%	38.1%	32.9%	28.6%	18.4%	9.6%	33.9%

Table 5.6 Plan Z's Performance as a Percentage Better (or Worse) than Bonds ($25,000 Initial Investment; No Additions)

Initial deposit	Yield premium	Rate scenario	Z-90	Z-80	Z-70	Z-60	Z-50	Z-40	Z-30	Z-20	Z-10	Average
$25,000	1.0%	GR	−5.2%	−4.7%	−4.2%	−3.6%	−3.1%	−2.6%	−2.0%	−1.5%	−1.0%	−3.1%
		RR	−37.5%	−31.4%	−24.7%	−17.4%	−9.5%	−0.9%	8.5%	18.6%	29.6%	−7.2%
		GF	28.4%	21.9%	15.7%	9.8%	4.2%	−1.1%	−6.1%	−10.9%	−15.5%	5.2%
		RF	133.2%	104.3%	78.9%	56.5%	36.8%	19.4%	4.1%	−9.3%	−21.1%	44.7%
		GU	8.2%	5.9%	3.6%	1.3%	−1.0%	−3.4%	−5.7%	−8.0%	−10.3%	−1.0%
		RU	32.5%	45.6%	54.5%	58.7%	57.7%	51.8%	41.4%	27.4%	10.7%	42.2%
		GRU	−4.5%	−3.6%	−2.8%	−2.1%	−1.4%	−0.8%	−0.2%	0.2%	0.7%	−1.6%
		RRU	−37.0%	−29.7%	−22.0%	−13.8%	−5.2%	3.9%	13.3%	23.2%	33.5%	−3.8%
		GFU	30.4%	24.0%	17.9%	11.9%	6.2%	0.7%	−4.6%	−9.7%	−14.6%	6.9%
		RFU	145.3%	117.0%	91.3%	67.9%	46.8%	27.8%	10.7%	−4.5%	−18.0%	53.8%
		GR/F	−7.6%	−4.6%	−1.8%	0.7%	3.0%	5.0%	6.8%	8.2%	9.3%	2.1%
		RR/F	−28.8%	−17.9%	−6.7%	4.3%	15.1%	25.4%	34.9%	43.5%	51.0%	13.4%
		GF/R	38.2%	30.6%	23.1%	15.6%	8.3%	1.1%	−6.0%	−12.8%	−19.5%	8.7%
		RF/R	126.1%	106.0%	85.5%	65.1%	45.1%	25.8%	7.5%	−9.5%	−25.1%	47.4%
	1.5%	Real-R/F	48.8%	40.1%	39.9%	38.1%	34.7%	29.8%	23.6%	16.0%	7.4%	30.9%
		Real-F/R	12.4%	13.2%	12.6%	10.7%	7.5%	3.2%	3.2%	−8.8%	−16.1%	4.2%
		Real-U	24.0%	24.9%	24.3%	22.3%	18.9%	14.5%	8.9%	2.6%	−4.5%	15.1%
Average all			29.8%	26.0%	22.7%	19.2%	15.5%	11.7%	8.1%	3.8%	−0.2%	15.2%
Average "real"			28.4%	26.1%	25.6%	23.7%	20.4%	15.8%	11.9%	3.3%	−4.4%	16.7%

The fact that most of the extreme results can be found in several of the same scenarios raises this question: Is looking at one scenario at a time, no matter how simplistic or realistic, how likely or unlikely, the best way to interpret the results? Wouldn't it be fairer to judge Plan Z's performance against all scenarios simultaneously? How likely is the future to resemble some one of these fabrications? Each is an idealized type, not a serious attempt at prognostication. To protect ourselves against picking favorites, for or against, why not average them? In doing so, we create a blend that might actually come closer to mimicking reality. After all, how plausible is it that rates will rise rapidly for the next 25 years? But we may well have 2, 5, or (who knows?) even 10 years of rapidly rising rates at some point. Averaging across all scenarios includes that possibility and each of the others in full measure without letting any one predominate.

How does Plan Z look from this perspective? When you look at its performance across all interest rate scenarios ("Average all" in Tables 5.3, 5.5, and 5.6), in only one case out of 27 does Plan Z actually underperform either cash or bonds—and then by a mere 0.2 percent, and when in its most marginal form, Z-10. Its average superiority over cash is actually 23.9 percent, and its advantage over bonds is 15.2 percent.* Table 5.7 summarizes.

Plan Z and Risk

A notion about which perhaps not enough has been said until now is risk. In its technical and everyday forms, there is no escaping it. There is a chance, whatever we decide, that the outcome will not meet our expectations. Judged by the strictures of risk, Plan Z is a plum, because the only risk associated with it is a *second-order,* or lower-level, risk. Look back at Tables 5.3, 5.5, and 5.6. The

* Once again, we should point out that these kinds of percentages are the average of Plan Z's lead or lag in each scenario and not a percentage of its average advantage (or disadvantage) in dollars. This evens out the results from each scenario so one huge loss or gain will not unduly lower or raise the overall average.

Table 5.7 Plan Z's Relative Performance, on Average

		Annual contribution	Initial deposit	
		Cash	Cash	Bonds
All ZB	Average All	15.7	32.0	15.2
All ZB	Average "Real"	21.8	33.9	16.7
Z-50	Average All	16.0	32.1	15.5
Z-50	Average "Real"	23.6	38.1	20.4

minus signs there *do not indicate a loss of money.* They show relative performance against cash or bonds. With Plan Z there is *no risk that you'll lose money,* only that in some unusual or unfavorable situations you might not make as much as in a situation more perfectly matched to your plan.

No government-backed fixed instrument can, in the end, hand you a loss—and that includes zero coupon bonds. Speculative vehicles may promise you a higher return, but you can also lose your shirt. Plan Z is unusual in that it is speculative *and* safe. It grants you the security of not having to worry about an ultimate loss (though there can be interim periods of adversity) while offering you the potential for magnificent gains (read on!) of a kind that no readily accessible fixed instrument can hope to deliver.

The Door to the Future

To provide some context for evaluating Plan Z, let's devise another game. Say you are asked to pay a fee to walk through a door and "win" a mysterious sum on the other side. In some cases, it's less than you've paid to play, in others more. Under these conditions, you'd be hard-pressed to know whether it was worth your while or not. But what if you were told that the expected payoff, on average, is in your favor—a fact based on your being able to play repeatedly—say, a thousand times? At times you would lose, but the great proportion of trials would favor you by far. More than that, the extent of your winnings would swamp whatever losses you incurred. Your decision would be clear-cut. Of course you'd play. But there's a catch. In actuality you can play only once. What do you do?

Let's change the game. Instead of one door, there are 17 (one for each of our scenarios). Again, there are different payoffs behind each. You know that you will, on average, come out ahead if you can walk through all 17. But once more, you can choose just one. Are the odds and payoff attractive enough for you to take that chance?

The answer to this question is another question: What are your real alternatives? If you don't like the odds Plan Z offers, you can play the ones given by cash or bonds. (Choosing not to play by hiding your money in your mattress is not a real option. What kind of odds do you get then?) On average, the performance of cash versus Plan Z is negative; so is the average performance of bonds (just replace every plus sign with a minus sign and vice versa in Tables 5.3, 5.5, and 5.6 to see). Although among some of the scenarios we have tested, cash or bonds come out ahead, those instances are far fewer than those where Plan Z prevails. Given a decision to invest in fixed instruments, the real question is this: How can you choose either over Plan Z?

Though Plan Z bests both in most cases, there is no guarantee it will do so in every particular case under every circumstance. However much Plan Z stacks the deck in your favor, there is always the chance you'll be dealt a bad hand. Who can say whether the period you invest in may not be the worst possible for the program you've selected? But this possibility exists no matter what kind of investment you undertake. There's a bad time for bonds, a bad time for stocks, a bad time for real estate, and a bad time for cash. Plan Z should not be held to a standard of certitude not asked of other investments. The relevant consideration is which investment strategy is likely to do best in the most cases and in the widest array of circumstances.

We all face a succession of doors leading to the future. No matter how many possibilities we foresee, at any one time there is only one door, and we are permitted to pass through it just once. As long-term investors, we do not have an endless number of attempts to find the ideal conditions to invest for the future. We generally have one shot and no say in what those conditions are. Seen in this light, the advantage that Plan Z confers *on average*—even in its most primitive form—is no small thing. Only when we look back over the period for which we are investing will we be certain which vehicle was best. But then it will be too late. Though Plan Z may not always offer the best performance, it remains the best bet *now* to do so. Hindsight may prove our decisions unwise, but true wisdom consists in rendering sound judgments *before* the verdict of history is in.

There is a Hindu saying: "The way out is by the door—why is it no one can see this?" The choice is yours.

ZB with Constant Duration Zeros

Any estimate of Plan Z at this point should be provisional since our demonstration of its abilities has only just begun. Thus far, we have seen only a plain vanilla version of Plan Z. It is time to try something a little fancier.

All simulations so far have employed zeros of a constant maturity, which is natural enough because most investors will have a specific maturity date in mind when they create their plan. But if we switch to zeros of a constant duration, we can draw on their consistently high volatility to improve our return.

In this round of simulations (Tables 5.8 through 5.13), for the sake of expedience we'll limit ourselves to the three realistic interest rate scenarios introduced earlier. We will also consider only three forms of Plan Z: Z-90, Z-50, and Z-10. Otherwise, the conditions are the same as in Tables 5.2 through 5.6.

Note that a 25-year investment in zeros of a constant maturity, the kind we simulated earlier in this chapter, is roughly equivalent to holding a constant duration zero of 13 years. That's the average duration of the zeros you would have had in your portfolio over that time (13 = (25 + 24 + 23 . . . + 1) ÷ 25). Thus, the 10-year

Table 5.8 Interest Rate Scenario: Real–Rising/Falling

Period	Annual contribution	Yield premium	Z %	Duration	Cash	Zeros	Difference
25 years	$2,000	1.5%	Z-90	10 years	$140,788	$188,202	33.7%
				20 years		$239,107	69.8%
				30 years		$341,381	142.5%
			Z-50	10 years		$176,381	25.3%
				20 years		$254,598	80.8%
				30 years		$466,671	231.5%
			Z-10	10 years		$149,181	6.0%
				20 years		$168,679	19.8%
				30 years		$210,191	49.3%

Table 5.9 Interest Rate Scenario: Real—Rising/Falling

Period	Initial deposit	Yield premium	Z %	Duration	Cash	Bonds	Zeros	Plan Z versus: Cash	Plan Z versus: Bonds
25 years	$25,000	1.5%	Z-90	10 years	$174,356	$177,997	$228,984	31.3%	28.6%
				20 years	↓	↓	$260,082	49.2%	46.1%
				30 years	↓	↓	$322,911	85.2%	81.4%
			Z-50	10 years	↓	↓	$220,615	26.5%	23.9%
				20 years	↓	↓	$315,375	80.9%	77.2%
				30 years	↓	↓	$572,084	228.1%	221.4%
			Z-10	10 years	↓	↓	$186,074	6.7%	4.5%
				20 years	↓	↓	$214,050	22.8%	20.3%
				30 years	↓	↓	$275,613	58.1%	54.8%

Table 5.10 Interest Rate Scenario: Real—Falling/Rising

Period	Annual contribution	Yield premium	Z %	Duration	Cash	Zeros	Difference
25 years	$2,000	1.5%	Z-90	10 years	$174,717	$172,687	−1.2%
				20 years		$157,674	−9.8%
				30 years		$151,206	−13.5%
			Z-50	10 years		$177,119	1.4%
				20 years		$180,042	3.0%
				30 years		$197,159	12.8%
			Z-10	10 years		$175,897	0.7%
				20 years		$178,870	2.4%
				30 years		$186,407	6.7%

Table 5.11 Interest Rate Scenario: Real—Falling/Rising

Period	Initial deposit	Yield premium	Z %	Duration	Cash	Bonds	Zeros	Plan Z versus:	
								Cash	Bonds
25 years	$25,000	1.5%	Z-90	10 years	$166,388	$219,044	$200,459	20.5%	−8.5%
				20 years			$202,702	21.8%	−7.5%
				30 years			$214,670	29.0%	−2.0%
			Z-50	10 years			$192,253	15.5%	−12.2%
				20 years			$222,120	33.5%	1.4%
				30 years			$289,272	73.9%	32.1%
			Z-10	10 years			$172,710	3.8%	−21.2%
				20 years			$182,993	10.0%	−16.5%
				30 years			$203,057	22.0%	−7.3%

Table 5.12 Interest Rate Scenario: Real—Undulating

Period	Annual contribution	Yield premium	Z %	Duration	Cash	Zeros	Difference
25 years	$2,000	1.5%	Z-90	10 years	$134,230	$155,613	15.9%
				20 years		$172,046	28.2%
				30 years		$210,827	57.1%
			Z-50	10 years		$155,307	15.7%
				20 years		$205,426	53.0%
				30 years		$335,792	150.2%
			Z-10	10 years		$139,936	4.3%
				20 years		$154,639	15.2%
				30 years		$184,664	37.6%

Table 5.13 Interest Rate Scenario: Real—Undulating

Period	Initial deposit	Yield premium	Z %	Duration	Cash	Bonds	Zeros	Plan Z versus: Cash	Plan Z versus: Bonds
25 years	$25,000	1.5%	Z-90	10 years	$138,834	$157,943	$175,230	26.2%	10.9%
				20 years	↓	↓	$200,975	44.8%	27.2%
				30 years	↓	↓	$257,519	85.5%	63.0%
			Z-50	10 years	↓	↓	$171,545	23.6%	8.6%
				20 years	↓	↓	$245,049	76.5%	55.2%
				30 years	↓	↓	$444,289	220.0%	181.3%
			Z-10	10 years	↓	↓	$147,237	6.1%	−6.8%
				20 years	↓	↓	$167,517	20.7%	6.1%
				30 years	↓	↓	$209,303	50.8%	32.5%

Table 5.14 Average Results Across All Scenarios

	Investment	Duration	Z–90	Z–50	Z–10	Average
ZB vs. Cash	$ 2,000 annual	10 years	16.1%	14.1%	3.7%	11.3%
		20 years	29.4%	45.6%	12.5%	29.2%
		30 years	62.0%	131.5%	31.2%	74.9%
		Average	35.8%	63.7%	15.8%	38.5%
	$25,000 deposit	10 years	26.0%	21.9%	5.5%	17.8%
		20 years	38.6%	63.6%	17.8%	40.0%
		30 years	66.6%	174.0%	43.6%	94.7%
		Average	43.7%	86.5%	22.3%	50.8%
		Average All	39.8%	75.1%	19.1%	44.7%
		Avg. 20 Yr	34.0%	54.6%	15.2%	34.6%
		Avg. 30 Yr	64.3%	152.8%	37.4%	84.8%
ZB vs. Bonds	$25,000 deposit	10 years	10.3%	6.8%	−7.8%	3.1%
		20 years	22.0%	44.6%	3.3%	23.3%
		30 years	47.5%	144.9%	26.7%	73.0%
		Average	26.6%	65.4%	7.4%	33.1%

constant duration zeros in these simulations actually represent a reduction in volatility compared with those in the previous set.

The pattern of the returns confirms the claim that zeros thrive on volatility. In most cases, Plan Z's lead over cash or bonds was extended as the duration of the zeros lengthened. Only once did its position fail to improve—again, a scenario in which rates largely climb (real—falling/rising). The average results across all scenarios are displayed in Table 5.14.

As you can see, Plan Z in this form is even more successful. By taking on the higher volatility and additional risk of constant duration zeros, you can boost the potential rewards considerably. (We will consider the care and handling of constant duration zeros in later chapters.)

To this point some readers may still be troubled by the fact that, although its merits outweigh any flaws, Plan Z has not vanquished its competitors in every scenario conjured thus far. Whether this is an unreasonable expectation or not, the underlying complaint is true. However, we have only scratched the surface of Plan Z. Each instance in this chapter has been a shot in the dark—and a single shot at that. We jotted down our strategy, shoved it in a bottle, cast it on the sea—then waited for an answer. But you don't have to sit passively for 25 years hoping that reality favors Plan Z. You can adopt a strategy that automatically adjusts to interest rates as they change. In Chapter 6 we introduce a method to accomplish this. The results can be astounding.

6

Powering Plan Z

The Variable Z Percentage

In this chapter we will look at a way of freeing Plan Z from reliance on a *fixed* Z percentage of the kind put forth in the previous chapter. In this way, Plan Z's performance can be significantly enhanced. At the same time we will show you how to incorporate your own market views (if any) to create a Z percentage appropriate for your temperament as well as your pocketbook.

The Variable Z Percentage (VZP)

Why would anyone want a variable Z percentage? As we have seen, ZB works well in most circumstances. But imagine that you could continually adjust the balance between your accounts so it was more nearly right all the time. There's no reason your Z percentage must always be the same. In changing circumstances, a fixed Z percentage can be a constraint. You can often squeeze something extra from a position by investing or liquidating more aggressively. For example, if you had $75 in zeros and $25 in cash and rates dropped suddenly so your zeros were worth $100, you would be sworn to sell off $6.25 worth to maintain your fixed 75/25 split. But you might be even better off if your Z percentage were now *lowered* to, say, 73 percent, so you would have to sell a few *extra* zeros to rebalance. If zero prices come back down, you'll need to buy some to reestablish this new 73/27 balance. But wouldn't it then be a good idea to change your Z percentage *again*, this time *raising* it to, say, 78 percent to force you to invest still *more* money in zeros when they are low in price? Should prices drop some more, you might increase your Z percentage to 81 to pour even more funds into zeros. Each time prices move significantly you would benefit from adapting your apportionment to the situation, wringing more out of each position by either selling more zeros at a higher price or lending more money at a higher rate. The question is, how can you do this intelligently according to a prescription or plan?

The solution is to allow each Plan Z investor to choose two things: (1) a range of Z percentages (called a Z Range), defined by the highest and lowest Z percentage he feels comfortable with (these are respectively his Z_{max} and Z_{min}), and (2) an interest rate range (I Range), within which he expects interest rates to move (bounded by his I_{max} and I_{min}).* Because he wants to buy zeros when they are low in price, his Z_{max} will be paired with his I_{max}, and because he wants to sell zeros at a high price, his Z_{min} will be associated with his I_{min}. Once formulated, his variable Z percentage (VZP) enables him to have a flexible cash-to-zero relationship. Even the mildest opinions on interest rates can create a map to guide investment when rates shift (as they are bound to).

How do you encode your appraisals in a single formula? You derive an equation for a line between two points, the two limiting positions defined by your Z_{max} and I_{max} on the one hand and your Z_{min} and I_{min} on the other. Whether he knows it or not, when Zachary

* This is putting the matter simply for now. A refinement is discussed in the final section of this chapter.

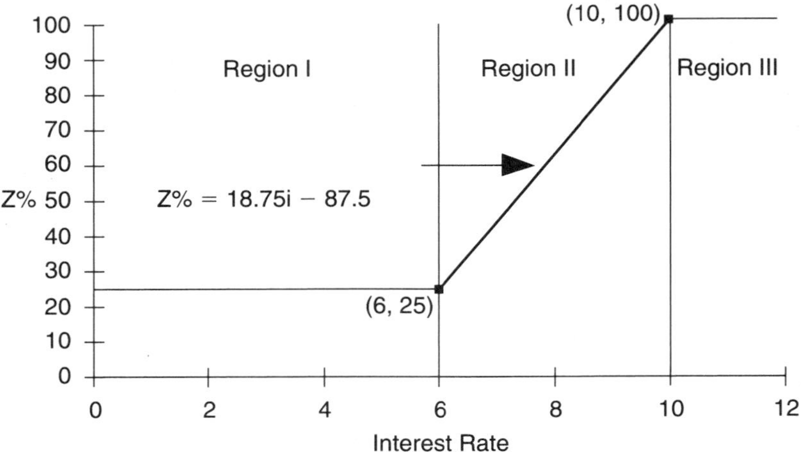

Figure 6.1 A picture of Zachary's VZP formula.

chooses a Z Range between 25 and 100 and foresees an I Range between 6 and 10 percent he is picking out two points on a graph with the coordinates (6, 25) and (10, 100). The line connecting them is described by the equation shown in Figure 6.1. This equation is also his VZP formula: $Z\% = 18.75i - 87.5$, where i is the current interest rate.* Every year, Zachary plugs the current interest rate into this equation and determines the Z percentage at which he should rebalance.**

As long as rates move within Zachary's I Range, his VZP formula will tell him how to adjust his Z percentage at rebalancing time. You can see that when rates are within Region I in Figure 6.1, at 6 percent or below, Zachary is doing dynamic balancing at a fixed Z percentage of 25. When interest rates move through Region II, however, he raises or lowers his Z percentage, depending on where they are. When they enter Region III, Zachary takes on a fixed Z percentage again.

* See Appendix A for complete directions on how to derive a VZP formula.

** Important: The rates in question should be short-term, not long-term. Keep short-term rates in mind when you select your I Range as well. One reason for keying off the short-term rate is that it is managed by the Federal Reserve whereas the long-term rate is determined responsively by the market. There is often a brief lag in the long-term rate. By following the short-term rate, you can often get a jump on what long rates will do.

An example might clarify how this approach amplifies dynamic balancing's "buy low, sell high" imperative. Let's conjure up an event that moves rates up so that the price of zeros falls in half. A fixed Z-25 investor who started out with $250 in zeros and $750 in cash would find that his whole portfolio is now valued at $875 and his zeros at only $125. To maintain his Z percentage of 25, he must increase his zero holdings to $218.75 by buying $93.75 worth. If he had been using a VZP formula much like that in Figure 6.1, the jump in rates would have simultaneously triggered an increase in his Z-percentage from 25 to something like 50 percent. This would have required him to reallocate *more* than $93.75 to zeros—as much as $300 more. This simple, mechanical procedure "forces" him to do precisely what he desires: increase his investment at higher yields. (Remember, when the price is lower, the angle to 100 is greater and so is the yield.) Similarly, if rates were to fall back to where they began, causing zero prices to double, the VZP investor would be forced to sell—that is, take profits—to an extent several times that of his fixed-Z counterpart. VZP *exaggerates* ZB's normal buy low, sell high mechanism by "automatically" adjusting an investor's Z percentage according to a preset, logical plan. This ratcheting up and down takes place time and again, squeezing more out of position after position. The cumulative effect, as we shall see, can be considerable.

VZP Computer Simulations

To illustrate how effective a variable Z percentage can be, let's trace the fortunes of three investors—one aggressive, one conservative, one "agnostic." All three will try their hands at dynamic balancing with zeros in two (now familiar) ways: by making $2,000 annual contributions and by depositing $25,000 without additions. Each will use four different kinds of zeros: first constant maturities, and then constant-duration zeros of 10, 20, and 30 years. We will base our simulations on the three "realistic" interest rate scenarios from Chapter 5.

Because many readers are probably in a similar frame of mind now, we will take the agnostic investor first. The agnostic has no strong views on interest rates, so he designates an I Range as broad as any to be found over the last several decades: between 4 and 20 percent. He is equally unwilling to commit himself totally to cash or zeros, preferring a middle course, so he limits his Z Range to between 25 percent and 75 percent. Even these bland assumptions are enough to formulate a VZP (in this case, $Z\% = 3.125i + 12.5$). They are also sufficient to generate some pretty impressive returns, in several cases two or three times those of cash or bonds (Tables 6.1 and 6.2). Only once in 48 trials did Plan Z finish behind the competition. When it came to annual contributions, the agnostic's average lead was 83.4 percent over cash and 81.6 percent against bonds. In the case of initial deposits, the figures are 114 percent more than cash and 90.3 percent better than bonds.

The conservative investor is risk-averse and therefore reluctant to commit much money to highly volatile zero coupon bonds, preferring instead a strong cash position at all times. She sets her Z percentage between 0 and 60. She is conservative too in her estimate of rates (though she need not be; the two assessments are independent) and considers it improbable that they will stray more than two points above or below whatever the rate is on the date she begins her Plan Z investing. Because there are two different starting rates in the scenarios we used, our conservative investor had two different VZP equations. As shown in Tables 6.3 and 6.4 in the case of the scenario Real-U, her $Z\% = 15i - 35$; in the other two scenarios it is $Z\% = 15i - 50$. Despite her relative restraint, the conservative investor also racks up some sizable gains, in some cases more than 10 times greater than her fixed-instrument alternatives. (Her average performance, in fact, is over one-and-a-half times that of cash or bonds.)

The aggressive investor is willing to go to extremes, to put all or nothing in either cash or zeros. His Z percentage therefore runs the gamut from 0 to 100. He's also willing to accept the risk of taking a stand on interest rates. Because his narrower interest rate selections make it possible for him to err in different ways, the

Table 6.1 The "Agnostic" Investor Tries Dynamic Balancing with Zeros

Investment	Selected rates	Selected Z%	Scenario	Type of zero	Cash	Bonds	Plan Z	Z vs. cash	Z vs. bonds
$2,000 annual	4% to 20%	Z-75 to Z-25	Real-R/F	Constant maturity	$140,788	$141,080	$218,219	55.0%	54.7%
				Duration = 10			$191,014	35.7%	35.4%
				Duration = 20			$306,712	117.9%	117.4%
				Duration = 30			$609,654	333.0%	332.1%
			Real-F/R	Constant maturity	$174,717	$178,929	$182,157	4.3%	1.8%
				Duration = 10			$182,925	4.7%	2.2%
				Duration = 20			$195,632	12.0%	9.3%
				Duration = 30			$223,344	27.8%	24.8%
			Real-U	Constant maturity	$134,230	$135,758	$172,974	28.9%	27.4%
				Duration = 10			$174,568	30.1%	28.6%
				Duration = 20			$263,989	96.7%	94.5%
				Duration = 30			$477,148	255.5%	251.5%

Table 6.2 The "Agnostic" Investor Tries Dynamic Balancing with Zeros

Investment	Selected rates	Selected Z%	Scenario	Type of zero	Cash	Bonds	Plan Z	Z vs. cash	Z vs. bonds
$25,000 deposit	4% to 20%	Z-75 to Z-25	Real-R/F	Constant maturity	$174,356	$177,997	$262,336	50.5%	47.4%
				Duration = 10			$244,649	40.3%	37.4%
				Duration = 20			$399,673	129.2%	124.5%
				Duration = 30			$802,163	360.1%	350.7%
			Real-F/R	Constant maturity	$166,388	$219,044	$236,429	42.1%	7.9%
				Duration = 10			$195,629	17.6%	−10.7%
				Duration = 20			$238,607	43.4%	8.9%
				Duration = 30			$323,395	94.4%	47.6%
			Real-U	Constant maturity	$138,834	$157,943	$204,118	47.0%	29.2%
				Duration = 10			$195,320	40.7%	23.7%
				Duration = 20			$323,979	133.4%	105.1%
				Duration = 30			$651,202	369.1%	312.3%

Table 6.3 The "Conservative" Investor Tries Dynamic Balancing with Zeros

Investment	Selected rates	Selected Z%	Scenario	Type of zero	Cash	Bonds	Plan Z	Z vs. cash	Z vs. bonds
$2,000 annual	6% to 10%	Z-60 to Z-0	Real-R/F	Constant maturity	$140,788	$141,080	$205,643	46.1%	45.8%
				Duration = 10			$190,520	35.3%	35.0%
				Duration = 20			$291,573	107.1%	106.7%
				Duration = 30			$508,277	261.0%	260.3%
			Real-F/R	Constant maturity	$174,717	$178,929	$189,195	8.3%	5.7%
				Duration = 10			$195,782	12.1%	9.4%
				Duration = 20			$224,183	28.3%	25.3%
				Duration = 30			$165,815	−5.1%	−7.3%
	5% to 9%		Real-U	Constant maturity	$134,230	$135,758	$221,943	65.3%	63.5%
				Duration = 10			$252,028	87.8%	85.6%
				Duration = 20			$556,079	314.3%	309.6%
				Duration = 30			$1,377,000	925.9%	914.3%

Table 6.4 The "Conservative" Investor Tries Dynamic Balancing with Zeros

Investment	Selected rates	Selected Z%	Scenario	Type of zero	Cash	Bonds	Plan Z	Z vs. cash	Z vs. bonds
$25,000 deposit	6% to 10%	Z-60 to Z-0	Real-R/F	Constant maturity	$174,356	$177,997	$242,667	39.2%	36.3%
				Duration = 10			$241,725	38.6%	35.8%
				Duration = 20			$371,564	113.1%	108.7%
				Duration = 30			$647,190	271.2%	263.6%
			Real-F/R	Constant maturity	$166,388	$219,044	$233,362	40.3%	6.5%
				Duration = 10			$206,047	23.8%	−5.9%
				Duration = 20			$265,237	59.4%	21.1%
				Duration = 30			$360,368	116.6%	64.5%
	5% to 9%		Real-U	Constant maturity	$138,834	$157,943	$278,407	100.5%	76.3%
				Duration = 10			$296,584	113.6%	87.8%
				Duration = 20			$736,509	430.5%	366.3%
				Duration = 30			$2,025,559	1,359.0%	1,182.5%

aggressive investor is granted three turns at each interest rate scenario. One conjecture will turn out to have been too high, one too low, and one almost exactly right. Because of the different requirements of the scenarios themselves, he actually has more than three VZP formulas. These will each be mentioned in turn.

In Tables 6.5 and 6.6, our aggressive investor's Z% = 12.5i − 100. In both tables he estimated rates at 8 to 16 percent when they actually ranged from a low of 3 percent to highs of 11 percent (in the Real-U scenario), 13 percent (in Real-F), and 17 percent (Real-R). In every case his forecast for interest rates missed the low end of interest rate activity entirely—that is, whatever transpired below 8 percent, he was locked into a fixed Z percentage of 0 (completely invested in cash) the whole time. Despite this misjudgment, his returns are healthy (between 40 and 54 percent above cash and bonds on average), except for one scenario (Real-F), where his performance dipped below that of bonds.

In Tables 6.7 and 6.8, our aggressive investor's hypotheses on rates turn out to be precisely correct. When rates are between 3 and 11 percent, his VZP formula is Z% = 12.5i − 37.5; when rates are 3 to 13 percent, it is Z% = 10i − 30; and when they range from 3 to 17 percent, Z% = 7.143i − 21.43. Once again, returns are hefty (an average of one-and-a-half to two times the size of cash or bonds), tending to mount as the volatility of the zeros increases.

In Tables 6.9 and 6.10, the aggressive investor's rate suppositions wind up being well on the low side. He thinks rates will stay between 3 and 7 percent (Z% = 25i − 75) but, depending on the scenario, they actually rise as much as 4 to 10 percentage points above his I_{max}. His miscalculation, however, turns out to be to his advantage, with returns in some instances that are truly stupendous. In no case is his average return less than five times greater than that of cash or bonds.

More Simulations

As a further test of VZP, we will run it through several other scenarios in addition to the "realistic" ones just discussed. For

Table 6.5 The "Aggressive" Investor Tries Dynamic Balancing with Zeros—and Guesses Interest Rates Too High

Investment	Selected rates	Selected Z%	Scenario	Type of zero	Cash	Bonds	Plan Z	Z vs. cash	Z vs. bonds
$2,000 annual	8% to 16%	Z-100 to Z-0	Real-R/F	Constant maturity	$140,788	$141,080	$201,846	43.4%	43.1%
				Duration = 10	↓	↓	$176,879	25.6%	25.4%
				Duration = 20			$242,478	72.2%	71.9%
				Duration = 30			$360,690	156.2%	155.7%
			Real-F/R	Constant maturity	$174,717	$178,929	$174,064	−0.4%	−2.7%
				Duration = 10	↓	↓	$183,570	5.1%	2.6%
				Duration = 20			$197,335	12.9%	10.3%
				Duration = 30			$215,570	23.4%	20.5%
			Real-U	Constant maturity	$134,230	$135,758	$151,591	12.9%	11.7%
				Duration = 10	↓	↓	$155,763	16.0%	14.7%
				Duration = 20			$192,901	43.7%	42.1%
				Duration = 30			$252,780	88.3%	86.2%

Table 6.6 The "Aggressive" Investor Tries Dynamic Balancing with Zeros—and Guesses Interest Rates Too High

Investment	Selected rates	Selected Z%	Scenario	Type of zero	Cash	Bonds	Plan Z	Z vs. cash	Z vs. bonds
$25,000 deposit	8% to 16%	Z-100 to Z-0	Real-R/F	Constant maturity	$174,356	$177,997	$275,290	57.9%	54.7%
				Duration = 10	↓	↓	$235,168	34.9%	32.1%
				Duration = 20	↓	↓	$344,590	97.6%	93.6%
				Duration = 30	↓	↓	$542,604	211.2%	204.8%
			Real-F/R	Constant maturity	$166,388	$219,044	$165,584	−0.5%	−24.4%
				Duration = 10	↓	↓	$174,717	5.0%	−20.2%
				Duration = 20	↓	↓	$188,037	13.0%	−14.2%
				Duration = 30	↓	↓	$206,090	23.9%	−5.9%
			Real-U	Constant maturity	$138,834	$157,943	$163,431	17.7%	3.5%
				Duration = 10	↓	↓	$165,894	19.5%	5.0%
				Duration = 20	↓	↓	$213,823	54.0%	35.4%
				Duration = 30	↓	↓	$292,126	110.4%	85.0%

Table 6.7 The "Aggressive" Investor Tries Dynamic Balancing with Zeros—and Guesses Interest Rates Exactly Right

Investment	Selected rates	Selected Z%	Scenario	Type of zero	Cash	Bonds	Plan Z	Z vs. cash	Z vs. bonds
$2,000 annual	3% to 17%	Z-100 to Z-0	Real-R/F	Constant maturity	$140,788	$141,080	$246,988	75.4%	75.1%
				Duration = 10	↓	↓	$224,300	59.3%	59.0%
				Duration = 20	↓	↓	$420,768	198.9%	198.2%
				Duration = 30	↓	↓	$927,495	558.8%	557.4%
	3% to 13%		Real-F/R	Constant maturity	$174,717	$178,929	$190,921	9.3%	6.7%
				Duration = 10	↓	↓	$191,119	9.4%	6.8%
				Duration = 20	↓	↓	$215,133	23.1%	20.2%
				Duration = 30	↓	↓	$256,048	46.6%	43.1%
	3% to 11%		Real-U	Constant maturity	$134,230	$135,758	$197,202	46.9%	45.3%
				Duration = 10	↓	↓	$208,857	55.6%	53.8%
				Duration = 20	↓	↓	$379,483	182.7%	179.5%
				Duration = 30	↓	↓	$794,907	492.2%	485.5%

Table 6.8 The "Aggressive" Investor Tries Dynamic Balancing with Zeros—and Guesses Interest Rates Exactly Right

Investment	Selected rates	Selected Z%	Scenario	Type of zero	Cash	Bonds	Plan Z	Z vs. cash	Z vs. bonds
$25,000 deposit	3% to 17%	Z-100 to Z-0	Real-R/F	Constant maturity	$174,356	$177,997	$303,901	74.3%	70.7%
				Duration = 10			$293,818	68.5%	65.1%
				Duration = 20			$561,445	222.0%	215.4%
				Duration = 30			$1,234,154	607.8%	593.4%
	3% to 13%		Real-F/R	Constant maturity	$166,388	$219,044	$254,104	52.7%	16.0%
				Duration = 10			$207,506	24.7%	−5.3%
				Duration = 20			$271,384	63.1%	23.9%
				Duration = 30			$386,309	132.2%	76.4%
	3% to 11%		Real-U	Constant maturity	$138,834	$157,943	$243,395	75.3%	54.1%
				Duration = 10			$241,602	74.0%	53.0%
				Duration = 20			$491,614	254.1%	211.3%
				Duration = 30			$1,147,898	726.8%	626.8%

Table 6.9 The "Aggressive" Investor Tries Dynamic Balancing with Zeros—and Guesses Interest Rates Too Low

Investment	Selected rates	Selected Z%	Scenario	Type of zero	Cash	Bonds	Plan Z	Z vs. cash	Z vs. bonds
$2,000 annual	3% to 7%	Z-100 to Z-0	Real-R/F	Constant maturity	$140,788	$141,080	$342,236	143.1%	142.6%
				Duration = 10	↓	↓	$349,451	148.2%	147.7%
				Duration = 20	↓	↓	$976,554	593.6%	592.2%
				Duration = 30	↓	↓	$3,076,575	2,085.3%	2,080.7%
			Real-F/R	Constant maturity	$174,717	$178,929	$224,733	28.6%	25.6%
				Duration = 10	↓	↓	$203,240	16.3%	13.6%
				Duration = 20	↓	↓	$228,452	30.8%	27.7%
				Duration = 30	↓	↓	$272,245	55.8%	52.2%
			Real-U	Constant maturity	$134,230	$135,758	$317,067	136.2%	133.6%
				Duration = 10	↓	↓	$336,597	150.8%	147.9%
				Duration = 20	↓	↓	$972,557	624.5%	616.4%
				Duration = 30	↓	↓	$3,198,529	2,282.9%	2,256.1%

Table 6.10 The "Aggressive" Investor Tries Dynamic Balancing with Zeros—and Guesses Interest Rates Too Low

Investment	Selected rates	Selected Z%	Scenario	Type of zero	Cash	Bonds	Plan Z	Z vs. cash	Z vs. bonds
$25,000 deposit	3% to 7%	Z-100 to Z-0	Real-R/F	Constant maturity	$174,356	$177,997	$324,258	86.0%	82.2%
				Duration = 10	↓	↓	$433,139	148.4%	143.3%
				Duration = 20	↓	↓	$1,053,995	504.5%	492.1%
				Duration = 30	↓	↓	$2,740,427	1,471.7%	1,439.6%
			Real-F/R	Constant maturity	$166,388	$219,044	$465,595	179.8%	112.6%
				Duration = 10	↓	↓	$276,159	66.0%	26.1%
				Duration = 20	↓	↓	$417,754	151.1%	90.7%
				Duration = 30	↓	↓	$657,471	295.1%	200.2%
			Real-U	Constant maturity	$138,834	$157,943	$457,468	229.5%	189.6%
				Duration = 10	↓	↓	$441,331	217.9%	179.4%
				Duration = 20	↓	↓	$1,488,379	972.1%	842.4%
				Duration = 30	↓	↓	$5,446,382	3,822.9%	3,348.3%

expediency, we have chosen the 7 "gentle" interest rate scenarios from Chapter 5 rather than use all 17. If anything, these seven are less volatile than the "rapid" scenarios we omitted, which should mean that VZP's capabilities will be somewhat understated.

As above, each investment requires the selection of an I Range, a Z range, and a zero duration. We tested all combinations of (1) three kinds of I Ranges: a narrow one that turns out low, a narrow one that winds up high, and a wide guess that spans the entire actual interest rate band and then some;* (2) zeros of three constant durations: 10 years, 20 years, and 30 years; and (3) two Z Ranges: a narrow one of 25 to 75 percent and a wide one of 0 to 100 percent. Results of making an initial $25,000 contribution (no further deposits) are shown in Tables 6.11, 6.12, and 6.13. The first displays dollar amounts and the second and third VZP's performance versus cash and bonds, respectively.

The first thing to notice is the considerable distance between VZP's average achievement and those of cash and bonds. Across all scenarios and strategies—however unlikely or ill-advised—VZP's average return is $285,638, 108.55 percent better than cash and 85.99 percent beyond bonds. There are just two moderately negative scenarios (GR and GRU), again both characterized by constantly rising rates.

All in all, VZP outperforms cash 88 percent of the time. Its lead when it comes out ahead is 125 percent, and its deficit when it falls behind is 12 percent. Versus bonds, VZP has the advantage 71 percent of the time. Its winning margin is 125 percent on average and its losing margin 9 percent.

Without exception, VZP's lead lengthened with the duration of the zeros that were employed. Were we to eliminate 10-year zeros—a peculiar choice anyway, because their duration is actually less than what zeros of constant maturity would average—then VZP's averaged result would turn out to be $342,449, 150.03 percent ahead of cash and 122.98 percent above bonds.

* "Low" means the I_{max} is roughly in the middle of the scenario's actual rate range, whereas the I_{min} is a full percentage point below the lowest actual rate. For the high guess, the I_{min} is close to the midpoint and the I_{max} one percentage point above the highest actual rate. The wide rate guess extended from the "low" I_{min} to the "high" I_{max}.

Table 6.11 Dollar Results of VZP including Seven Other Interest Rate Scenarios

Rate guess	Constant duration	Z Range	GR	GF	GU	GRU	GFU	GR/F	GF/R	R-R/F	R-F/R	R-U	Average
Low	10 years	25–75%	119,176	132,836	126,545	115,169	181,521	164,607	139,386	289,219	223,408	260,444	175,231
		0–100%	121,281	141,910	132,320	116,238	202,439	177,665	154,285	368,817	256,346	386,768	205,807
	20 years	25–75%	104,979	151,301	129,968	97,280	225,291	178,568	157,306	519,238	292,804	558,619	241,535
		0–100%	103,306	167,438	138,047	93,839	266,184	193,262	182,425	766,043	366,145	1,168,731	344,542
	30 years	25–75%	92,508	172,390	134,310	82,780	281,460	199,751	183,442	1,119,699	424,731	1,443,848	413,492
		0–100%	88,012	197,576	144,684	75,963	350,229	211,547	218,678	1,740,145	554,116	3,939,093	752,004
High	10 years	25–75%	116,878	114,914	115,974	114,751	149,580	163,109	127,707	229,776	186,556	218,012	153,726
		0–100%	116,653	106,198	111,068	115,362	137,525	175,040	129,588	227,775	177,204	269,376	156,579
	20 years	25–75%	110,364	122,100	117,893	107,658	167,113	190,111	143,446	352,101	217,795	409,090	193,767
		0–100%	114,172	109,050	113,263	114,764	146,684	222,180	151,864	314,199	194,118	609,841	209,014
	30 years	25–75%	104,248	129,784	120,492	101,681	188,083	229,257	166,545	653,971	280,044	921,363	289,547
		0–100%	111,754	112,001	115,652	114,241	156,864	287,810	180,484	439,501	216,820	1,511,697	324,682
Wide	10 years	25–75%	118,022	123,565	121,053	115,345	166,008	164,149	133,709	252,621	205,437	230,004	162,991
		0–100%	118,947	122,820	121,143	116,716	169,612	177,608	142,628	284,773	218,579	304,748	177,757
	20 years	25–75%	107,641	135,955	123,458	103,447	196,954	185,715	151,637	423,014	259,394	450,118	213,733
		0–100%	108,616	135,272	124,795	106,610	204,824	213,871	172,808	531,873	297,336	787,862	268,387
	30 years	25–75%	98,214	149,650	126,751	93,575	235,661	217,953	178,607	873,116	366,351	1,074,751	341,463
		0–100%	99,223	149,045	129,386	98,144	249,274	265,500	216,553	1,163,433	445,229	2,356,413	517,220
		Average	108,555	137,434	124,822	104,642	204,184	200,984	162,839	586,073	287,912	938,932	285,638
		Cash	113,296	101,512	107,237	114,571	126,938	132,612	109,527	174,356	166,388	138,834	
		Bonds	113,814	126,666	122,744	113,439	157,310	120,372	147,862	177,997	219,044	157,943	

Table 6.12 VZP versus Cash

Rate guess	Constant duration	Z Range	GR	GF	GU	GRU	GFU	GR/F	GF/R	R-R/F	R-F/R	R-U	Average
Low	10 years	25–75	5.19%	30.86%	18.00%	0.52%	43.00%	24.13%	27.26%	65.88%	34.27%	87.59%	33.67%
		0–100	7.05%	39.80%	23.39%	1.45%	59.48%	33.97%	40.86%	111.53%	54.07%	178.58%	55.02%
	20 years	25–75	−7.34%	49.05%	21.20%	−15.09%	77.48%	34.65%	43.62%	197.80%	75.98%	302.36%	77.97%
		0–100	−8.82%	64.94%	28.73%	−18.10%	109.70%	45.73%	66.56%	339.36%	120.05%	741.82%	149.00%
	30 years	25–75	−18.35%	69.82%	25.25%	−27.75%	121.73%	50.63%	67.49%	542.19%	155.27%	939.98%	192.63%
		0–100	−22.32%	94.63%	34.92%	−33.70%	175.91%	59.52%	99.66%	898.04%	233.03%	2,737.27%	427.70%
High	10 years	25–75	3.16%	13.20%	8.15%	0.16%	17.84%	23.00%	16.60%	31.79%	12.12%	57.03%	18.30%
		0–100	2.96%	4.62%	3.57%	0.69%	8.34%	31.99%	18.32%	30.64%	6.50%	94.03%	20.17%
	20 years	25–75	−2.59%	20.28%	9.94%	−6.03%	31.65%	43.36%	30.97%	101.94%	30.90%	194.66%	45.51%
		0–100	0.77%	7.43%	5.62%	0.17%	15.56%	67.54%	38.65%	80.21%	16.67%	339.26%	57.19%
	30 years	25–75	−7.99%	27.85%	12.36%	−11.25%	48.17%	72.88%	52.06%	275.08%	68.31%	563.64%	110.11%
		0–100	−1.36%	10.33%	7.85%	−0.29%	23.58%	117.03%	64.78%	152.07%	30.31%	988.85%	139.32%
Wide	10 years	25–75	4.17%	21.72%	12.88%	0.68%	30.78%	23.78%	22.08%	44.89%	23.47%	65.67%	25.01%
		0–100	4.99%	20.99%	12.97%	1.87%	33.62%	33.93%	30.22%	63.33%	31.37%	119.51%	35.28%
	20 years	25–75	−4.99%	33.93%	15.13%	−9.71%	55.16%	40.04%	38.45%	142.62%	55.90%	224.21%	59.07%
		0–100	−4.13%	33.26%	16.37%	−6.95%	61.36%	61.28%	57.78%	205.05%	78.70%	467.48%	97.02%
	30 years	25–75	−13.31%	47.42%	18.20%	−18.33%	85.65%	64.35%	63.07%	400.77%	120.18%	674.13%	144.21%
		0–100	−12.42%	46.83%	20.65%	−14.34%	96.37%	100.21%	97.72%	567.27%	167.58%	1,597.29%	266.72%
		Average	−4.18%	35.39%	16.40%	−8.67%	60.85%	51.56%	48.67%	236.14%	73.04%	576.30%	108.55%

Table 6.13 VZP versus Bonds

Rate guess	Constant duration	Z Range	GR	GF	GU	GRU	GFU	GR/F	GF/R	R-R/F	R-F/R	R-U	Average
Low	10 years	25–75	4.71%	4.87%	3.10%	1.53%	15.39%	36.75%	−5.73%	62.49%	1.99%	64.90%	19.00%
		0–100	6.56%	12.03%	7.80%	2.47%	28.69%	47.60%	4.34%	107.20%	17.03%	144.88%	37.86%
	20 years	25–75	−7.76%	19.45%	5.89%	−14.24%	43.21%	48.35%	6.39%	191.71%	33.67%	253.68%	58.03%
		0–100	−9.23%	32.19%	12.47%	−17.28%	69.21%	60.55%	23.38%	330.37%	67.16%	639.97%	120.88%
	30 years	25–75	−18.72%	36.10%	9.42%	−27.03%	78.92%	65.94%	24.06%	529.05%	93.90%	814.16%	160.58%
		0–100	−22.67%	55.98%	17.87%	−33.04%	122.64%	75.74%	47.89%	877.63%	152.97%	2,394.00%	368.90%
High	10 years	25–75	2.69%	−9.28%	−5.52%	1.16%	−4.91%	35.50%	−13.63%	29.09%	−14.83%	38.03%	5.83%
		0–100	2.49%	−16.16%	−9.51%	1.70%	−12.58%	45.42%	−12.36%	27.97%	−19.10%	70.55%	7.84%
	20 years	25–75	−3.03%	−3.60%	−3.95%	−5.10%	6.23%	57.94%	−2.99%	97.81%	−0.57%	159.01%	30.18%
		0–100	0.31%	−13.91%	−7.72%	1.17%	−6.75%	84.58%	2.71%	76.52%	−11.38%	286.11%	41.16%
	30 years	25–75	−8.40%	2.46%	−1.83%	−10.37%	19.56%	90.46%	12.64%	267.41%	27.85%	483.35%	88.31%
		0–100	−1.81%	−11.58%	−5.78%	0.71%	−0.28%	139.10%	22.06%	146.91%	−1.02%	857.12%	114.54%
Wide	10 years	25–75	3.70%	−2.45%	−1.38%	1.68%	5.53%	36.37%	−9.57%	41.92%	−6.21%	45.62%	11.52%
		0–100	4.51%	−3.04%	−1.30%	2.89%	7.82%	47.55%	−3.54%	59.99%	−0.21%	92.95%	20.76%
	20 years	25–75	−5.42%	7.33%	0.58%	−8.81%	25.20%	54.28%	2.55%	137.65%	18.42%	184.99%	41.68%
		0–100	−4.57%	6.79%	1.67%	−6.02%	30.20%	77.68%	16.87%	198.81%	35.74%	398.83%	75.60%
	30 years	25–75	−13.71%	18.15%	3.26%	−17.51%	49.31%	81.07%	20.79%	390.52%	67.25%	580.47%	118.01%
		0–100	−12.82%	17.67%	5.41%	−13.48%	58.46%	120.57%	46.46%	553.63%	103.26%	1,391.94%	227.11%
		Average	−4.62%	8.50%	1.69%	−7.75%	29.80%	66.97%	10.13%	229.26%	31.44%	494.48%	85.99%

Table 6.14 Peaks and Troughs in Actual (Short-Term) U.S. Interest Rates Since 1978

	Date	Rate %	Comment
Trough	Early 1978	7	—
Peak	Early 1980	17	10% upswing in a 2-year span
Trough	Late 1980	8.5	A drop of over 8% in less than a year
Peak	Early 1981	18	Up more than 9% in under a year
Trough	Late 1981	12.5	A decline of 5% within a year
Peak	Early 1982	15	A 2.5% rise in less than a year
Trough	Early 1983	8.5	A fall of over 6% in a year
Peak	Mid-1984	11.5	Up 3% in 1½ years
Trough	Mid-1986	5.75	Down almost 6% in 2 years
Peak	Mid-1989	10	Up 4% in 3 years
Trough	Mid-1992	3.75	Down over 6% in 3 years

Anatomy of a "Killing"

Let's pause to appreciate the mechanism behind VZP by taking apart the remarkable result from Table 6.10 in which a $25,000 initial deposit turned into $5,446,382 after 25 years.

The natural reaction is: How is this possible? First, let's understand that it *is* possible. In defense of the underlying interest rate scenario (Real-U), those who feel that several oscillations between 5 and 10 percent over 25 years represent far more volatility than one would likely find in reality are directed to Table 6.14, which shows how extreme the actual moves in (short-term) U.S. interest rates have been over the last 15 years.

According to Merton's law*: "Whatever is, is possible." The dramatic shifts listed in Table 6.14 have happened and so can happen again. Their example places the burden of proof on those who may claim that fluctuations like those in Real-U are impossible. It has been said that the past does not repeat itself—but sometimes it rhymes.

Let's look at the $5 million-plus VZP payoff year by year. Table 6.15 details interest rates, the starting and ending positions in cash and zeros, the percentage change in equity, and the cumulative

* Sociologist Robert K. Merton.

compound rate of return. Figure 6.2 shows the year-end value of Plan Z, cash, and bonds in this scenario.

To read the sequence of events recorded in Table 6.15:

1. Begin with a given year's "starting allocation."
2. Then see what happened to rates from that year to the next. The change in rates determines the "ending allocation." If the long-rate goes up, zero prices drop (and if the long-rate falls, zero prices rise). The cash account always earns the short-term rate, whatever it may be. (The ending allocation should always equal the total shown in "year-end total.")
3. One year's ending allocation becomes the next year's starting allocation but first it is rebalanced according to the new Z percentage that the VZP formula dictates (keying off the short-term rate). Thus, the *ending* total of $99,270 in Year 6 is the identical sum that *starts off* Year 7, just distributed differently because of the new Z-percentage (only $3,309 was invested in zeros instead of $82,967).
4. The Z percentage for any given year is determined by plugging in the short-term rate for that year in place of the variable "i" of the relevant VZP formula. In Year 6, the Z percentage was 70.5 because the short-term rate was 5.82 and Z% = 25 (5.82) − 75 = 70.5. It became 3.25 in Year 7 when the short-term rate plummeted to 3.13 because in that year Z% = 25 (3.13) − 75 = 3.25.

Although our aggressive investor started this scenario with an off year (in which his holdings declined to $21,510 from his original $25,000), he endured only nine losing years overall and was able to enjoy 16 winning ones (including six out of the first seven years). By Year 4, his annual compound return was already in double digits, a lofty perch from which it never fell—despite the fact that for the first five years, he did no rebalancing and remained entirely invested in zeros.

Table 6.15 Anatomy of a "Killing"

Year	Starting rates		Z %**	Starting allocation		Ending allocation		Year-end total	This year's change	CRR*
	Short-term	Long-term		Zeros	Cash	Zeros	Cash			
1	7.00	8.50	100.0	$25,000	–	$21,510	–	$21,510	−14%	−14%
2	10.27	9.37	100.0	$21,510	–	$23,845	–	$23,845	11%	−2%
3	7.82	9.32	100.0	$23,845	–	$29,419	–	$29,419	23%	6%
4	7.37	8.87	100.0	$29,419	–	$37,722	–	$37,722	28%	11%
5	9.15	8.25	100.0	$37,722	–	$52,421	–	$52,421	39%	16%
6	5.82	7.32	70.5	$37,015	$15,406	$82,967	$16,303	$99,270	89%	26%
7	3.13	4.63	3.3	$3,309	$95,962	$1,387	$98,969	$100,356	1%	22%
8	6.49	7.99	87.3	$87,483	$12,873	$68,725	$13,707	$82,432	−18%	16%
9	7.68	9.18	100.0	$82,433	–	$138,721	–	$138,721	68%	21%
10	6.06	7.56	76.5	$106,170	$32,551	$101,428	$34,524	$135,952	−2%	18%
11	8.91	8.01	100.0	$135,952	–	$90,685	–	$90,685	−33%	12%
12	10.75	9.85	100.0	$90,685	–	$158,723	–	$158,723	75%	17%
13	6.56	8.06	89.0	$141,290	$17,433	$227,290	$18,577	$245,867	55%	19%
14	5.09	6.59	52.2	$128,353	$117,513	$79,705	$123,492	$203,197	−17%	16%
15	7.10	8.60	100.0	$203,198	–	$245,225	–	$245,225	21%	16%
16	9.11	8.21	100.0	$245,225	–	$531,832	–	$531,832	117%	21%
17	4.13	5.63	28.4	$150,825	$381,007	$47,039	$396,759	$443,798	−17%	18%
18	8.67	10.17	100.0	$443,798	–	$673,288	–	$673,288	52%	20%
19	9.86	8.96	100.0	$673,288	–	$1,604,832	–	$1,604,832	138%	24%
20	4.56	6.06	39.0	$626,872	$977,960	$251,677	$1,022,579	$1,274,256	−21%	22%
21	8.17	9.67	100.0	$1,274,256	–	$1,232,644	–	$1,232,644	−3%	20%
22	8.65	10.15	100.0	$1,232,644	–	$4,389,706	–	$4,389,706	256%	26%
23	4.28	5.78	32.1	$1,408,441	$2,981,266	$1,688,295	$3,108,966	$4,797,261	9%	26%
24	3.83	5.33	20.7	$993,484	$3,803,776	$384,007	$3,949,399	$4,333,406	−10%	24%
25	7.53	9.03	100.0	$4,333,406	–	$5,446,382	–	$5,446,382	26%	24%

*The equivalent annual Compound Rate of Return since inception.
**Z% = 25 (i) −75.

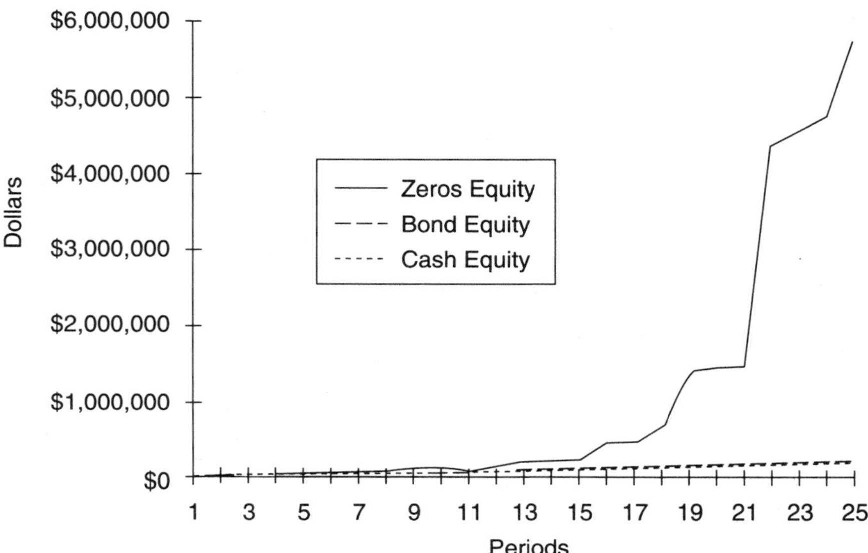

Figure 6.2 Anatomy of a "killing."

Until Year 6, rates stayed above his chosen I_{max} of 7 percent, which meant his Z percentage was, for the time being, fixed at his chosen maximum of 100. Without a cash position of any kind, he was unable to do any buying or selling. But his total equity grew nonetheless, because rates fell for six straight years.

Rates finally changed direction in Year 7, soaring 3.36 percent. But our investor was not seriously hurt by collapsing zero prices because he had parked almost 97 percent of his previous gains in cash. His Z percentage had been drastically reduced, from 70.5 to 3.3, precisely in accord with his VZP formula, when rates fell the year before. Although his cash appreciated a mere 3.13 percent in Year 7 and his zeros lost a great deal of their value, his net worth actually rose a percent anyway, because he had so much cash and so few zeros. By then he had over $100,000 on account and a compound annual rate of return of 22 percent. In three of the next four years, he lost money as interest rates largely increased. Because rates were consistently at or near his I_{max} in this period, his Z percentage was fairly high, and a good proportion of his funds were vulnerable to the ravages of rising rates. But by the same token, the fact that he was entirely invested in zeros helped him in Year 12 when rates finally did fall and he more than recouped the losses he'd suffered in the previous two years.

Two years in particular accounted for a huge portion of his profits in dollar terms. Over the course of Year 19, he made nearly $1 million. Fully invested in zeros when interest rates plunged 2.9 percent, the price of his extra-volatile 30-year zeros was jacked up 138 percent. The other big gain came in Year 22, when he took similar advantage of a massive 4.37 percent rate drop to reap a 256 percent gain and added $3,157,062 to his portfolio. Both years, it must be admitted, witnessed extraordinarily violent interest rate shifts. Yet movements of this type are not entirely unheard of (see Table 6.14). Significant as the roles played by Years 19 and 22 may be, before either, our investor already had a compound rate of return of 20 percent. Had he instead maintained only that level of success for the full 25 years, he would still have made $2.38 million.

The key factors in this "killing": (1) a number of huge swings in rates; (2) the selection of highly volatile 30-year constant-duration zeros (using 25-year zeros in an otherwise identical simulation resulted in $2,821,013, 20-year zeros $1,488,379, and 15-year zeros a "mere" $801,449); and (3) several beautifully timed switches completely into and out of zeros, the result of the investor's aggressively defined Z Range and his fortunate "forecast" of interest rates. The latter kept him almost fully invested in zeros when rates were high and pushed him into cash when they were low. It turns out that several other more-restrictive Z Ranges (0–20, 40–60, 25–75, 50–100, and 80–100) all grossly underperform this particular all-or-nothing approach, though some did manage as much as $1.4 million. Not only was this aggressive investor able to take advantage of a number of steep declines in interest rates, but his VZP formula also caused him to sidestep several potentially devastating losses by lessening his Z percentage at critical times.

Ideally enacted, Plan Z will "force" the sale of zeros when rates are near their lows and the purchase of zeros when rates are at or near their highs. By that standard, the aggressive investor in this example performed superbly. Interest rates fell into the low end of his specified I Range of 3 to 7 percent on five occasions, meaning he cashed out of zeros in a big way each time because VZP forced his Z percentage to zero or close to it. Four times out of five, rates promptly soared, causing zero prices to become "bargains" again—just after he had sold them at high prices. Those same high rates are exactly what caused VZP to then raise his Z percentage, directing him to invest that much more in zeros at their bargain levels once again.

In the end, credit for this scenario's success should go to VZP itself. The final equity of $5,446,382 is far ahead of results using other methods. In the same circumstances (same interest rate scenario, same duration zeros), a fixed Z-50 tactic (Table 5.13) would have generated $444,289, while a straight investment in zeros, bought and held for the period (equivalent to a fixed Z percentage of 100), would have yielded just $172,464 (still 9 percent better than bonds and 24 percent more than cash).

Selecting the "Right" Interest Rate Range

One question remains: Why did our aggressive investor do better when he guessed "low" than when he picked interest rates almost exactly right? What can this case tell us about the best strategy for determining an I_{max} and I_{min}?

Clearly, if an investor's specified I Range is entirely above or below actual rates, he will, for all practical purposes, be stuck with a fixed Z percentage. (If they are always higher than his selected range, his Z percentage will be identical to his Z_{max}. If they are below, VZP will always rebalance at his Z_{min}.) What happens if his Z_{max} and Z_{min} correspond precisely with the actual extremes? Then he will have some advantage over a fixed Z percentage to the extent that these extremes are repeatedly attained, causing VZP to maximize his buying and selling. But if interest rates only infrequently

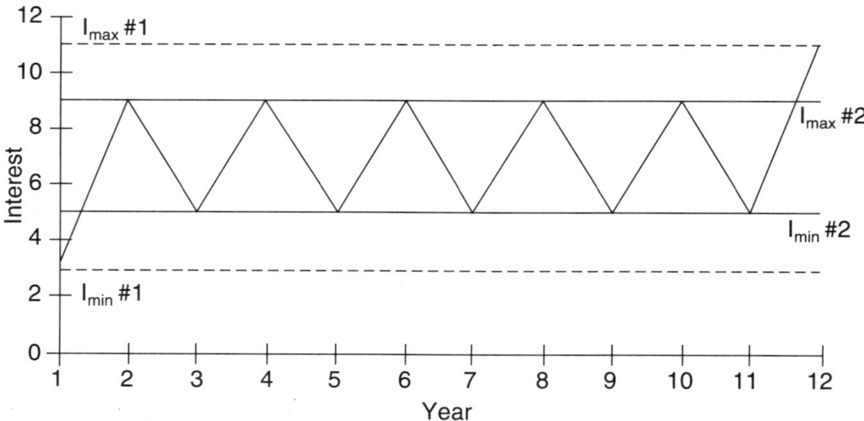

Figure 6.3 The more correct I Range guess is not necessarily the more profitable one.

reach the vicinity of the I_{max} and I_{min} his Z percentage will rarely approach his Z_{min} or Z_{max}, remaining constrained instead within a relatively narrow range. This point is illustrated in Figure 6.3.

Other things being equal, the investor who picked I_{max} and I_{min} #2 in Figure 6.3 will outperform the investor who selected the more extreme values because interest rates touch his Z_{max} and Z_{min} more frequently. He will repeatedly take maximum profits as VZP pushes him from one (relatively) extreme Z percentage to another again and again. The investor who picked I_{max} and I_{min} number 1 will be buying and selling at the same time but in lesser quantities because his Z percentage will be more moderate at these turning points than number 2's. If, however, investor 1 had selected a wider Z Range than investor 2, investor 1 might actually have prevailed. This means you can compensate to some extent for a broad I Range by selecting a more aggressive Z Range. In other words, the greater the span of your Z Range, the narrower your I Range can be.

If you want the best possible VZP performance, follow these guidelines:

1. Try to pick the interest rate range you think will be highly trafficked (this ensures that VZP will be engaged as much

as possible. You don't want rates floating above or below your range but moving through it again and again).

2. Select the most aggressive (widest) Z percentage you are comfortable with (this will exaggerate the dynamic of buying and selling that much more).
3. If there are two or more interest rate zones you feel are equally likely to be active, choose the one that is relatively lower (because in the lower range, each percentage point represents a greater portion of the whole, making for greater volatility. For example, the swing in zero prices when rates move from 5 to 6 percent is much greater than when they go from 12 to 13 percent).

To summarize: The object in picking interest rates is not to predict the absolute poles but to be where the "action" is, to select an I_{min} and I_{max} that describe a range likely to be more frequently traversed than any other. Try to concentrate your Z percentage into a reasonable fraction of the anticipated range rather than attempting to encompass it. Because we know that 0 percent is the absolute lower bound on rates and we have no inkling what the upper bound may be, we have yet another reason to believe that if you want to shoot high with Plan Z, *it's best to aim low.* A third reason: If you guess wrong, aiming low will keep you in higher-yielding zeros instead of lower-yielding cash: An error will force you to spend more time either at your Z_{max} (if you guessed too low) or your Z_{min} (too high) than is optimal. So if you must err (and it is likely you will), it is best to guess low. By causing VZP to over-invest in zeros rather than cash you will at least earn the higher rate associated with long-term instruments.

VZP in Review

By just looking at the results, you can see that VZP is a clear improvement over ZB (dynamic balancing with zeros), just as ZB was an advance over dollar-cost averaging. This is to be expected since the rules that drive each are progressively more powerful and effective. Each extends its predecessor's strengths or eliminates some weakness. Dollar-cost averaging helps you buy cheap; dynamic balancing enables you to sell dear as well; VZP makes it possible to do both in a situation-sensitive way. Its flexibility makes it a dynamic form of dynamic balancing.

In the next chapter, we will introduce a form of Plan Z that fastens on another variable—time—adjusting it to specific conditions according to each investor's temperament and outlook.

7

Controlling Time

The Variable Zero Duration

Now that we've seen how well VZP worked when we made one aspect of Plan Z flexible, why not liberate another? The candidate in this chapter is time. If we allow Plan Z free play along the duration axis (length of investment) instead of the cash axis (amount of investment), the result is the variable zero duration, or VZD.

VZD operates almost exactly the way VZP does. But instead of a high and low Z percentage (Z_{max} and Z_{min}), you choose a maximum and minimum zero duration (D_{max} and D_{min}), which establishes your D Range.* Whereas VZP fixed your zero duration and varied your Z percentage, the variable zero duration (VZD) fixes your Z percentage and allows your zeros' duration to change. Like VZP, VZD boosts yields beyond those any fixed form of Plan Z can generate. VZP squeezes more out of each rebalancing cycle by adjusting the

* Despite the name, you don't have to be "deranged" to try this.

amount of cash invested in zeros; VZD accomplishes much the same by shifting the amount of *time* for which you invest. VZP lends more dollars when interest rates are high; VZD lends money for a longer time at high rates. Under VZP, each rebalancing called for the shifting of funds and the simultaneous establishment of a new Z percentage. VZD trades at a fixed Z percentage but changes the *kind* of zeros it employs, swapping durations as the investor's personal formula directs.

From a speculative standpoint, the only question facing fixed-instrument investors is whether to be in bills or bonds—in other words, whether to lend short or long. The variable Z percentage determines when you should husband cash and when you should lend long-term. The variable zero duration, by contrast, defines what long-end *means*, whether 5, 10, 15, or 20 years into the future.

Essentially, VZD does right what dollar-cost averaging with zeros couldn't. We've stressed two points in this book so far: (1) Buying cheap is not our objective, but lending a lot of money when interest rates are high and lending a small amount when interest rates are low *is*. (2) When rates are high, it is better to lend for a longer time; when rates are low, it is better to lend for a shorter time. The first point was directly addressed by VZP; the second will be—by VZD.

How does VZD work? As interest rates go up, the duration of your zeros automatically goes up as well—as determined by your VZD formula*; and when rates go down, the duration of your zeros drops with them. In its action VZD is more like the elevator game used to describe ZB (in Chapter 5) than anything yet discussed in this book, because it really has your money moving from a fast (high-duration) to a slow (low-duration) vehicle as the situation dictates. The reason we want to modulate the volatility of our zeros—the point of varying their duration—is to take advantage of rising and falling rates to different ends. Remember Table 2.4? We saw there that every 1 percent drop in the interest rate can push a 30-year zero's price up nearly 33 percent while nudging the price of

* The VZD formula is identical to the VZP formula, except for the substitution of durations for Z percentages. See Appendix A.

Table 7.1 VZD with I Range from 3% to 10% and D Range from 9 to 30 Years

When i is	VZD will call for ownership of
3% or less	9-year zeros
4%	12-year zeros
5%	15-year zeros
6%	18-year zeros
7%	21-year zeros
8%	24-year zeros
9%	27-year zeros
10% or more	30-year zeros

a 5-year zero just 5 percent higher. On the other hand, if rates go up 1 percent, they'll drive down the price of a 30-year zero by around 25 percent while a 5-year zero's price will decrease just 4 or 5 percent.

If VZD were a car, we would want to install an automatic transmission that runs in overdrive when it goes forward but can only go slowly in reverse. VZD's objective is to be in overdrive (the 30-year zero) when rates are moving forward (that is, falling) and move haltingly (via the 5-year zero) when rates are going backward (rising).

Assuming you had selected an I Range from 3 to 10 percent and a D Range from 9 to 30 (that is, you decided the duration of your zeros should be no more than 30 years and no less than 9), then you would find yourself owning zeros of different durations under the different conditions shown in Table 7.1.

Like VZP, VZD not only wrests more profit from certain positions, it also automatically protects you from loss, limiting the consequences of potentially adverse situations. It does so by moving into zeros of a shorter duration that will not decline so much in value (as a percentage) if interest rates retrace their steps and undo a favorable move. Say you stated the preferences noted in Table 7.1 and rates went from 9 to 7 percent. Two things would happen: Your 27-year zeros would increase in value by 70 percent because of the interest rate decline, and your VZD formula would call for a switch to zeros with a duration of 21 years. If rates should hop back

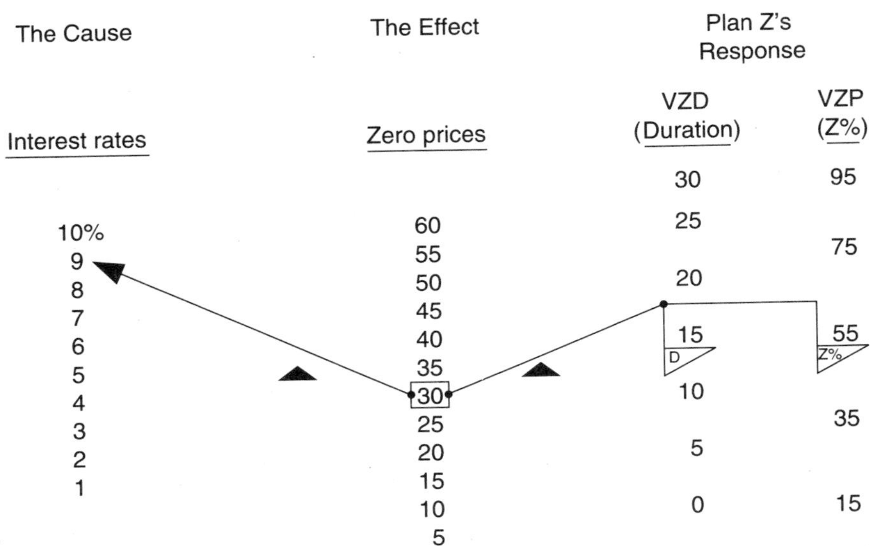

Figure 7.1 Two "seesaws," connected by the price of zeros, illustrate how Plan Z responds to interest rate fluctuations.

up to 9 percent, you will be holding less volatile zeros and "give back" less in losses than you made in profit on the way down. Of course, should rates fall farther instead—say to 5 percent—you won't make quite as much with 21-year zeros as you would have with the longer-duration instruments you just traded in. But they will still turn in a 40 percent profit. And then, with rates at 5 percent, VZD will advise you to change duration still again—this time to 15-year zeros. If rates *now* jump back up 2 percent, you'll return only about 28 percent of what you had gleaned the round before. (In fact, if rates keep oscillating in a 2 percent range between 9 and 7 percent, you'll repeatedly make 40 percent and give back only 28 percent.)

VZP pulls money out of your zeros directly; VZD achieves the same objective for your plan by reducing the duration of the zeros in it. When VZD switches from 30- to 15-year zeros, it is fully invested in zeros, but they are now of a "lesser" sort, closer by halfway to cash. The mechanism is different from VZP but the effect is nearly the same.

Figure 7.1 depicts a mechanical analogy of how VZP and VZD work.

As rates (at the left in Figure 7.1) rise or fall, zero prices move inversely at the other end of the seesaw that connects them. Through the action of VZP or VZD (the seesaw at right), an adjustment is made in Plan Z—raising or lowering either the Z percentage or zero duration, whichever plan is in use.

VZD Simulations

The ensuing computer simulations reveal VZD's abilities. In format and assumptions (term, deposit, interest rate scenarios, and interest rate guesses), these examples are identical to Tables 6.11 through 6.13. The only difference: The investors choose different kinds of parameters because of their different requirements. In Tables 7.2 through 7.4, three kinds of interest rate guesses (low, high, and wide) were combined with three duration ranges (0–15, 15–30, and 0–30—that is, low, high, and wide) and three Z percentages (20, 50, and 80—low, medium, and high).

As you can see, VZD generated an average of $211,437, which was 57.62 percent better than cash and 40.61 percent ahead of bonds. These results place VZD alongside VZP as a more effective version of Plan Z, though it falls shy of VZP's average return of $285,638 by 26 percent. However, it manifests some redeeming features that VZP does not share. It may not amass sums quite as large as VZP, but it piles up its somewhat more modest gains with greater consistency. Its results are more closely clustered around the average. So you don't get as many very large returns with VZD, but you don't get large "losses," either. (Remember, a "loss" means a result that fails to equal a cash or bond investment—*not* necessarily an actual loss of dollars.)

Both plans do very well overall. Under the best circumstances, VZP will do a bit better. But, in less favorable states of affairs, VZD will excel at "damage control."

VZD Tactics

A tip when using VZD: Avoid a high D Range (e.g., 15 to 30 years). First of all, it entails a greater risk of loss (relative to cash or bonds)

Table 7.2 VZD: Summary of Simulated Results

Rate guess	Duration range	Z%	GR	GF	GU	GRU	GFU	GR/F	GF/R	R-R/F	R-F/R	R-U	Average
Low	0–15 years	20	$113,575	111,475	114,063	115,242	143,480	145,499	122,499	240,401	200,934	205,674	151,284
		50	113,991	128,190	124,690	115,956	171,602	163,547	142,113	350,795	252,187	337,777	190,085
		80	114,405	147,247	135,751	116,314	204,107	179,146	161,211	462,389	297,384	504,393	232,235
	15–30 years	20	107,420	118,055	115,547	107,458	158,762	157,618	132,231	380,923	247,733	316,712	184,246
		50	99,136	147,773	127,213	96,118	217,279	184,978	159,797	658,091	339,389	633,487	266,326
		80	91,451	184,554	137,491	84,384	290,110	193,753	173,660	674,905	344,300	751,193	292,580
	0–30 years	20	108,264	117,273	116,658	110,734	157,210	160,672	136,922	405,055	263,743	367,873	194,440
		50	101,103	145,354	130,478	104,029	212,532	194,662	175,892	849,268	410,025	999,212	332,256
		80	94,385	179,775	143,507	96,400	281,108	211,439	205,532	1,189,445	492,645	1,833,718	472,795
High	0–15 years	20	115,961	103,670	110,494	116,838	134,935	146,108	116,305	191,039	167,919	162,372	136,564
		50	120,069	106,981	115,538	120,297	147,747	168,144	126,998	215,453	169,925	203,364	149,452
		80	124,312	110,385	120,779	123,825	161,599	192,422	138,340	239,139	171,568	251,954	163,432
	15–30 years	20	111,958	113,116	114,238	111,028	150,438	155,450	124,291	253,369	189,754	216,411	154,005
		50	109,974	132,928	124,927	105,232	192,031	188,014	144,820	343,470	211,973	332,518	188,589
		80	108,020	156,030	135,749	98,962	242,149	215,345	161,808	367,778	214,154	398,516	209,851
	0–30 years	20	115,440	104,490	111,944	116,525	140,439	158,334	122,076	221,217	170,507	198,899	145,987
		50	118,727	109,098	119,306	119,417	162,858	202,187	142,336	288,587	175,531	324,317	176,236
		80	122,102	113,880	127,042	122,253	188,098	252,188	164,293	352,479	179,038	502,855	212,423
Wide	0–15 years	20	115,971	109,139	113,760	117,245	139,794	146,610	120,747	213,699	186,394	185,677	144,904
		50	120,096	121,616	124,147	121,261	161,211	168,641	138,765	279,650	217,938	277,035	173,036
		80	124,361	135,453	135,292	125,277	185,438	191,639	158,151	352,798	250,707	397,926	205,704
	15–30 years	20	109,660	115,554	114,803	108,951	154,080	156,028	127,710	297,520	213,199	257,707	165,521
		50	104,407	140,144	125,917	99,972	202,920	185,562	151,243	446,359	263,158	449,771	216,945
		80	99,386	169,686	136,515	90,566	262,612	203,597	167,007	468,627	271,094	540,136	240,923
	0–30 years	20	112,845	112,371	115,423	114,129	148,396	158,746	129,296	273,449	205,932	261,700	163,229
		50	112,169	130,758	128,285	113,005	185,978	198,478	160,616	445,271	266,469	565,128	230,616
		80	111,493	151,995	141,797	111,345	230,813	235,537	192,490	621,004	321,330	1,033,480	315,128
	Average		111,136	130,259	124,495	110,473	186,212	182,013	148,043	410,451	247,960	463,326	211,437
		Cash	113,296	101,512	107,237	114,571	126,938	132,612	109,527	174,356	166,388	138,834	
		Bonds	113,814	126,666	122,744	113,439	157,310	120,372	147,862	177,997	219,044	157,943	

Table 7.3 VZD versus Cash

Rate guess	Duration range	Z%	GR	GF	GU	GRU	GFU	GR/F	GF/R	R-R/F	R-F/R	R-U	Average
Low	0–15 years	20	0.25%	9.81%	6.37%	0.59%	13.03%	9.72%	11.84%	37.88%	20.76%	48.14%	15.84%
		50	0.61%	26.28%	16.28%	1.21%	35.19%	23.33%	29.75%	101.19%	51.57%	143.30%	42.87%
		80	0.98%	45.05%	26.59%	1.52%	60.79%	35.09%	47.19%	165.20%	78.73%	263.31%	72.44%
	15–30 years	20	−5.19%	16.30%	7.75%	−6.21%	25.07%	18.86%	20.73%	118.47%	48.89%	128.12%	37.28%
		50	−12.50%	45.57%	18.63%	−16.11%	71.17%	39.49%	45.90%	277.44%	103.97%	356.29%	92.99%
		80	−19.28%	81.81%	28.21%	−26.35%	128.54%	46.11%	58.55%	287.08%	106.93%	441.07%	113.27%
	0–30 years	20	−4.44%	15.53%	8.79%	−3.35%	23.85%	21.16%	25.01%	132.31%	58.51%	164.97%	44.23%
		50	−10.76%	43.19%	21.67%	−9.20%	67.43%	46.79%	60.59%	387.09%	146.43%	619.72%	137.29%
		80	−16.69%	77.10%	33.82%	−15.86%	121.45%	59.44%	87.65%	582.19%	196.08%	1220.80%	234.60%
High	0–15 years	20	2.35%	2.13%	3.04%	1.98%	6.30%	10.18%	6.19%	9.57%	0.92%	16.95%	5.96%
		50	5.98%	5.39%	7.74%	5.00%	16.39%	26.79%	15.95%	23.57%	2.13%	46.48%	15.54%
		80	9.72%	8.74%	12.63%	8.08%	27.31%	45.10%	26.31%	37.16%	3.11%	81.48%	25.96%
	15–30 years	20	−1.18%	11.43%	6.53%	−3.09%	18.51%	17.22%	13.48%	45.32%	14.04%	55.88%	17.81%
		50	−2.93%	30.95%	16.50%	−8.15%	51.28%	41.78%	32.22%	96.99%	27.40%	139.51%	42.55%
		80	−4.66%	53.71%	26.59%	−13.62%	90.76%	62.39%	47.73%	110.94%	28.71%	187.04%	58.96%
	0–30 years	20	1.89%	2.93%	4.39%	1.71%	10.64%	19.40%	11.46%	26.88%	2.48%	43.26%	12.50%
		50	4.79%	7.47%	11.25%	4.23%	28.30%	52.47%	29.96%	65.52%	5.49%	133.60%	34.31%
		80	7.77%	12.18%	18.47%	6.71%	48.18%	90.17%	50.00%	102.16%	7.60%	262.20%	60.54%
Wide	0–15 years	20	2.36%	7.51%	6.08%	2.33%	10.13%	10.56%	10.24%	22.56%	12.02%	33.74%	11.75%
		50	6.00%	19.80%	15.77%	5.84%	27.00%	27.17%	26.69%	60.39%	30.98%	99.54%	31.92%
		80	9.77%	33.44%	26.16%	9.34%	46.09%	44.51%	44.39%	102.34%	50.68%	186.62%	55.33%
	15–30 years	20	−3.21%	13.83%	7.06%	−4.91%	21.38%	17.66%	16.60%	70.64%	28.13%	85.62%	25.28%
		50	−7.85%	38.06%	17.42%	−12.74%	59.86%	39.93%	38.09%	156.00%	58.16%	223.96%	61.09%
		80	−12.28%	67.16%	27.30%	−20.95%	106.88%	53.53%	52.48%	168.78%	62.93%	289.05%	79.49%
	0–30 years	20	−0.40%	10.70%	7.63%	−0.39%	16.90%	19.71%	18.05%	56.83%	23.77%	88.50%	24.13%
		50	−0.99%	28.81%	19.63%	−1.37%	46.51%	49.67%	46.65%	155.38%	60.15%	307.05%	71.15%
		80	−1.59%	49.73%	32.23%	−2.82%	81.83%	77.61%	75.75%	256.17%	93.12%	644.40%	130.64%
	Average		−1.91%	28.32%	16.09%	−3.58%	46.70%	37.25%	35.17%	135.41%	49.03%	233.73%	57.62%

Table 7.4 VZD versus Bonds

Rate guess	Duration range	Z%	GR	GF	GU	GRU	GFU	GR/F	GF/R	R-R/F	R-F/R	R-U	Average
Low	0–15 years	20	−0.21%	−11.99%	−7.07%	1.59%	−8.79%	20.87%	−17.15%	35.06%	−8.27%	30.22%	3.43%
		50	0.16%	1.20%	1.59%	2.22%	9.09%	35.87%	−3.89%	97.08%	15.13%	113.86%	27.23%
		80	0.52%	16.25%	10.60%	2.53%	29.75%	48.83%	9.03%	159.77%	35.76%	219.35%	53.24%
	15–30 years	20	−5.62%	−6.80%	−5.86%	−5.27%	0.92%	30.94%	−10.57%	114.01%	13.10%	100.52%	22.54%
		50	−12.90%	16.66%	3.64%	−15.27%	38.12%	53.67%	8.07%	269.72%	54.94%	301.09%	71.78%
		80	−19.65%	45.70%	12.01%	−25.61%	84.42%	60.96%	17.45%	279.17%	57.18%	375.61%	88.72%
	0–30 years	20	−4.88%	−7.42%	−4.96%	−2.38%	−0.06%	33.48%	−7.40%	127.56%	20.41%	132.92%	28.73%
		50	−11.17%	14.75%	6.30%	−8.30%	35.10%	61.72%	18.96%	377.12%	87.19%	532.64%	111.43%
		80	−17.07%	41.93%	16.92%	−15.02%	78.70%	75.65%	39.00%	568.24%	124.91%	1,061.00%	197.43%
High	0–15 years	20	1.89%	−18.15%	−9.98%	3.00%	−14.22%	21.38%	−21.34%	7.33%	−23.34%	2.80%	−5.06%
		50	5.50%	−15.54%	−5.87%	6.05%	−6.08%	39.69%	−14.11%	21.04%	−22.42%	28.76%	3.70%
		80	9.22%	−12.85%	−1.60%	9.16%	2.73%	59.86%	−6.44%	34.35%	−21.67%	59.52%	13.23%
	15–30 years	20	−1.63%	−10.70%	−6.93%	−2.13%	−4.37%	29.14%	−15.94%	42.34%	−13.37%	37.02%	5.34%
		50	−3.37%	4.94%	1.78%	−7.23%	22.07%	56.19%	−2.06%	92.96%	−3.23%	110.53%	27.26%
		80	−5.09%	23.18%	10.60%	−12.76%	53.93%	78.90%	9.43%	106.62%	−2.23%	152.32%	41.49%
	0–30 years	20	1.43%	−17.51%	−8.80%	2.72%	−10.72%	31.54%	−17.44%	24.28%	−22.16%	25.93%	0.93%
		50	4.32%	−13.87%	−2.80%	5.27%	3.53%	67.97%	−3.74%	62.13%	−19.86%	105.34%	20.83%
		80	7.28%	−10.09%	3.50%	7.77%	19.57%	109.51%	11.11%	98.03%	−18.26%	218.38%	44.68%
Wide	0–15 years	20	1.90%	−13.84%	−7.32%	3.36%	−11.13%	21.80%	−18.34%	20.06%	−14.91%	17.56%	−0.09%
		50	5.52%	−3.99%	1.14%	6.90%	2.48%	40.10%	−6.15%	57.11%	−0.50%	75.40%	17.80%
		80	9.27%	6.94%	10.22%	10.44%	17.88%	59.21%	6.96%	98.20%	14.46%	151.94%	38.55%
	15–30 years	20	−3.65%	−8.77%	−6.47%	−3.96%	−2.05%	29.62%	−13.63%	67.15%	−2.67%	63.16%	11.87%
		50	−8.27%	10.64%	2.59%	−11.87%	28.99%	54.16%	2.29%	150.77%	20.14%	184.77%	43.42%
		80	−12.68%	33.96%	11.22%	−20.16%	66.94%	69.14%	12.95%	163.28%	23.76%	241.98%	59.04%
	0–30 years	20	−0.85%	−11.29%	−5.96%	0.61%	−5.67%	31.88%	−12.56%	53.63%	−5.99%	65.69%	10.95%
		50	−1.45%	3.23%	4.51%	−0.38%	18.22%	64.89%	8.63%	150.16%	21.65%	257.81%	52.73%
		80	−2.04%	20.00%	15.52%	−1.85%	46.72%	95.67%	30.18%	248.88%	46.70%	554.34%	105.41%
	Average		−2.35%	2.84%	1.43%	−2.61%	18.37%	51.21%	0.12%	130.59%	13.20%	193.35%	40.61%

Table 7.5 VZD: Averaged Results, by Range Category

D range	Low I range		High I range		Wide I range		Total
Low (0–15)	$191,201	+	$149,816	+	$174,548	=	$171,855
High (15–30)	247,717	+	184,148	+	207,796	=	213,220
Wide (0–30)	333,164	+	178,215	+	236,324	=	249,234

than the other duration ranges. Fully 18 of the 30 instances in which VZD was outdistanced by its competitors involved high D Ranges (the wide range was beaten 12 times and the low range not once). There's an obvious trade-off between the low and wide D Ranges. The latter gives far more profit on average (see Table 7.5) but with more instances of losses, whereas the former offers less profit, but does so with no losses at all (again, these are "losses" only *relative* to bonds and cash). The high D Range has nothing to recommend it. It is somewhat more profitable than the low D Range but not nearly as safe. Compared to the wide range, it is both less profitable *and* a greater risk.

What accounts for the problems of the high D Range? Its most conservative posture—the refuge it takes when rates have descended—is the 15-year zero. This effectively prevents any investor who employs it from significantly lessening the risk of holding zeros. For however long zero prices zoom skyward, he will remain stuck with 15-year zeros. Thus, when zero prices collapse, his equity is likewise dragged along. Except for unusual cases (such as an exceptionally prescient rate forecast by a high D Range investor or a bizarre choice of parameters by a wide range investor), a wider D Range (something approaching 0 to 30 years) is both more profitable and less risky than a high one, and much more profitable (if more risky) than a low one. It accomplishes this by working both ends of the buy low, sell high imperative, affording the possibility of full protection when rates rise and full participation when they fall.

Freeing the elements of Plan Z as far as we can, making them adaptable to real conditions, pays off in several ways. VZP and VZD are significant improvements on their fixed counterparts. A question: If this trick works so well for Z percentages and durations separately and singly, what would happen if we let both vary simultaneously within the same plan? In the next chapter we develop the final and finest version of Plan Z, one capable of many things, including bringing the high duration range—which we have just buried—back to life.

8

Ultimate Z

The Variable Plans Combined

Because Z percentages and durations are independent of one another, it is a simple matter to vary both at the same time. Their joint liberation in one plan, the next step on Plan Z's evolutionary ladder, is more multiplicative than additive in its effects—the reason we dub this version VZ^2.

VZ² Simulations

Before we explore the whys and wherefores of VZ^2, let's look at what it can do. Tables 8.1 through 8.9 show the results of simulations performed across the 10 interest rate scenarios we have used in the two previous chapters. In all cases here, we set the Z Range to 0 to 100, a position (as we shall see) that is both the most aggressive and the most defensive available to us. As with prior

VZP and VZD simulations, we track a $25,000 deposit for 25 years. Separate tables (8.1, 8.4, and 8.7) depict each of three different D Ranges: low (0–15 years), high (15–30 years), and wide (0–30 years). For all tables, our hypothetical investor selects two I Ranges: the one over which he wants his duration to vary (call this his I_d Range) and another that will account for adjustments in his Z percentage (his I_z Range). We have juggled all possible combinations of low, high, and wide I Ranges. (These last three terms are defined just as they were in chapters 6 and 7.)

The average outcome for all three D Ranges (Tables 8.1, 8.4, and 8.7) is $321,262, better than either VZP or VZD on its own. Tables 8.2, 8.5, and 8.8 compare the low, high, and wide D Ranges to cash, and Tables 8.3, 8.6, and 8.9 depict the same ranges versus bonds.

One interesting fact jumps out immediately. In the last chapter we admonished readers to stay clear of a high D Range when using VZD because it did not generate returns on a par with a wide D Range and also incurred a disproportionate share of "losses" (relative to cash and bonds). In the context of VZ^2, however, the high D Range's reputation is resurrected with an average return of $396,977, compared to $194,445 for the low range and $371,363 for the wide range. What made the difference? The VZP component of VZ^2 rides to the rescue of the high D Range by drastically reducing the risk of holding high-duration zeros. The way it accomplishes this is a model for how VZ^2 works in general.

If you recall, the problem with a 15 to 30 D Range for VZD was that it kept the investor in a fairly long-duration zero at all times, thwarting any defensive action, however dire the circumstances. But now the variable Z percentage can do the work the duration (still) cannot. We know that the Z percentage is moved in the same direction as durations are when interest rates go up or down. So as the VZD component is reducing the duration (in accord with the chosen D Range), the VZP formula is simultaneously shrinking the Z percentage (as specified in the Z Range). Should interest rates sink and zero prices soar, the duration will hit the D_{min} (in this case 15 years) and hold there no matter how high prices go.

Table 8.1 VZ²: Low D Range, with the Gamut of Other Possible Parameters

D Range	I Range for Z%	I Range for duration	GR	GF	GU	GRU	GFU	GR/F	GF/R	R-R/F	R-F/R	R-U	Average
		Cash	113,296	101,512	107,237	114,571	126,938	132,612	109,527	174,356	166,388	138,834	
		Bonds	113,814	126,666	122,744	113,439	157,310	120,372	147,862	177,997	219,044	157,943	
0–15 years	Low	Low	$114,827	150,781	142,203	116,922	215,714	200,144	187,833	484,486	358,632	896,172	286,771
		High	127,218	112,705	124,384	124,913	170,292	209,901	146,271	254,530	172,453	287,020	172,969
		Wide	125,830	137,330	139,646	124,420	193,531	211,914	174,503	353,966	269,925	547,794	227,886
	High	Low	115,405	107,612	117,199	115,752	159,051	196,700	140,036	259,978	174,853	324,934	171,152
		High	117,900	104,874	113,430	117,701	146,620	186,793	129,473	249,469	163,249	198,906	152,842
		Wide	116,665	106,240	115,299	116,831	151,645	191,381	134,466	255,101	169,662	251,893	160,918
	Wide	Low	115,118	127,467	129,565	116,491	183,289	201,513	164,928	367,855	266,113	567,382	223,972
		High	122,477	108,728	118,799	121,054	156,141	198,197	137,711	252,433	168,705	240,703	162,495
		Wide	121,165	120,834	127,031	120,791	169,782	202,384	153,948	298,406	217,215	378,424	190,998
		Average	119,623	119,619	125,284	119,431	171,785	199,881	152,130	308,469	217,867	410,359	194,445

Table 8.2 VZ^2 versus Cash (Low D Range)

D Range	I Range for Z%	I Range for duration	GR	GF	GU	GRU	GFU	GR/F	GF/R	R-R/F	R-F/R	R-U	Average
0–15 years	Low	Low	1.35%	48.54%	32.61%	2.05%	69.94%	50.92%	71.49%	177.87%	115.54%	545.50%	111.58%
		High	12.29%	11.03%	15.99%	9.03%	34.15%	58.28%	33.55%	45.98%	3.65%	106.74%	33.07%
		Wide	11.06%	35.28%	30.22%	8.60%	52.46%	59.80%	59.32%	103.01%	62.23%	294.57%	71.66%
	High	Low	1.86%	6.01%	9.29%	1.03%	25.30%	48.33%	27.86%	49.11%	5.09%	134.04%	30.79%
		High	4.06%	3.31%	5.78%	2.73%	15.51%	40.86%	18.21%	43.08%	−1.89%	43.27%	17.49%
		Wide	2.97%	4.66%	7.52%	1.97%	19.46%	44.32%	22.77%	46.31%	1.97%	81.43%	23.34%
	Wide	Low	1.61%	25.57%	20.82%	1.68%	44.39%	51.96%	50.58%	110.98%	59.94%	308.68%	67.62%
		High	8.10%	7.11%	10.78%	5.66%	23.01%	49.46%	25.73%	44.78%	1.39%	73.37%	24.94%
		Wide	6.95%	19.03%	18.46%	5.43%	33.75%	52.61%	40.56%	71.15%	30.55%	172.57%	45.11%
		Average	5.58%	17.84%	16.83%	4.24%	35.33%	50.73%	38.90%	76.92%	30.94%	195.58%	47.29%

Table 8.3 VZ² versus Bonds (Low D Range)

D Range	I Range for Z%	I Range for duration	GR	GF	GU	GRU	GFU	GR/F	GF/R	R-R/F	R-F/R	R-U	Average
0–15 years	Low	Low	0.89%	19.04%	15.85%	3.07%	37.13%	66.27%	27.03%	172.19%	63.73%	467.40%	87.26%
		High	11.78%	−11.02%	1.34%	10.11%	8.25%	74.38%	−1.08%	43.00%	−21.27%	81.72%	19.72%
		Wide	10.56%	8.42%	13.77%	9.68%	23.03%	76.05%	18.02%	98.86%	23.23%	246.83%	52.84%
	High	Low	1.40%	−15.04%	−4.52%	2.04%	1.11%	63.41%	−5.29%	46.06%	−20.17%	105.73%	17.47%
		High	3.59%	−17.20%	−7.59%	3.76%	−6.80%	55.18%	−12.44%	40.15%	−25.47%	25.94%	5.91%
		Wide	2.50%	−16.13%	−6.07%	2.99%	−3.60%	58.99%	−9.06%	43.32%	−22.54%	59.48%	10.99%
	Wide	Low	1.15%	0.63%	5.56%	2.69%	16.51%	67.41%	11.54%	106.66%	21.49%	259.23%	49.29%
		High	7.61%	−14.16%	−3.21%	6.71%	−0.74%	64.65%	−6.87%	41.82%	−22.98%	52.40%	12.52%
		Wide	6.46%	−4.60%	3.49%	6.48%	7.93%	68.13%	4.12%	67.65%	−0.83%	139.60%	29.84%
		Average	5.10%	−5.56%	2.07%	5.28%	9.20%	66.05%	2.89%	73.30%	−0.54%	159.81%	31.76%

Table 8.4 VZ²: High D Range, with the Gamut of Other Possible Parameters

D Range	I Range for Z%	I Range for duration	GR	GF	GU	GRU	GFU	GR/F	GF/R	R-R/F	R-F/R	R-U	Average
15–30 years	Low	Low	$90,276	193,255	151,082	92,493	318,784	227,863	242,806	1,386,541	600,465	4,222,507	752,607
		High	108,381	160,293	145,296	104,937	261,562	253,335	206,023	762,368	320,623	1,407,750	373,057
		Wide	98,913	176,002	148,115	98,130	285,442	240,019	223,246	962,478	436,309	2,419,389	508,804
	High	Low	111,754	112,001	124,437	112,798	191,970	287,810	180,484	419,090	192,444	990,272	272,306
		High	114,194	109,136	120,107	114,297	175,906	267,072	163,882	396,953	176,041	537,657	217,525
		Wide	112,966	110,556	122,216	113,576	182,316	276,789	171,744	408,837	185,138	772,938	245,708
	Wide	Low	100,482	147,391	139,351	102,099	244,752	274,543	226,304	1,035,696	457,200	2,554,181	528,200
		High	111,254	132,378	132,782	109,322	211,765	266,389	188,503	581,639	260,741	955,667	295,044
		Wide	105,724	139,674	135,876	105,343	225,511	269,205	205,437	730,633	338,925	1,539,061	379,539
		Average	105,994	142,298	135,474	105,888	233,112	262,558	200,937	742,693	329,765	1,711,047	396,977

Table 8.5 VZ^2 versus Cash (High D Range)

D Range	I Range for Z%	I Range for duration	GR	GF	GU	GRU	GFU	GR/F	GF/R	R-R/F	R-F/R	R-U	Average
15 to 30 yrs	Low	Low	−20.32%	90.38%	40.89%	−19.27%	151.13%	71.83%	121.69%	695.24%	260.88%	2,941.41%	433.38%
		High	−4.34%	57.91%	35.49%	−8.41%	106.05%	91.03%	88.10%	337.25%	92.70%	913.98%	170.98%
		Wide	−12.70%	73.38%	38.12%	−14.35%	124.87%	80.99%	103.83%	452.02%	162.22%	1,642.65%	265.10%
	High	Low	−1.36%	10.33%	16.04%	−1.55%	51.23%	117.03%	64.78%	140.36%	15.66%	613.28%	102.58%
		High	0.79%	7.51%	12.00%	−0.24%	38.58%	101.39%	49.63%	127.67%	5.80%	287.27%	63.04%
		Wide	−0.29%	8.91%	13.97%	−0.87%	43.63%	108.72%	56.81%	134.48%	11.27%	456.74%	83.34%
	Wide	Low	−11.31%	45.20%	29.95%	−10.89%	92.81%	107.03%	106.62%	494.01%	174.78%	1,739.74%	276.79%
		High	−1.80%	30.41%	23.82%	−4.58%	66.83%	100.88%	72.11%	233.59%	56.71%	588.35%	116.63%
		Wide	−6.68%	37.59%	26.71%	−8.05%	77.65%	103.00%	87.57%	319.05%	103.70%	1,008.56%	174.91%
		Average	−6.45%	40.18%	26.33%	−7.58%	83.64%	97.99%	83.46%	325.96%	98.19%	1,132.44%	187.42%

Table 8.6 VZ^2 versus Bonds (High D Range)

D Range	I Range for Z%	I Range for duration	GR	GF	GU	GRU	GFU	GR/F	GF/R	R-R/F	R-F/R	R-U	Average
15–30 years	Low	Low	−20.68%	52.57%	23.09%	−18.46%	102.65%	89.30%	64.21%	678.97%	174.13%	2,573.44%	371.92%
		High	−4.77%	26.55%	18.37%	−7.49%	66.27%	110.46%	39.33%	328.30%	46.37%	791.30%	141.47%
		Wide	−13.09%	38.95%	20.67%	−13.50%	81.45%	99.40%	50.98%	440.73%	99.19%	1,431.81%	223.66%
	High	Low	−1.81%	−11.58%	1.38%	−0.57%	22.03%	139.10%	22.06%	135.45%	−12.14%	526.98%	82.09%
		High	0.33%	−13.84%	−2.15%	0.76%	11.82%	121.87%	10.83%	123.01%	−19.63%	240.41%	47.34%
		Wide	−0.75%	−12.72%	−0.43%	0.12%	15.90%	129.94%	16.15%	129.69%	−15.48%	389.38%	65.18%
	Wide	Low	−11.71%	16.36%	13.53%	−10.00%	55.59%	128.08%	53.05%	481.86%	108.73%	1,517.15%	235.26%
		High	−2.25%	4.51%	8.18%	−3.63%	34.62%	121.30%	27.49%	226.77%	19.04%	505.07%	94.11%
		Wide	−7.11%	10.27%	10.70%	−7.14%	43.35%	123.64%	38.94%	310.47%	54.73%	874.44%	145.23%
		Average	−6.87%	12.34%	10.37%	−6.66%	48.19%	118.12%	35.89%	317.25%	50.55%	983.33%	156.25%

Table 8.7 VZ²: Wide D Range, with the Gamut of Other Possible Parameters

D Range	I Range for Z%	I Range for duration	GR	GF	GU	GRU	GFU	GR/F	GF/R	R-R/F	R-F/R	R-U	Average
0–30 years	Low	Low	92,603	189,032	155,759	99,524	310,599	245,689	270,676	1,272,143	689,443	5,750,690	907,616
		High	124,401	117,169	132,414	122,502	203,785	288,717	179,847	393,159	180,464	657,795	240,025
		Wide	111,185	156,796	149,931	112,352	249,435	273,838	231,060	655,691	377,550	2,041,706	435,954
	High	Low	111,754	112,001	124,437	112,985	191,309	287,810	180,484	419,090	192,444	990,272	272,259
		High	116,701	106,349	116,210	116,409	161,386	251,150	150,463	379,519	163,116	314,520	187,582
		Wide	114,194	109,136	120,107	114,684	172,835	267,072	163,882	399,467	178,513	537,657	217,755
	Wide	Low	101,762	145,758	141,320	106,438	240,508	284,165	237,243	964,205	475,190	2,890,090	558,668
		High	120,494	111,645	124,107	119,495	178,373	270,418	164,985	387,783	173,640	462,550	211,349
		Wide	112,682	130,917	134,800	113,726	204,802	276,490	198,874	531,073	278,513	1,128,669	311,055
		Average	111,753	130,978	133,232	113,124	212,559	271,705	197,502	600,237	300,986	1,641,550	371,363

Table 8.8 VZ^2 versus Cash (Wide D Range)

D Range	I Range for Z%	I Range for duration	GR	GF	GU	GRU	GFU	GR/F	GF/R	R-R/F	R-F/R	R-U	Average
0 to 30 yrs	Low	Low	−18.26%	86.22%	45.25%	−13.13%	144.69%	85.27%	147.13%	629.62%	314.36%	4,042.13%	546.33%
		High	9.80%	15.42%	23.48%	6.92%	60.54%	117.72%	64.20%	125.49%	8.46%	373.80%	80.58%
		Wide	−1.86%	54.46%	39.81%	−1.94%	96.50%	106.50%	110.96%	276.06%	26.91%	1,370.61%	217.80%
	High	Low	−1.36%	10.33%	16.04%	−1.38%	50.71%	117.03%	64.78%	140.36%	15.66%	613.28%	102.55%
		High	3.01%	4.76%	8.37%	1.60%	27.14%	89.39%	37.38%	117.67%	−1.97%	126.54%	41.39%
		Wide	0.79%	7.51%	12.00%	0.10%	36.16%	101.39%	49.63%	129.11%	7.29%	287.27%	63.12%
	Wide	Low	−10.18%	43.59%	31.78%	−7.10%	89.47%	114.28%	116.61%	453.01%	185.59%	1,981.69%	299.87%
		High	6.35%	9.98%	15.73%	4.30%	40.52%	103.92%	50.63%	122.41%	4.36%	233.17%	59.14%
		Wide	−0.54%	28.97%	25.70%	−0.74%	61.34%	108.50%	81.58%	204.59%	67.39%	712.96%	128.97%
		Average	−1.36%	29.03%	24.24%	−1.26%	67.45%	104.89%	80.32%	244.26%	80.89%	1,082.38%	171.08%

Table 8.9 VZ^2 versus Bonds (Wide D Range)

D Range	I Range for Z%	I Range for duration	GR	GF	GU	GRU	GFU	GR/F	GF/R	R-R/F	R-F/R	R-U	Average
0–30 years	Low	Low	−18.64%	49.24%	26.90%	−12.27%	97.44%	104.11%	83.06%	614.70%	214.75%	3,540.99%	470.03%
		High	9.30%	−7.50%	7.88%	7.99%	29.54%	139.85%	21.63%	120.88%	−17.61%	316.48%	62.84%
		Wide	−2.31%	23.79%	22.15%	−0.96%	58.56%	127.49%	56.27%	268.37%	72.36%	1,192,69%	181.84%
	High	Low	−1.81%	−11.58%	1.38%	−0.40%	21.61%	139.10%	22.06%	135.45%	−12.14%	526.98%	82.07%
		High	2.54%	−16.04%	−5.32%	2.62%	2.59%	108.64%	1.76%	113.22%	−25.53%	99.14%	28.36%
		Wide	0.33%	−13.84%	−2.15%	1.10%	9.87%	121.87%	10.83%	124.42%	−18.50%	240.41%	47.44%
	Wide	Low	−10.59%	15.07%	15.13%	−6.17%	52.89%	136.07%	60.45%	441.70%	116.94%	1,729.83%	255.13%
		High	5.87%	−11.86%	1.11%	5.34%	13.39%	124.65%	11.58%	117.86%	−20.73%	192.86%	44.01%
		Wide	−0.99%	3.36%	9.82%	0.25%	30.19%	129.70%	34.50%	198.36%	27.15%	614.61%	104.69%
		Average	−1.81%	3.40%	8.54%	−0.28%	35.12%	125.72%	33.57%	237.22%	37.41%	939.33%	141.82%

Normally, there is no way for VZD, alone, to capture the profits in rising zero prices once rates have fallen below its designated I_{min}. Past that point there's nothing it can do. But when a variable Z percentage is used in concert with a variable duration, the variable Z percentage picks up where the variable duration leaves off, continuing to reduce the Z percentage (if you've picked the right I Ranges) long after the duration has become "stuck." If your duration has already been reduced to its minimum of, say, $D_{min} = 15$, you will continue to hold 15-year zeros, but you will hold fewer and fewer of them as they rise because VZP will simply continue to sell them off.

The caveat (mentioned parenthetically above) is as follows: VZ^2 won't work unless its VZP half remains free to operate past the point where its VZD half grinds to a halt. As a rule, when using a high D Range, the I_{min} for the Z Range (called the Iz_{min}) must be lower than the I_{min} for the D Range (the Id_{min}). If that's so, you can confidently specify an aggressive D Range emphasizing only the most volatile, long-term zeros. Of course, you should be sure that your Z_{min} is low, too; otherwise VZP will be hampered in its "rescue" efforts, leaving you with a relatively high proportion of your plan in zeros. Thus, another rule: If your D Range is high, your Z_{min} should be low.

If you use a high Z Range, say 50 to 100 percent, you could run into a similar problem. Soaring rates could make zero prices plummet, forcing you to keep half your money in them. This means you'll be continually hindered from realizing your paper gains, flirting with the possibility you'll give back your profits as fast as you earned them, if and when rates change tack.

For VZP, a Z Range of 0 to 100 is more effective than a narrow one because a Z_{min} of zero lets you liquidate completely. But there's a clear trade-off: You need to be heavily invested in zeros to chalk up a big score, but you also have to be able to cut your Z percentage drastically in order to sell just as heavily. An extreme Z Range of 0 to 100 answers both calls. But now VZ^2 allows you to divide the labor. One variable can take more responsibility for buying, the other for selling. You can, for example, maintain a high Z Range (such as

Table 8.10 Comparison of Plans Having *at Least One* I_{min} Set *Low*, with Plans Having *Neither* I_{min} Set *Low*

	All programs (average)	**1 or both I Ranges low (average)**	**Neither I Range low (average)**
Table 8.1, D range: 0–15	$194,445	$216,550	$166,814
Table 8.4, D range: 15–30	396,977	486,995	284,455
Table 8.7, D range: 0–30	371,363	482,904	231,932
Average	$320,928	$395,483	$227,733

50 to 100) and load up on zeros at all times because your variable duration will permit you to cut down in another way.

VZ²'s success is due to the fact that it makes the use of high-powered, high-duration, high-volatility zeros safe. If you select a low Z_{min} and make sure your Iz_{min} (the one that determines your Z_{min}) is lower than your Id_{min} (the one that sets your D_{min}), you will enjoy greater volatility and the likelihood of enhanced returns without increasing risk. Similarly, you may choose a high Z Range without fear—but only if you set your D_{min} low and your Id_{min} lower than your Iz_{min}. You should also avoid setting *both* your D and Z Ranges high. One or the other—it doesn't matter which—will be fine. The other, meanwhile, must be set low. Thus, another guideline: The minimum setting of *at least one of the two* should be put at or close to 0.

You can find confirmation of these principles in the tables themselves. In every case, the combination of a high I Range for both D and Z had the poorest result by a good margin (it averaged $152,842 across all scenarios in Table 8.1, $217,525 in Table 8.4, and $187,582 in Table 8.7). Notice too that the low-low combination corroborates the observation at the end of Chapter 6 on the advisability of aiming low when picking an I Range. Every program consisting of two low I Ranges had a better average outcome across all the rate scenarios than any other on the same table (the leader in Table 8.1 at $286,771, Table 8.4 at $752,607, and Table 8.7 at $907,616). This fact also underscores the importance of having at least one of your I_{min}s low. Table 8.10 assembles the result of all the programs that do so (data comes from the first four and the seventh lines of Tables 8.1, 8.4, and 8.7).

Strategies with at least one low I Range were 73.6 percent higher on average than those that employed only high and/or wide I Ranges. If we were to rule out high I Ranges altogether and look only at the combinations low-low, low-wide, wide-low, and wide-wide, the average results derived from Tables 8.1, 8.4, and 8.7 respectively are $232,407; $542,288; and $553,323. Clearly, aiming low pays off.

VZP and VZD are tools that magnify dynamic balancing's effects, ways of automatically adjusting our chosen plan to particular conditions as they go. Operating along separate axes, they initiate more aggressive plans as zeros get cheaper (and safer), and more conservative ones as zeros get higher priced (and more susceptible to a tumble). VZ^2 gives your "automatic pilot"—VZD or VZP—an automatic copilot to help out in emergencies. Let's take a graphic look at what this means in different situations.

Suppose we select discontinuous (non-overlapping) I Ranges. We let our D Range be 15 to 30 over an I Range of 8 to 10 percent and establish a Z Range of 0 to 100 over a range of 2 to 4 percent (see Figure 8.1). As rates rise from 2 to 4 percent and zeros get cheaper, we gradually go from having no investment in zeros to a total commitment. Because we are below the I_{min} for D, we are in 15-year zeros. At this stage, VZ^2 is operating like a form of *VZP* with a constant duration of 15. If rates drive upward through the 4 to 8 percent range, then it will resemble *ZB-100* when it uses a zero of that same constant duration. Neither the Z percentage nor the variable duration can change because we are at Z_{max} and D_{min} throughout this middle stretch. If interest rates shoot higher still, to between 8 and 10 percent, Plan Z will still call for a Z_{max} of 100, but now the duration variable will become adjustable. Now we're employing something very like *VZD* with a D Range of 15 to 30 and a fixed Z percentage of 100.

Consider a more reasonable set of I Ranges (Figure 8.2) that slightly overlap. We let our Z Range be 0 to 100 again but this time over a broader I Range of 2 to 8 percent. Our D Range is still 15

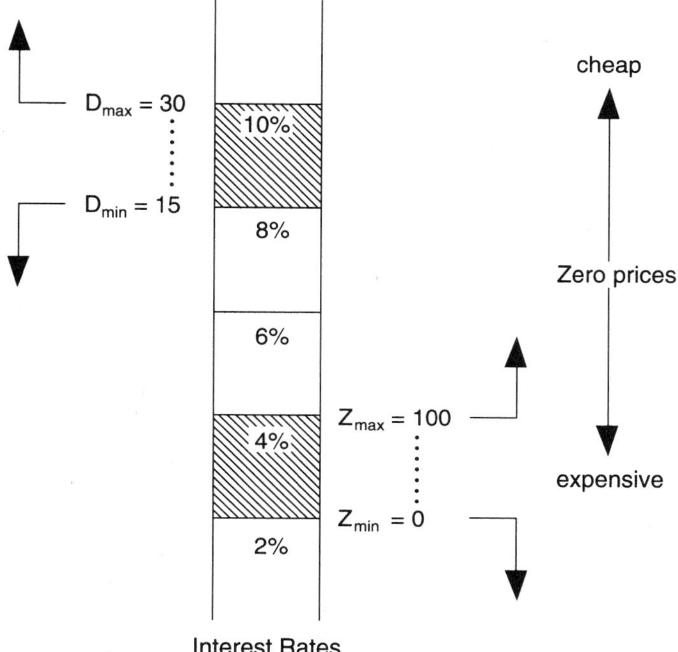

Figure 8.1 The I Ranges for duration and Z% do not have to overlap.

to 30 but over a wider and lower I Range of 6 to 10 percent. As rates move between 2 and 6 percent, we are fixed at a D_{min} of 15. VZ^2 has "turned off" its VZD unit and is operating as though it were VZP with a constant-duration zero. The Z percentage will go as low as 0 and up to about 66.67 when rates hit 6 percent. Above 6 percent, VZD is actuated and VZ^2 starts working on all cylinders. Between 6 and 8 percent (represented by the crosshatched rectangle in Figure 8.2), the Z percentage will modulate between 66.67 and 100 percent while the duration will go from a D_{min} of 15 to as high as 22.5 years, halfway to its D_{max}. Above 8 percent, VZP reaches its maximum value and becomes ZB-like, stuck at a Z percentage of 100, as VZD continues functioning by moving between durations of 22.5 and 30 years.

We suggest you use VZ^2 diagrams of this sort when you formulate your own plans to help you visualize the way your two variables will interact.

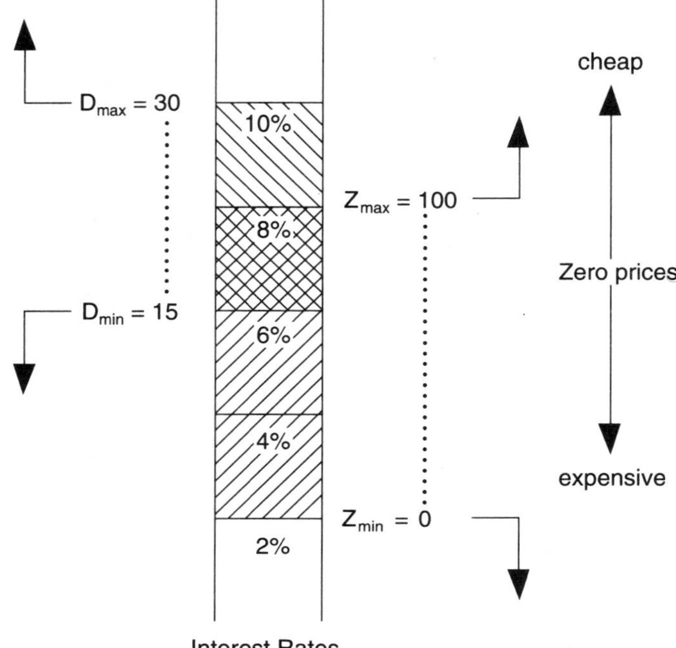

Figure 8.2 The two I Ranges (for duration and Z%) may overlap.

Universal Plan Z

The reader may have noticed that VZ^2 is the ultimate Plan Z; no model is more effective, reliable, and consistent. It is also the universal form of Plan Z because it can, with the proper settings, mimic any other form.* Set Z_{min} to equal Z_{max} and put both at 50 and you've neutralized the variable Z percentage mechanism so VZ^2 works like VZD. Assign D_{min} and D_{max} to some constant number and you've canceled the variable duration and turned VZ^2 into VZP. Under various circumstances it can be made to resemble ZB as well—and in fact it probably will function like one or more of these earlier versions of Plan Z at limited times under almost every investor's plan.

* Excepting the use of constant maturities. But this is no detriment. See Chapter 9.

The Value of VZ^2

Every version of Plan Z, from the discredited ZA through VZ^2, seeks to capitalize on the unpredictable trajectory of interest rates by means of a system that keys off their movement, whichever direction they take. ZB implicitly spreads an infinite I Range within which rebalancing occurs at a fixed percentage. The variable forms, VZP and VZD, employ an explicit, finite I Range in the hope that its limited range will coincide with some part of the course of actual rates and thus trigger the aggressive buying and selling needed to enhance yield. But there's an inherent trade-off in this latter tactic. The wider your I Range, the more likely you are to "catch" reality, but the more "spread out" are the buy-and-sell signals it conveys. A change of 1 percent means less in an extended I Range, causing only a modest adjustment in your Z percentage or duration. On the other hand, if you narrow your I Range to concentrate the aggressiveness of its action, you take the chance that actual rates may miss a significant portion of your range or even bypass it altogether.

What VZ^2 does is multiply the chances that your I Range will be actuated without necessarily diluting its effect. It allows you to spread your net wider than you could with either VZP or VZD alone (giving you two guesses instead of one) but without diminishing the potential for aggressiveness—in fact, aggressiveness will be increased where both I Ranges overlap, simultaneously engaging both variable components so VZ^2 is functioning at full force. A key choice you face with VZ^2 is whether you want to *magnify* the capacities of its constituent parts by telescoping their two I Ranges or *extend* their capacities by pulling the two I Ranges apart.

Thus far, we have only presented and interpreted Plan Z; the point, however, is to use it.

Part III

Implementing Plan Z

9

Putting Plan Z into Practice: Issues, Ideas, Tactics, and Techniques

Let's review two things before we consider applying Plan Z: namely, what you can expect of it and what it expects of you.

Plan Z: A Long-Term Investment

We cannot state it emphatically enough: Plan Z is a *long-term* investment plan. The universe of investment possibilities is huge, and Plan Z is in no way intended to supplant them all. Chiefly a new strategy in the generally steady and relatively safe world of traditional fixed investments, Plan Z aims to boost the yields of these usually stodgy investments, giving them returns more often associated with more venturesome vehicles. As such, Plan Z is intended for the safety-conscious investor considering fixed instruments, annuities, or something similar.

Plan Z Demands Discipline

Plan Z requires a long-term commitment. Zero coupon bonds, as we have seen, can be extremely volatile. But ultimately their price will rise. Plan Z is designed to succeed *in the long run.* In its more aggressive versions, Plan Z is like a thrilling amusement park ride—good fun while you stay in your seat but dangerous should you try to rise halfway through. (Of course, if you do exceptionally well, you can cash out early.)

Long-term commitment need not be a strenuous requirement. After all, *you* are the one establishing the length of your investment period. The only obligation you are bound to uphold is one you set yourself.

You should be prepared to stand by Plan Z through thick and thin. It is possible that it may not do as well as some other fixed instruments in its early years. But in most cases it will, given time, catch up. One of the trials of investing in Plan Z is enduring its irregular pace—up two steps, down three, up five, down two—while competing investments are stepping along at a slower but more regular clip. You have to be patient. Remember, *you* decided to get rich slow.

Professionals in the market have a saying: "They always come in at the top." This means that when the tide comes in, people get excited and jump in—just as it's about to reverse. And when the tide goes out, they get demoralized and discouraged and go home—just when it's about to come in again. Many professionals play the market by going *contrary* to public behavior. You need patience, perspective, and discipline to avoid going along with the mob, buying at the top and selling at the bottom.

You should have a firm grasp of the mechanics of Plan Z (or, for that matter, any investment) before handing over your hard-earned dollars—which is why this book takes pains to clarify how Plan Z works and what it can and cannot do. It's your money; you must see the connections yourself rather than rely on the representations of others.

Although we hope this book will inspire you to start Plan Z right away, results will most likely *not* be immediate. This calls for self-knowledge and self-discipline to ensure that you get neither demoralized nor carried away.

In the rest of this chapter, we will systematically explore the issues involved in putting Plan Z into practice. First, let's gain some perspective by sorting the various aspects of Plan Z and the factors that affect it into two groups: those that are in your control and those that are not. We are guided in this by an oft-cited prayer attributed to Reinhold Niebuhr that holds much wisdom for investors, parents, golfers, and other strivers:

> God, grant me the serenity to accept the things I cannot change, the courage to change the things I can, and the wisdom to know the difference.

Things NOT in Your Control

Prominent among the things you cannot control are interest rates—specifically, the timing, degree, direction, and frequency of their fluctuations. However, a Plan Z investor has less to fear from making a wrong bet on interest rates than those who invest in other fixed instruments. It doesn't matter as much to him what direction rates take in the short term as long as they are volatile in the long run.

The other matter beyond your control is whether the economy undergoes inflation or deflation. Inflation is the result of a depreciation of the currency, which consumers experience as a general decline in purchasing power. Deflation, the opposite phenomenon, is experienced as an increase in purchasing power.

Whether we have inflation or deflation is important because over the long haul the stock market tends to keep pace with inflation whereas fixed instruments generally do not. The difference is that equities represent actual goods. In most cases, when you buy a share of stock you're buying an interest in a firm that sells a product or a service, something that has real earning capacity. Under inflationary conditions, a company could presumably raise its prices to increase its earnings and offset any decrease in purchasing power. This would protect shareholders from feeling the full effect of inflation.

But fixed instruments have no such mechanism working in their behalf. The amount an investor gets paid back is expressed and contracted for in the currency, in dollars. If the value of that currency decreases, it will not buy as much as it once did. The only thing the investor is guaranteed is a nominal sum of dollars, not how much he will be able to buy with that money.

Having said this, we should note that today, through long and bitter experience, the fixed instrument markets have become somewhat sophisticated about dealing with inflation. Interest rates themselves tend to reflect the inflation rate and take it into account. If investors demand a real return of 5 percent when inflation is at 2 percent, then someone who lends his money will require 7 percent in order to be compensated for the 2 percent loss in purchasing power and still earn a 5 percent yield in real terms. Thus, the interest rates that fixed instruments bear (i.e., your income) tend to reimburse you for inflation, although—for complex reasons beyond the scope of this book—not the full amount (e.g., your principal remains fixed, and thus loses value in real terms). So some attrition of real value will occur when you invest in fixed instruments in inflationary times.

Some people might balk at investing in fixed instruments on the grounds that inflation will eat up some of their interest. But we don't know for a fact whether we will have inflation or deflation (or neither). Since it is never a good idea to put all your eggs in one basket,* you might play it safe by putting some money in precious metals or natural resource companies as protection against the possibility of inflation and buy some zero coupon bonds as a deflationary hedge. (Some other diversification strategies are mentioned in Chapter 11.)

Plan Z is not exempt from the bite of inflation, but it is less likely to be hurt to the same extent as other fixed investments. If

* Even if, as Mark Twain suggests, you "WATCH THAT BASKET."

a dollar buys just half or a quarter of what it used to buy, it's still better to have more of them. And Plan Z is designed to give you more dollars than most other similarly safe investments.

In the end, it is impossible to tell what the precise implications of inflation are for Plan Z because it is a *trading* plan. One of the advantages of Plan Z is that it may actually profit from scenarios that might be considered disastrous, because disasters are usually accompanied by volatility, and Plan Z thrives on volatility. The worst case, a severely inflationary economy in which interest rates fall shy of compensating you for your loss of purchasing power, would almost certainly be accompanied by abnormal volatility in the economy, in interest and inflation rates both, such that the prices of zero coupon bonds might frequently swing by as much as 20, 40, 80, or 150 percent. And Plan Z has the capacity to capitalize on that, enough perhaps to more than recoup your loss of purchasing power.

Thus, though it provides no defense against inflation as such, Plan Z is prepared to benefit from the side effects of inflation or most other kinds of calamitous financial circumstances. Although no one can guarantee that Plan Z will outperform all other investments under all conditions, it is one of the few investment programs possessing the safety of government-derived securities (and perhaps the only one) that has even a prayer of profiting from adversity. The high inflation scenario just related is generally understood to mean certain disaster for bond holders. It can be certain disaster for money market investors, people who hold cash, too. It is *not* certain disaster for Plan Z and, in fact, it has a good chance of working out well, even in real terms.

As for deflation, the U.S. has not encountered any on an annual basis for several decades, and it seems unlikely any time soon. Deflation struck during the 1930s when interest rates dropped to below 1 percent as prices fell by nearly 10 percent. An interest rate of 1 percent—which seems to us extraordinarily low—actually represented a real return of 11 percent. For every hundred dollars invested you got back only $101. But that $101 bought as much as $111 had the year before.

Deflation, unlike inflation, is noted for the absence of volatility. Inflation promotes speculation by investors attempting to catch up with their fading purchasing power. However, purchasing power improves during deflation, so investors don't feel compelled to speculate because merely standing pat brings positive results. Without going too much into economic theory, inflation destroys wealth, thereby stimulating a rush into what would normally be judged unsound investments by those frantic to preserve capital. This destabilizes areas of the economy, leading to volatility. Deflation, however, tends to dampen speculative fires: Why take high risks when the safest investment—even stashing cash in your mattress—provides a real return? Deflation is also the ultimate guarantor of falling interest rates and, as the simulations in previous chapters have shown, the latter have a beneficial effect on Plan Z.

Also out of your control are disruptive world events—large-scale tragedies and catastrophes, such as flood, famine, and war that promote political or economic instability. We have represented these kinds of events in our "realistic" scenarios through the introduction of interest rate "spikes" (discussed in Chapter 5). The point here is that, again, Plan Z is poised to benefit from these disasters insofar as they lead to interest rate volatility.

Things in Your Control

With Plan Z you have a say in (1) how much you invest and in what form—annual contributions, initial deposit, or both; (2) how long a period your plan covers; (3) what variant of Plan Z you employ; (4) what percentage of your money you keep in your zero balance (and, with VZP and VZD, what interest rate range you choose); (5) how frequently and under what circumstances you rebalance; (6) the duration of your portfolio (that is, the average time to maturity of your zeros); and (7) what kind of zeros you buy, in what form, and from whom.

Each of these points (except 3 and 4, which we address in the next chapter) will now be visited in some detail.

Deciding How Much to Invest and When

We have seen (in Chapter 2) that to avail yourself of the power of compounding, the sooner you start, the better. Everyone knows the story, true or false, of how the island of Manhattan was bought for $24. We have not verified the computations, but the epilogue has it that if the sum had been allowed to compound at a 10 percent annual rate, it would by now be roughly equivalent to the market value of Manhattan's real estate. The moral: When you factor in compound interest, the Indians drove a pretty good bargain after all. Because time is the most important element in compounding, it is important for any savings plan to load up as much and as early as possible. As we saw, making deposits early can outweigh the effects of both (a) subsequent contributions that are many times larger than that initial investment, and (b) higher interest rates that come at a future date. So the best time to invest is almost always: *now.*

How much should you invest? There is no minimum amount required to start Plan Z. As we shall soon see, there is an investment vehicle appropriate to Plan Z to match every budget. So don't think you can't afford it. It is true that the more you squirrel away, the more you are liable to claim at the end. But you don't have to put every penny you own into it. The rule is this: Invest what you can—no more, no less. What Plan Z asks is just sound investment policy. *You should never, never at any time invest money you cannot afford to tie up.*

By its nature, long-term investing is an exercise in thrift. This now-vanishing custom can be cultivated. Work up a budget, figure out how much you can readily spare, and save it. If it still seems too much, put in only half as much. Do whatever you have to so long as you save. As Andrew Tobias has pointed out, because of taxes, you have to make more than whatever you spend in order to replace it. Thus, a penny saved is *more* than a penny earned. It may be worth a good deal more if you put that penny to work in Plan Z.

Many investors may have little or no choice about how much they have to invest in Plan Z and when. If you have a small IRA, your maximum annual contribution is limited by law. Others will be governed by their day-to-day finances, investing what they can when they have it. Clearly, there is no single detailed piece of advice valid for all, but we can formulate a few guidelines.

1. If you have the luxury of deciding whether to jump or ease into Plan Z, you should recall that, everything else being equal, it is generally best to put as much money to work as soon as possible. This means that if you have, say, $25,000 earmarked for Plan Z, you will generally be better off allocating the entire amount at once. *Unless you expect rates to rise immediately,* there is no benefit to holding back any part of it.
2. Presumably, your investment funds are not being kept in a can but are currently invested elsewhere. If they are in a passive investment like a CD or money market fund, then the tip just offered remains sound. If, however, you must liquidate a stock market portfolio or other investment, think twice. We don't suggest you arbitrarily liquidate it simply to fund Plan Z. If you were already dissatisfied and planning to sell, fine. But there's no need to be *overly* anxious about hopping aboard Plan Z—it's a long-term plan.
3. Plan Z should constitute no more than a reasonable portion of your total portfolio—not all of it, not even close. (The principles of sound portfolio management are touched on in Chapter 11.) Do not put all your savings into Plan Z (or any other single investment).
4. If you have a specific objective in mind and can estimate closely how much you will need (perhaps a top private college for your child at around $150,000 in today's dollars), then you can use the simulations as a rough guide to how much you should invest. You can even make an adjustment for inflation. Thus, $150,000 after 20 years of 3 percent annual inflation would require $270,000 in current dollars. This is about how much VZP garnered on average after 25 years on the basis of a $25,000 deposit.

5. Keep in mind the reliability of your future income. Are you a civil servant? Then your wages are fairly secure. A pro football player? Don't count on 20 years of the same earnings. Expect a trust fund to mature soon? Then put a little extra into your plan.
6. If you have strong views about the course of interest rates,* then by all means adjust your plan accordingly. Recall that, generally speaking, a period of falling rates tends to be more favorable to Plan Z than rising rates. So if you expect the former, accelerate your commitment to Plan Z. If you expect rising rates for the next few years, you may prefer to sit on the sidelines or "feed" your investment funds into Plan Z gradually over the period.

Choosing the Length of Your Plan

Time is on the side of Plan Z. The longer it is in force, the greater its chance of encountering periods of unusual volatility, and the more opportunity compounding has to work. Plainly, you should invest for as long as you can. Once again, though, many investors will find this issue determined by their circumstances. (Age can be decisive, because the time spans Plan Z requires represent substantial fractions of a normal working lifetime.) If, for example, your purpose is to finance college tuition for a child just a few years old, then your planned investment period will have to be 15 to 20 years. If you are planning for retirement at a particular date, that fact will fix your investment span within narrow limits. If your horizon is much less than 15 years, then you cannot expect Plan Z to reach its full potential. It might—if you get lucky and hit a period of highly volatile or rapidly falling interest rates right off the bat. But luck is not a reliable element of Plan Z or any other investment plan.

* The author publishes a regular monthly market letter providing an ongoing analysis of and outlook for interest rates (as well as the economy, stock market, inflation, precious metals, and currency markets). The annual subscription rate is $195. For an introductory single copy of the current issue send $5 to "MORRY on the MARKET," 50 Broadway, Suite 3700, New York, NY 10004 or call (212) 785-3900.

The suggested minimum investment period is 15 years, preferably 20, and ideally 25 to 30 or more.

Here's something to keep in mind: Your available time span could well be longer than you think if your goal is to generate funds that will themselves be spent over time. If, for example, your child will enter college in 16 years, you will need money from 16 to 20 years from now. If you plan to retire in 13 years, you will be needing capital and income during a period starting 13 years from now and extending for (we hope) many years beyond. The point is that, in many instances, you don't need to plan your investment to fully mature or end on a specific date, as long as it will make available some capital when and as you need it *after* that date. (Some specific techniques for accommodating this need will be discussed later.)

Deciding When to Rebalance

In all our simulations thus far, we have used annual rebalancing for the sake of simplicity and to make consistent comparisons. But there is no law that says you must follow suit. Nothing prevents you from rebalancing semiannually, quarterly, or monthly, although there are some potential drawbacks to rebalancing too frequently, namely: (a) it demands more of your time and attention, (b) it may create excessive transaction costs, and (c) it may result in premature buying and selling. The last point is the most serious and requires a little explanation.

As traders, our object is to buy (relatively) low and sell (relatively) high. In general, when zero prices rise, Plan Z sells and when prices fall, it buys. In a perfect system, we would wait until prices reach the exact top to sell and then suspend buying until prices hit the absolute bottom. But few investors of any kind have a hope of doing this on a regular basis. That's the whole point of a "mechanical" rule: It ensures as far as possible that, without relying on foreknowledge or luck, we consistently sell *relatively* high, compared to the prices at which we buy and buy *relatively* low, compared to the prices at which we sell.

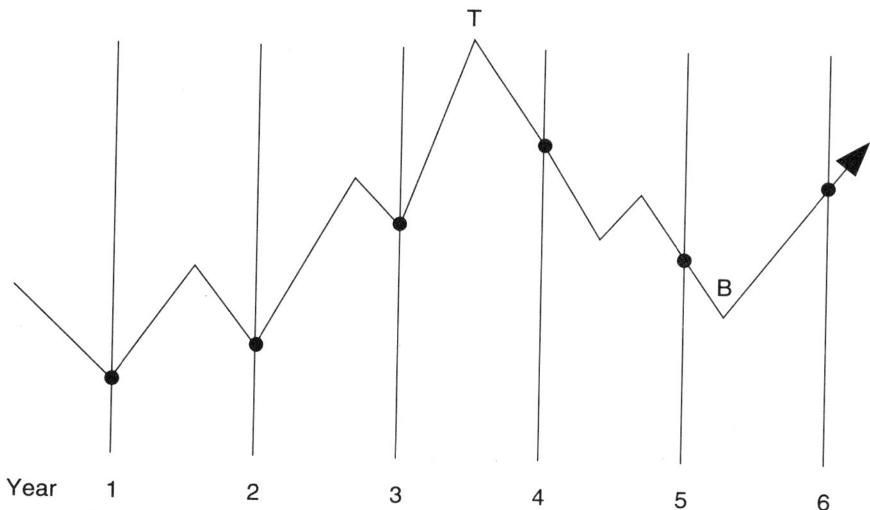

Figure 9.1 Rebalancing too frequently or too infrequently can result in missing opportunities.

If you rebalance infrequently, the bottom (or top) may come and go before you have a chance to buy (or sell). However, if you rebalance too frequently, you will sell some zeros far too early and cheaply and buy others far too early and too dear. Because significant trends in interest rates (which determine zero prices) usually last from 6 months to a few years, one year is probably a fair interval between rebalancings. If you preferred to rebalance every 6 or 18 months, no one could strongly argue the point with you. But move much beyond these limits and you risk the possibility that you will entirely miss an opportunity to sell at high prices or buy at low prices.

Figure 9.1 is a chart of zero prices. A top occurs between Years 3 and 4 and a bottom between 5 and 6. If we rebalance annually, we will never sell at the precise peak, but we will sell fairly near the top in Year 3 and again in Year 4. We will also buy some in Year 5 close to the bottom.* Suppose, though, that we

* You can tell whether Plan Z will buy or sell at any given rebalancing by comparing the price of zeros since the last transaction. If the price has gone up from then, it must sell. If it has gone down, it will invariably buy.

rebalanced only every other year. We'd sell in Year 2 and Year 4, advantageously avoiding one of our premature sales, the one in Year 3. But then we'd wind up missing the vicinity of the low in Year 5—a great buying opportunity—and have to wait until Year 6, after prices had risen substantially, before we could buy again. On the other hand, had we chosen to rebalance semiannually, we would have come much closer to selling at the top between years 3 and 4. But we would have fewer zeros left to sell at that level, because we made *five* premature sales in Years 1, 1½, 2, 2½, and 3. Likewise, we would buy some zeros extremely close to their absolute low price between years 5 and 6. But we'd be able to buy only a few, having already bought too early on three previous occasions: Years 4, 4½, and 5.

The problem with rebalancing too often is that it means you will almost certainly be buying or selling before either action is optimal. In fact, the more frequently you rebalance, the closer you approach the average price instead of the *best* one. When you rebalance every week or every day or every month, the optimal buying or selling point becomes no more important than any other and is averaged in with all the rest. By the time you reach it, you either have few zeros left to sell or little cash with which to buy.

Assuming that you decide to rebalance yearly, when do you rebalance? The most natural time would be at or shortly after the calendar year's end. However, should Plan Z acquire a large following, this could mean a sudden surge in buying or selling concentrated around the turn of the year.* If zero prices had risen during the year, Plan Z would call for selling and, if a sizable number of people follow Plan Z, that could reduce prices, forcing many to sell a bit cheaper than they would have otherwise. The opposite situation might occur in years when zero prices fall and Plan Z calls for buying. Given this, we strongly suggest you avoid the obvious

* This prospect is diminished by the vastness of the total zero market. As of mid-1992, $144 billion of U.S. Treasury bonds had been stripped to create zeros. Of these, $14 billion were derived from 10-year bonds, $5 billion from 20-year bonds, and $124 billion from 30-year bonds. There were also $450 billion of Treasuries outstanding suitable for conversion to zeros but not yet stripped. This does not include corporate, municipal, and other zeros.

year-end rebalancing date and use your own birthday or anniversary or some other personally significant time of year in order to more evenly spread buying and selling by Plan Z participants and minimize any detrimental effect on zero prices. (You might alternatively use an 8-, 11-, or 13-month rebalancing period instead of 12.)

There's another method an investor might use to decide when to rebalance: keying directly off changes in the interest rate instead of the calendar. Because Plan Z aims to take advantage of rate fluctuations, it might seem to make sense to rebalance only after meaningful changes occur in the rates themselves rather than to act at arbitrary time intervals. If, for example, you decide to rebalance whenever rates rise or fall by a half percent, you might find yourself rebalancing several times a year. If rates change only slightly over the year, you won't have to rebalance just because the calendar says to. This sounds good, but . . .

For one thing, the selection of a specific rate criterion, whether a half percent or other, is itself arbitrary and risks a mismatch with reality. If rates stay between 6.1 and 6.9 percent for an extended time after you've rebalanced at 6.5 percent, you'll do no rebalancing at all and perhaps pass up some opportunities to buy low or sell high. On the other hand, if rates zigzag back and forth vigorously in a brief span, an annual rebalancer might miss out entirely whereas an investor who keys off rates will catch each move that meets his standard. When rates fall or rise in a steady trend—that's a different story. If his criterion is too sensitive, someone who keys off rates will buy or sell every step along the way, far too frequently. Professionals like to say that the big money is made in the big move. But keying off rates means you never catch the big move because you're too busy with small ones (if your criterion is small), or you do little or no rebalancing at all (if it is too big).

Using time as a basis for rebalancing is a good idea *because* it is random (that is, not correlated) with respect to price.

A compromise of techniques is possible: Adopt the policy of rebalancing yearly *and* whenever rates move by *more than a large distance* (say 2 or 3 percentage points). This way, you retain the advantages of annual rebalancing and are still able to capture unusual mid-year shifts (such as a "spike") as well. It is possible that you may yet act too soon by buying or selling after a 2 or 3 percent move that grows to 4 or 5 by year's end. But these rare instances may be outweighed by the times mid-year rebalancing helps you catch a move you would otherwise have missed.

As we have seen, rebalancing can be counterproductive if you do it too often. In addition, when you buy individual zeros through a broker, you incur transaction costs. So why not eliminate marginal rebalancing altogether? For example, when your account is 49 percent in zeros and your Z percentage calls for 50, then you might consider skipping that year's rebalancing entirely. Why bother? By establishing a threshold and acting only when a shift of funds of some significance (perhaps 5 percent or more of your zero account) is called for, you can avoid relatively meaningless transactions.

Selecting the Right Maturity Length (Duration)

You have a fundamental choice: Hold zeros with a constant maturity *date*, ones that always mature in the same year; or keep zeros with a constant maturity *length* (i.e., constant duration zeros), ones that are always the same distance from maturity no matter what the calendar says. The risk with the latter method is that your zeros never mature—they will not be held long enough to reach par. If there's a rise in rates, prices can drop so far that they won't even approach par by the time you want to cash out. We call this possibility *closeout risk*. The higher the volatility of your zeros as you approach the intended end date of your plan, the greater your closeout risk.

Generally, as a zero's maturity length decreases, so does its volatility. A portfolio of constant-duration zeros keeps a constant maturity length, so its volatility never changes. If you have chosen long-duration zeros,* swapping them every year to retain the same high level of volatility, then they will be perpetually susceptible to

* The longest term available for a zero coupon bond is 30 years because that is the longest bond issued by the U.S. Treasury.

large swings in price. This is the thing to do if you want volatility throughout the life of your plan.

If you want to minimize your closeout risk, there's something else you can do besides pick constant maturities: stick with long-term zeros for most of the way and convert them to short-term zeros when it becomes appropriate, much in the way some adjustable-rate mortgages can be converted to conventional or fixed-rate mortgages. (A discussion of closeout risk and recommendations for handling it are given in the next chapter, along with some words on the relative merits of constant maturities versus constant durations.)

Deciding What Kind of Zeros to Use

In considering the kind of zeros you want in your plan, you have two questions to answer: (1) Do you want to buy individual zero coupon bonds or shares in a mutual fund? (2) Do you prefer corporate, municipal, or government zeros? But before we contemplate these matters, a few words on zeros in general are in order.

The reader should not be confused by the myriad names for different kinds of zero coupon bonds: CATs, TIGRs, LIONs, COUGRs, and other acronyms, feline and otherwise. There are basically just a few kinds of zeros (Treasury, government agency, corporate, and "munis") and only two ways of creating or packaging them—derive them or issue them whole. The many non-Treasury bonds and their various means of escrowing, trustee-ing, and guaranteeing—along with the ingenuity of the brokerage firms that market them—account for the upsurge in acronyms.

For the vast majority of Plan Z investors, one piece of advice should free them from concern about distinctions among the various species of zeros: Stick to those backed by the U.S. Treasury. Whatever animal your broker offers you, ask if a direct obligation of the Treasury is behind it. If not, pass.

1. *Mutual funds.* Several zero coupon bond funds have been established in the last few years. Most retail brokers can refer you to them. Some are advertised in financial publications such as *Inves-*

tor's Business Daily, the *Wall Street Journal*, and *BARRON'S*. Most of these funds tend to be passive and do not employ a formula or procedure remotely like Plan Z. One fund, Benham Capital Management (800-321-8321), is uniquely positioned to facilitate the implementation of Plan Z in most of its variations.* Benham offers a family of zero coupon bond funds called the Benham Target Maturities Trusts (BTMT). At the time of this writing, there were five funds, each with a different targeted maturity spaced at five-year intervals, one maturing in 1995, another in 2000, and the others in 2005, 2010, and 2015.** Telephone transfers are available at no charge (for your IRA), even for small amounts. (Check with Benham in case this has changed.) For your cash account, Benham also offers a safe money market fund that consistently receives the highest safety ratings from the money market rating agencies.

When you invest in a zero fund, you do not directly own a zero coupon bond. Instead, you own shares in a mutual fund, a large collection of zero coupon bonds. This allows you to benefit from tax laws that distinguish between capital gains and dividends earned by share prices. Besides this, there is little difference between owning zeros directly and owning shares in a fund. In the case of BTMT, the price of your shares will be virtually identical to those of a zero coupon bond of the same maturity. So a deposit of $1,000 into BTMT fund 2015 is the equivalent of purchasing $1,000 worth of government-derived zero coupon bonds set to mature in 2015.

No disadvantages attach to owning shares in a zero fund and some particular advantages accrue. For example, Benham allows you to switch increments as large or small as you like. If you have a small IRA account with a couple of thousand dollars, rebalancing may require you to switch only a few dollars at a time. If you tried this in your own account through a broker, you might have to pay $250 to $400 for a single zero coupon bond. Even if you have a

* The author has no pecuniary interest in Benham nor any prospect of gaining from the use of its services by readers of this book. He is merely a satisfied customer.

** One of the things Benham enables you to do is readily maintain a constant-duration version of Plan Z. Although its funds are spaced at five-year intervals, it's a simple matter to create intermediate maturities merely by weighting deposits in two separate funds. (More on this in Chapter 10.)

moderately sized account and wish to move no more than $650, what do you do when the price of a zero is $500? One zero is not enough and two are too much. With Benham, you can specify the amount you want to the penny and they will transfer, on the basis of a phone call, exactly what you request.

As already mentioned, the alternative to a mutual fund is purchasing individual zero coupon bonds directly through a brokerage house. You will then have a commission to pay and the risk of poor execution to consider, via something familiar to many investors called the bid-asked spread. This is the difference between the highest bid and the lowest offering price for an item in the current open market. Suppose that at current rates, the theoretical value of a particular zero is 25. It may well be that no one is offering to sell one at the moment at that price. But someone may be offering a few at 26. If you wish to buy now you will have to pay the higher figure and accept a slightly lower yield as a result. Likewise, it is possible that at the moment you wish to sell, no one is bidding more than 24 for this bond, so you will have to accept a lower price. As large investors, mutual funds are in a better position to buy or sell wholesale or direct, the way your broker does, and small investors in such funds benefit.

A particular advantage of BTMT is that it facilitates the precise adjustment of your zeros' duration. As mentioned previously, the BTMT family holds zeros that mature in any of five or six distinct years at five-year intervals: 1995, 2000, to 2020. But suppose your retirement year is 2012 and you have decided on plan ZB-50 using a constant maturity date that coincides with your planned retirement. What do you do?

You could ask your broker to buy zeros that mature in 2012. But when it's time to rebalance, you may find it difficult to buy or sell zeros of that maturity in precisely the quantity you want at a fair price. Few may happen to be available for sale or wanted by other investors at the moment, so you may have to bid up (or offer down) the price, to your own detriment, in order to transact your purchase or sale. Much more convenient would be the creation of a "synthetic" duration of 2012 by splitting your zero investment between BTMT's 2010 and 2015 funds in a 60:40 proportion. Your zero account will then behave almost exactly as if it were invested in a zero that matures in 2012. Because the gap between BTMT's funds is five years, each year brings you 20 percent closer to the next fund. So it's very easy to figure out the proportion required to achieve any desired duration.

2. *Corporate and municipal zeros.* Corporate zeros are generally *issued* as zeros rather than being stripped from existing bonds. They tend to exhibit a higher interest rate than government bonds of the same maturities (usually an extra half to one percent) because they entail more risk (corporations *do* go bankrupt). Sound investing in corporate bonds requires encyclopedic knowledge and close attention. Businesses change, companies become more or less safe, and the interest rates they pay their creditors wavers. You have to monitor your corporation and its credit rating as well as the rest of the market.

Corporate bonds introduce a new element of uncertainty into Plan Z. Shaky corporate performance may lead a bond to fall in price even while government bonds are soaring. Because government bonds are regarded as having effectively no risk, they can be expected—without any second thoughts or concerns—to automatically reflect the interest market purely and directly. With corporate bonds, the link is less direct and results more doubtful.

Plan Z users have good reason to stick to the safest possible choices. Plan Z already has a good deal of volatility and interim risk. One of the most attractive features of Plan Z is that it can give you a higher yield with no additional ultimate risk. So why bother with corporate bonds? Plan Z gives you a good shot at getting the kind of effective yield most corporate bonds pay (and even more) while assuring you the safety of government instruments. Naturally, we don't wish to discourage experienced investors. But others should be wary. If you do not have a thorough knowledge of the corporate bond market, do not assume you can walk away with a higher yield at no cost to yourself. Remember, risk and reward are trade-offs. Plan Z may provide a partial waiver to this ironclad law of investing, and most readers should probably be satisfied with that.

Zeros derived from municipal bonds should also be avoided, for three reasons: (a) Contrary to popular opinion, defaults by municipalities are not unheard of. (b) Why complicate matters when you know that Treasuries are as close to risk-free as you can get? (c) Because Plan Z is expected to be used mainly in retirement and other tax-exempt accounts, the tax-free aspect of munis loses its inherent appeal. In fact, it becomes a liability, since munis yield *less* than Treasuries, and carry more risk.

Taxes

Mel Brooks once played the role of an accountant who had written a book entitled *Taxes, Taxes, Taxes: What Do They Want From Us?* Well, we know what they want, particularly when it comes to zero coupon bonds. The IRS treats a zero as though it traveled untroubled along its hypothetical growth curve, accruing value at a steady rate. If you are not in a tax-exempt account, you must pay tax on that accrued value year by year.* So, although interest rates may rise and the price of your zero fall, the IRS will judge it to have risen x number of percent, whatever the curve shows. And you must pay the tax due. Of course, there are years when the zero will rise in price and the IRS's valuation will be below the actual value, so your tax will be less than what it might be if it were based on a current market valuation.

The problem with paying taxes on zeros is that they do not throw off any cash flow, so the imputed tax (as it's called) must be paid with money taken from your other resources. For this reason, we anticipate that most readers will wish to implement Plan Z in some kind of tax-exempt vehicle, whether an Individual Retirement Account, a 401(k), or perhaps a small pension fund. Only in such an account can funds be compounded with the fullest force without

* A couple of corporate zero coupon bonds were granted exceptions when the IRS ruling was made a decade or so ago. These are not taxable until they mature. There are only a couple of specific issues to which these "grandfathered" exceptions apply, so it is not a significant factor for the zero coupon bond market or Plan Z.

being diminished by periodic withdrawals for tax payment. Nor do such accounts require support with funds from another source, funds you will not be able to replenish until your zero account matures many years hence.

As the law now stands, up to $10,000 may be given as a gift from one individual to another without any tax implications. Parents might want, if they are able, to take advantage of this to set up a nest egg for their offspring. If this appeals to you, be sure to speak with your tax advisor before you take any steps.

Implementation: An Overview

By now, you should have most of the basic issues involved in using Plan Z well in hand. But how do they fit together? Basically, there are three parts to doing Plan Z: setup, maintenance, and closeout.

The first step in setting up Plan Z is a three-part self-assessment.

1. You need to clarify your goals, decide what is most important, then ask yourself how much money you'll need and when.
2. The next question is how much money you have to invest. What does your current portfolio look like? Do you have a budget or savings plan? If not, you would doubtless do better if you set something up. What kind of earnings can you expect over the life of your plan? Where will current and future contributions (if any) come from? How much can you afford to tie up?
3. Finally, how much risk are you willing to tolerate? Does your temperament (and financial circumstances) tell you to take the safest possible course? Or are you willing to let Plan Z rip and see what it can do, keeping in mind that that might increase risk? Although personal finance, facts, and forecasts should play a major role in this decision, consult your gut as well.

Keep in mind that there are only two kinds of risk associated with Plan Z*: the risk of interim volatility (what we will call r^1) and closeout risk (r^2). The former refers to fluctuations in your equity between the time you start your plan and maturity—a form of market risk that attends any zero coupon investment. The latter is the risk associated with holding highly volatile high-duration zeros as the end of your plan approaches, and is peculiar to Plan Z. Interim risk is out of your control. But its significance is temporary. Closeout risk can represent a genuine problem, but it is within your control. You do not have to expose yourself to any more of it than you want when you tailor Plan Z to your needs—or when you use end-game tactics (presented later in this chapter) designed specifically to minimize its effects.

The next step is picking the program (the version of Plan Z with the appropriate parameters) that is right for you, a topic we will cover completely in the next chapter.

After you select a plan and know how much you are committing for how long and what to expect, it is time to open your accounts. You are taking a fateful step, the first one to this point with serious ramifications. Investigate all your options. Call brokers and funds. Ask for prospectuses. Read them carefully and assess their performance, service, and fees. (Remember the questions at the end of Chapter 4; beware of funds or pundits that tout the value of dollar-cost-averaging with zeros.) Make sure you are giving your money to trustworthy and capable people with a strong track record. Do not act hastily.

Once you have opened (at least) two accounts, you have to maintain them. This means keeping records as well as making the ongoing decisions that Plan Z requires. You will have to deal with the statements that your accounts generate. Do not dismiss them; they can be useful documentation of your program's progress (and necessary for tax purposes).

* Remember, with government-backed zeros there is no performance risk, no realistic chance of a decrease in the nominal value of your investment. In other words: You can't lose money.

The one active element of maintenance is rebalancing. The particulars depend on the program you undertake, but in no case should it be onerous. Plan Z is designed to work fairly automatically. Every year or so you plug in a number or two, make a couple of phone calls to initiate some transactions, and you're done till next time. (A more detailed look at rebalancing appears in the next section.)

Maintenance also entails troubleshooting. Three kinds of problems (real and imagined) can arise: (1) Results after a time appear disappointing. Perhaps you question whether you picked the correct version or the proper parameters or even whether Plan Z in any form is right for you. (2) Interim adversity strikes, and you realize you underestimated your capacity to tolerate risk. (3) A personal emergency requires an unanticipated withdrawal—or, an unexpected gift of some sort poses a different problem: when and how to make a substantial deposit.

Let's consider each in turn.

1. Discouragement may be a consequence of exaggerated expectations, especially at the outset. Be clear that Plan Z is not a get-rich-quick scheme, nor does it guarantee fabulous wealth. It is intended to enhance the yield offered by typical fixed instruments. It draws on the standard inventory of mechanical trading rules, adds some wrinkles of its own, and blends both with an insight into the special nature of zero coupon bonds. The result is a strategy that injects a judicious amount of speculation into an otherwise tepid brew. Plan Z does hold the potential for stellar results. But lottery jackpot–type returns are not common. The possibility that they will occur is real, and this fact rightfully and reasonably makes Plan Z more attractive. But do not be misled. We have, of necessity, dwelled on such returns out of proportion to their probability. Spectacular yields, though not unheard of, do not constitute the basis of Plan Z's value. Its "normal" benefit is spectacular enough. It fairly claims to beat the street, to offer better-than-average returns. Do not enter Plan Z with the idea that your $25,000 will become $5 million as a matter of course. It might. But it's not very likely. If you expect too much—especially too much, too soon—you will almost certainly

be disappointed with the otherwise admirable returns Plan Z is inclined to provide. It would be sad if you were to abandon Plan Z before it could flourish. (Even some of our multimillion-dollar examples did not bear fruit until they had run more than a dozen years.) If you remember that Plan Z is primarily a safe program that can't seriously hurt you, that it is supposed to give you an edge on the rest of the fixed-instrument market, then there's a good chance this problem will not come up at all.

But what if you run into rising rates at the start—the perfect prescription for Plan Z to underperform? Even this is not a justification for jumping ship. Several years of high rates are very likely to set in motion economic forces that will reverse that trend. There's a saying in the markets: "High (or low) prices are their own best cure." Economic extremes often summon into play counterforces that oppose, correct, and eventually "cure" them.

Because volatility is greatest in the early years of Plan Z, that is when the most discipline is required. Should a program start off slow because of rising rates, a withdrawal is not necessarily advisable. It might, in fact, be better to *make a deposit* because you are actually being presented with an opportunity to buy cheap. It seems counterintuitive, but since we know that zeros will ultimately reach par (it might take until the very end, but it will happen), it is good policy to make deposits after a bad stretch and make withdrawals following a good one. And as Plan Z investors, we should actually embrace what appear to be difficult times because they are only temporary. A firm called Clayton Brokerage had a reputation for doing some of the best fundamental research in the commodities industry. Their motto was "Change equals opportunity." We would paraphrase that and say: Adversity equals opportunity. We know that, with zeros, the bad times will pass. The further they drop, the higher they'll have to climb. So we should welcome adversity, viewing every decline in our equity as an opportunity to buy cheap and better position ourselves for a guaranteed move up.

If, however, you notice that rates are fluctuating nicely and you are rebalancing in both directions (sometimes selling, sometimes buying zeros) but your Z account's growth rate seems lower than it should be, then your Z percentage or Z Range, zero duration, D Range, or D_{max} (whatever you are using) may be too low, too limited, or too conservative. Consider ramping up one or more of them.

Finally, it may be the case that rates have been primarily stable or biased upward without sufficient compensatory volatility. Because the course of interest rates is not in your control, there is really no advice to be offered here (short of suggesting you apply for the chairmanship of the Federal Reserve). Although the U.S. Treasury bonds that Plan Z recommends are guaranteed to perform as promised and Plan Z itself guarantees no loss in nominal terms over the long haul, there are a few scenarios, and more than a few brief instances, when Plan Z will not perform as well as some other fixed investment. Given enough time, Plan Z will work. Over a realistic span, it will deliver in the vast majority of cases—with higher average returns than any comparably secure plan. But it cannot be expected to come through every single time.

2. Interim volatility shock can be preempted by a sober self-assessment at the start. But if you have taken your best shot at picking a program and still can't sleep nights, if you understand that zeros *must* rise in price, if you have sworn an oath of fidelity to Plan Z and yet lie awake as agitated as the equity in your zero account, then it is fair to say you have misjudged your risk tolerance. It's time to trim your program's sails, either by switching to a version that is less aggressive or by withdrawing funds to a level you can live with.

3. Things happen. If you must meet some unforeseen obligation, you may have no choice but to close Plan Z or reduce it. We can make a few suggestions. First, withdraw your money proportionally. If you have 25 percent of your equity in cash and 75 percent in zeros, take 25 percent of what you need from the cash account and the rest from the zeros, keeping your program intact as far as possible. If, however, you feel confident that your need for cash is temporary, then make a loan to yourself by withdrawing funds from the cash account only, repaying the loan with a cash deposit when you can. This eliminates any chance that you'll sell

zeros at a bad time. If you need more cash than you have on account, tamper with your zeros as little as you can. Later, restore the zero account before the cash account. It is the engine that drives Plan Z. Try to keep it running close to normal.

It is conceivable that you might have an unforeseen development that augments your cash (an inheritance, merit bonus, lottery jackpot) leaving you wondering how best to add money to Plan Z. If you find yourself burdened with extra cash, you can do one of two things: either deposit it proportionally so as to preserve the current balance between zeros and cash, or put it all in cash and await the next rebalancing before entering the zero market. (If you very recently rebalanced, put the money in proportionally.) If you are considering stepping up your investment in a big way, you might want to reduce the aggressiveness of your program just for that reason alone. Or you could switch plans entirely, put all your money into a more conservative version, and perhaps step up its aggressiveness gradually over several years.

A final word on deposits in general. To the extent that (a) rates have been falling, (b) the economy is in the doldrums, or (c) inflation is low, the greater the likelihood that rates will soon rise. So you might want to ease into Plan Z by depositing funds in several pieces over several years or by using a low Z_{max} and increasing it incrementally. Conversely, to the extent that (a) rates have been rising, (b) the economy has been overheating, or (c) inflation has been very high, the odds favor Plan Z (falling rates are likely soon). This would suggest a more rapid deployment into your plan, or perhaps even a more aggressive version of it than first intended.

We don't mean to give the impression that Plan Z requires elaborate fine-tuning. It's basically a one-decision operation. Start it up, make a note to adjust it once a year, then leave it alone. We would actually caution against tinkering. The more you modify it, the greater the chance for a miscalculation to creep in or for sober thought to be overruled in the heat of the moment. If you are an incorrigible hands-on guy or gal, then you might try to regulate your intrusions in the following way: Rather than open Plan Z's hood whenever you feel like it, permit yourself to "let off steam" by making limited changes at rebalancing time. Allow yourself some leeway to alter your Z percentage or duration by a small amount (say 5 percent or 3 years, depending on the parameter you're puttering with) if you feel it's a good idea at the time. Plan Z is, remember, a *plan*—it is not meant to be flown by the seat of your pants. So if you *must* tinker, *plan for that too,* so it won't get out of hand.

The last stage of Plan Z investing is closing out your various zero and cash accounts. You are encouraged to permit Plan Z to run as long as you can to give it the time it needs to do its best possible job. But you are free to close out at any time you are satisfied with results to that point. Understand that the risk you take on at closeout—that is, the possibility that volatility will significantly diminish your profits just before you realize them—is a special case of interim volatility. As you approach closeout, the fluctuations Plan Z normally undergoes are no longer temporary but final and can do permanent damage (or, for that matter, good) to your account. So you may not want to be as aggressive toward the end of your plan because what was once interim volatility can become terminal. In this connection, constant maturities present no problem because they are designed to mature on schedule. Constant durations are the unruly ones. If you find them intolerable, you can (as mentioned earlier) convert to constant maturities. Or you may wish to accelerate your maturities or use one of the other techniques to be introduced in Chapter 10.

Plan Z: Step by Step

Let's look in some detail at how Plan Z unfolds by considering the case of Zelda, who, after a rigorous self-examination, has decided to shift all $10,000 in her IRA from CDs and bonds to Plan Z, specifically to VZ^2.

To account for the possibility that she might one day come across another attractive investment, Zelda decides to set her Z_{max} to 80. That way, she'll always have at least 20 percent of her money in cash, "dry powder" available for diversification opportunities. She feels comfortable with a Z_{min} of 20 because then she'll earn the higher long-term rate on at least some part of her money at all times. Since she also wants a Z_{min} low enough that she won't feel overinvested should zero prices collapse, her Z range of 20 to 80 feels comfortable.

She is after results, so there's no reason for her to avoid setting her D_{max} to the most aggressive level possible: 30 years. But she opts for a D_{min} of 5 years, following the same reasoning that led her to choose a Z_{min} of 20—she wants some protection on the downside. Her designated D Range is, therefore, 5 to 30. In other words, she plans to hold zeros that range between 5 and 30 years' duration.

Now Zelda must pick two interest rate ranges.* She decides to cast her net wide along the duration axis because she doesn't feel confident that rates will stay in a narrow range—or that she could guess what that range would be, if they did. Using the recent past as a guide, Zelda picks an Id Range of 3 to 13 percent. Applying the shortcut in Appendix A, she derives the following formula to guide her in setting her duration: $D = 2.5i - 2.5$ (which can be further simplified to $D = 2.5(i-1)$). After checking to see if this is correct, she moves on to her Iz Range. Zelda heeds the advice to "aim low" and specifies an Iz_{min} of 2.5 and an Iz_{max} of 6. Again, using the shortcut in Appendix A she arrives at her personal equation: $Z\% = 20i - 40$ (or $Z\% = 20(i-2)$).

Zelda's next move is to pick up the newspaper or call her broker to find out the current rate of a one-year T-bill (or the 90-day T-bill or the 3-month CD rate—it doesn't matter as long as it is a short-term rate and she consistently uses the same measure for every rebalancing). She learns the current rate is 5 percent and plugs this value into her two formulas:

a.
$$\begin{aligned} Z\% &= 20\,(i-2) \\ &= 20\,(5-2) \\ &= 20\,(3) \\ &= 60 \end{aligned}$$

b.
$$\begin{aligned} D &= 2.5\,(i-1) \\ &= 2.5\,(5-1) \\ &= 2.5\,(4) \\ &= 10 \end{aligned}$$

* It's theoretically possible to pick as many as you can reasonably follow by having discontinuous ranges that cover different portions of the interest rate spectrum.

This tells Zelda to start her plan by purchasing $6,000 worth of zeros (that's 60 percent of the $10,000 she's allocated to Plan Z), all of 10 years' duration.

After a year, it's time to rebalance. She checks the one-year T-bill rate again and sees that it's risen to 7 percent. She inspects her brokerage statement, which now reads:

Cash account (with interest)	$4,250
Zero account	5,050
	$9,300

The total value of her program has fallen by 7 percent. "I asked for a more lively investment," she says to herself, "and it seems I got it." She recomputes her D and Z percentages based on the new interest rate with the following results:

a. $Z\% = 20\,(i-2) = 100$ b. $D = 2.5\,(i-1) = 15$

Zelda's new Z percentage of 100 is above her established Z_{max} of 80. This tells her to go up to her Z_{max} and no farther. She orders her broker to sell her 10-year zeros (now 9-year zeros, actually) and buy $7,440 worth of 15-year zeros (an amount equal to 80 percent of her total Plan Z equity), keeping $1,860 in her money market fund.

At the end of the second year, the interest rate has again risen, this time to 9 percent. Zelda's Z percentage is now 140—still well above her Z_{max}—and her D, she computes, is 20. Her statement records another loss:

Cash account (with interest)	$2,000
Zero account	5,900
	$7,900

Still at her Z_{max}, Zelda must begin Year 3 with 20 percent of her account in cash (or $1,580). Her instructions to her broker: "Sell my 15-year zeros (now 14-year zeros) and use the proceeds plus \$420 from the money market fund to buy 20-year zeros, leaving \$1,580 in cash."

In the following year, rates drop back down to 6 percent, so Zelda's accounts look like this:

Cash account (with interest)	\$1,725
Zero account	10,375
	\$12,100

Rising rates in the first two years caused losses, but the very same phenomenon had, through the agency of VZ^2, put Zelda into 20-year zeros that were sensitive to interest rates now going the other way. This enabled her to more than recoup her early losses. The new interest rate dictates that she readjust her Z percentage and duration again when she rebalances.

Eventually Zelda will arrive at Year 20 or so of her 25-year program and the issue of closing out will arise. She may decide to stay the course and, when she sells zeros on her 25th and final rebalancing, refrain from repurchasing any and end her plan in cash. But what if her zero account has just experienced two or three good years in a row, and Zelda's account shows a much higher balance than she'd hoped for? She'd hate to see those excellent returns degenerate into merely good or average ones. So she can, if she wants, cash out now. Or she can compromise: If she reduces her Z_{max} (or her D_{max}), either at once or gradually over the next few years, then Plan Z will still have a little room in which to operate, but Zelda will, in effect, have taken out some insurance against losing what Plan Z has helped her build.

One critical question remains: What kind of Plan Z (which form and which settings) should YOU choose? This (and a few subsidiary matters as well) will be addressed next.

10

Picking a Plan

When it comes to selecting the type of Plan Z you want, three considerations predominate: (1) the length of your investment span, (2) the interim volatility (r^1) you are willing to accept in view of the reward you seek, and (3) the level of closeout risk (r^2) you prefer.

1. The time you have to invest says a great deal about your attitude to r^1 and r^2. The younger the investor, the more he or she can afford an aggressive program—with its greater risks and rewards. There are three reasons for thinking so. First, a younger investor has more time, so the odds of a favorable final result are much improved. In fact, for a young adult in his or her mid-20s to early 30s, the odds of a less-than-good result are almost nil: It is difficult to imagine that unfavorable interest rate fluctuations will persist for 30 or 40 years. Second, more time means more compounding. Finally, younger people have more years of productive

earning power before them, so interim adversity will affect a smaller portion of their eventual life's savings.

Conversely, the older the investor, the more conservative his or her outlook. As a group, they have less time to wait for results, less time to allow for compounding, and less opportunity to replace or add to earnings—along with a more immediate need for the use of investment funds. These create powerful pressures to conserve savings and resist risk.

2. Interim risk volatility is a nonissue, more a matter of psychological comfort than financial prudence. With most investments, market risk is where the action and the danger is; not so with zeros or Plan Z. Meandering price levels do not threaten loss *in the long run.* In fact, it is interim volatility that provides the very basis for the speculation that Plan Z grafts onto the normally and still-safe action of zero coupon bonds. Nonetheless, you can to some extent control the degree of interim volatility you are likely to experience through your selection of a plan and its parameters.

3. As mentioned before, closeout risk can be managed (in a fashion) by using zeros of a constant maturity. Because this way all your zeros mature at the end of the investment period, your plan automatically converts itself completely to cash, and doubts and risks regarding volatility, interest rate fluctuations, and zero prices cease to be of concern. ZB and VZP are the only versions of Plan Z that use constant maturities. If your time horizon is relatively short, say around 12 to 15 years, and your outlook deeply conservative, they are choices you might want to consider.

There is good reason to doubt, though, whether constant maturities make sense for any Plan Z investor, no matter how risk-sensitive or short of time. To understand why, let's first reexamine what closeout risk is.

Consider the fortunate fellow who has $500,000 in his VZP account a year before he is set to retire. Good for him! One problem. His aggressive course leaves him holding 30-year zeros. One uptick of a percent or more and his bundle could shrink by half and possibly more. Here he is, on the eve of his program's maturity, and he's playing "double or nothing" with his retirement stake! Blame the high-duration zeros. He probably wouldn't have done as well without them. But now they threaten the very achievement they helped build.

As much anxiety as this anecdote might evoke—and the prospect of seeing your life's savings in commotion shortly before you are counting on them most is not to be minimized—still, it is a mistake to assume that the only way to avoid closeout risk is to employ constant maturities. There are three reasons for thinking so: (1) Closeout risk (as we shall soon see) can be minimized. You do not have to march your zeros toward maturity one year at a time. (2) One of the preeminent virtues of Plan Z, especially in its latter incarnations (most prominently VZ^2), is its ability to smooth the equity stream (a phenomenon to be investigated in the next section). In this light, the concerns about closeout risk prompted by ZB, VZP, and VZD turn out to have been slightly exaggerated. (3) For all its concern with preserving profits, the use of constant maturities forfeits the possibility of extended profits just because of its conservatism. You can make so much more with other strategies that the additional funds alone may make greater risk tolerable. The claim that ZB is safer than other versions doesn't wash, either. VZ^2, for example, does "poorly" (which is to say, less well than cash or bonds) in fewer instances.

So how can you limit closeout risk without caving in to constant maturities?

Allocate Less Money

You can switch to a more aggressive plan but devote less of your capital to it. This would give you some chance at a windfall but limit the damage should conditions turn out unfavorable at the end. By choosing a more aggressive form, an investor can give himself at least a shot at the 500 to 1,000 percent returns that favorable interest rate scenarios can sometimes provide. A return like that on even 10 or 20 percent of your portfolio is equivalent to doubling the value of the whole.

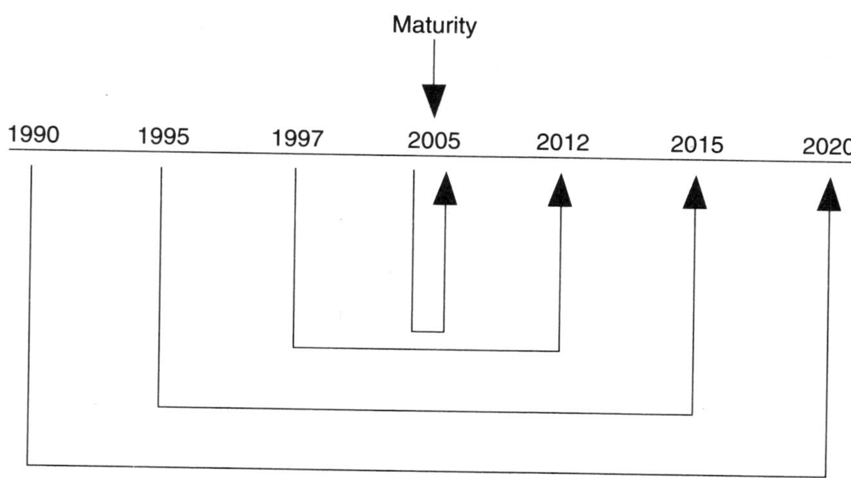

Figure 10.1 Accelerated maturation.

Cut Back Your Parameters

Perhaps the simplest way to ensure that the volatility of your constant-duration zeros is gradually subdued is to lower your Z_{max} (if you are using VZP or VZ^2) or your D_{max} (with VZD or VZ^2) over the latter portion of your plan. If you are using constant durations with ZB, you can lower your Z percentage.

Accelerate Maturation

You can avail yourself of zeros with a duration longer than your investment period and still have them mature on time. Trade high-duration (say 30-year) zeros, but march them forward in double-time, making them mature in just half the time (in this case, 15 years) as in Figure 10.1. Suppose you started in 1990 with a mind to retiring in 2005. In your first year, you buy 30-year zeros. As you move nearer to 2005, you switch to zeros that mature at dates proportionally closer to your target date with each rebalancing. In 1990 you hold zeros maturing in 2020. In 1995, you plan to hold zeros maturing in 2015. Similarly, at regular intervals, you advance the maturity date of your zeros so they converge on the maturity date from a point in the future, just as you converge on it from the other direction.

(By the way, you can also perform this process in reverse—"decelerated maturation"—in order to ease into Plan Z.)

Serial Plan Z

An alternative to accelerated maturation, if you have enough time, is to deploy two successive versions of Plan Z. A young adult with 30 or 40 years until retirement might implement VZP, VZD, or VZ^2 over the first 20 or so years and then switch his accumulated earnings into a constant maturity for the remainder. (This can also enable you to maintain a low-volatility form of Plan Z well past your original closeout date.)

Stepladdering

You can use VZD or VZ^2 as though it were something like a constant maturity. Set your D Range wide at the start, then narrow it in stages. It might hold at 0 to 30 for the first five years, 0 to 25 for the next five, and so on until you reach 0 to 5. This way, you lower the average duration in stages.

Floor Return

By enforcing a *floor*, or minimum return on your cash account, you can ease into or out of Plan Z. For example, rather than arrange for Plan Z to expire close to your retirement date, you can aim it at an expiration date well beyond retirement in order to let Plan Z stay active and volatile. When retirement eventually comes, you simply convert to using a floor return on the cash portion. How does this work? Just set your own floor, that is, a minimum acceptable return to be produced by the cash portion of your account, and put it up relatively high, say at 10 percent. This means you are demanding 10 percent income from your cash balance regardless of the real-world interest rate. When interest rates are below your 10 percent (as they are likely to be), you will have to sell sufficient zeros to provide you with the difference. In this way, you will be generating cash income while gradually liquidating your zero holdings in an orderly and timely way. When rates are low, you will be forced to sell relatively more of your (high-priced) zeros to subsidize the 10 percent return you are demanding from your cash account. When rates are higher, you will need to sell fewer (low-priced) zeros. So you will be selling more zeros at higher prices and fewer at low prices—moving more money out of the long-term investment when rates are low, keeping more there when rates are high. You will have incorporated an automatic "sell high" procedure into your orderly liquidation of zeros while generating retirement income.

An institution or an individual who is extremely risk-averse can also use this approach in reverse to ease into, rather than out of, Plan Z. By setting a relatively low *ceiling* return, you can reverse the flow of funds. Instead of subsidizing the cash return, you will draw on the interest your cash account earns and use it to purchase zero coupon bonds—steadily building a start-up position for Plan Z. Let's say you put all your money in cash and set a 3 percent *ceiling*. When rates are below it, you'd retain all interest income in the cash account. Anything above your ceiling would be skimmed and used to buy zeros. In the first few years, zeros would represent only a small portion of your total investment, so the volatility of your portfolio would be minimal. Once again, a valuable by-product of this procedure is the well-timed purchase of zeros. Because you are always retaining a constant 3 percent growth in the money market fund, as interest rates rise you will have proportionally more to invest in zeros. When rates are at 4 percent, you'd keep 3 percent of your interest in cash, leaving you with 1 percent to invest in zeros. But if rates move up to 10 percent, a full 7 percent would be available for the same purpose. You'd have seven times as much to invest, and you'd be investing heavily precisely when zeros were cheap. As we saw in Chapter 4, the important consideration when investing in zeros is to put more dollars in at higher rates and fewer at lower rates. This is precisely the mechanism at work here, something the floor and ceiling return approaches accomplish *automatically.*

The ceiling return method has one drawback. It takes time to create a meaningful position in zeros this way. So, if you are anxious to get started on Plan Z right away, it is not for you. Entities (for example, pension funds) that have longer time horizons than individuals do might prefer the leisurely introduction to Plan Z that a ceiling return affords, for two reasons. First, the zero account is unlikely to contribute much volatility to the portfolio until a lengthy period of steady growth has passed. This insulates the initial capital allocated to Plan Z from interim loss. Second, pension funds have special fixed obligations for 20, 30, 40, 50, even 100 years into the future. The ability to actually "fix" the return on the cash account may be helpful in providing a certain, reliable minimum. This approach affords an increased level of stability, a way for pension funds to plan ahead to meet, and possibly exceed, certain of their known future obligations. At the same time, the fund will be moving toward a position from which it will be able to take advantage of Plan Z, but by gradually using future revenues (interest earned), never exposing *initial* capital to risk, not even the risk of interim adversity.

Plan Z: Types and Characteristics

You know *your* needs, characteristics, and risk profile; what about Plan Z's? Which are the riskier (and therefore potentially more rewarding) versions? Which are more or less reliable and consistent? Which is right for you? First, some general principles:

1. For any plan using a fixed Z percentage, the higher the Z percentage, the more aggressive the position.
2. For any plan using constant durations, the longer the maturity length, the more aggressive (and riskier) it is.
3. For VZP, the wider the Z Range, the more aggressive the plan. If two Z Ranges are equally broad, the one with the higher Z_{max} is the more aggressive one. Thus, a Z Range

from 75 to 100 is more aggressive than one from 25 to 50 because its Z_{max} is higher.

4. With VZD, the higher your average duration, the greater the risk you are accepting. However, the average of the range you specify may not be the one you actually wind up with if your I Range mismatches actual rates. You could pick a D Range of 20 to 30 (theoretical average: 25 years) but hold 20-year zeros almost all the time if conditions never meet your interest rate criteria for switching.
5. For a particular average duration, the wider the D Range, the more aggressive the plan. For example, both a 14- to 16-year and a 0- to 30-year D Range have the same theoretical average of 15, but the latter is far more aggressive.
6. There is no simple way to categorize an I Range as aggressive or conservative, except at the extremes, because defining an I Range as one thing or another depends on how rates actually turn out. Your "effective" range will be that portion of your specified I Range which overlaps actual interest rates to the greatest degree. If you designate a band of 5 to 10 percent and rates move between 7 and 15 percent, *your* I Range will prevent you from taking action when rates are above 10 percent, and *actual* rates will forestall any action below 7 (because they never get that low). Generally speaking, we can say that a *narrow* I Range is aggressive because it means you plan to frequently switch from your maximum to your minimum Z percentage (or duration). A wide I Range is conservative, because it means you intend to make relatively minor adjustments to your Z percentage (or duration) as rates fluctuate.
7. With Z percentages or D Ranges, a wide range means more volatility and risk. Thus, the most aggressive stance possible would be a high and wide Z Range, say 0 to 100 (or a high and wide D Range) combined with a relatively narrow I Range.

Table 10.1 expresses these principles as they apply to each form of Plan Z. You can see at a glance which settings are likely

Table 10.1 Summarized Characteristics of Various Plan Types

Plan Z type	Conservative	Aggressive	Effective	Ineffective
ZB/constant maturity	Low Z%	High Z%	Z% in mid-range	Z% < 5 or Z% > 95
ZB/constant duration	Either low Z% or low D	Neither low Z% nor low D	Moderate Z% and high D	Z% < 5 or Z% > 95 or D < 5
VZP/constant maturity	Wide I Range and low Z Range	Narrow I Range and high or wide Z Range	High and/or wide Z Range	Z_{max} < 20 or narrow Z Range (Z_{max}–Z_{min} < 10%)
VZP/constant duration	Low D, wide Z Range, wide I Range	High D, narrow I Range, wide Z Range	Wide Z Range and medium I range	Very narrow Z Range ≈ ZB; very narrow or very wide I Range; very low Z_{max} (< 25)
VZD	Z% < 60 and low D Range (0–15) and wide I Range	Wide D Range (0–30) with high D_{max} and Z% = 50 to 80 and moderate I Range	Almost anything except ineffective parameters	Narrow D Range or ultra-low Z% (< 20) or too narrow I Range
VZ^2	Conservative VZP and conservative VZD	Aggressive VZP and aggressive VZD	Conservative VZP and VZD or aggressive VZP and VZD	Conservative VZP with aggressive VZD or aggressive VZP with conservative VZD

to produce the best and worst results as well as which are the most conservative and aggressive.

Observe that as you move down Table 10.1, from the earlier versions of Plan Z to the later ones, the prescriptions—what you need to do and be aware of—get more complex. That's to be expected, because the later versions of Plan Z all have more "moving parts": with ZB you just had to pick a Z percentage, while VZP requires a Z Range and an I Range, VZD a D Range and an I Range, and VZ^2 both. But as you move down the table, something else happens: Plan Z gets less fussy about when it will work and why, to the point where VZD and VZ^2 fare well in most cases in almost any formulation. This phenomenon is a direct outcome of the flexibility introduced in VZP and VZD and multiplied in VZ^2. In this respect, as in many others, VZ^2 is the culmination of Plan Z.

The material in Table 10.1 is presented from a different perspective in Table 10.2. You can find the type of Plan Z that matches

Table 10.2 Suggested Plans and Parameters for Different Time Horizons and Risk-Acceptance Levels

Risk Acceptance	Time to Invest		
	Short-term (10–15 yrs)	**Medium-term (15–20 yrs)**	**Long-term (20–30+ yrs)**
Low (conservative)	• ZB/CM: Z% = 80	• ZB/CM: Z% = 60 to 80*	• ZB/CM: Z% = 40 to 60*
	• VZP: $Z_{max} < 60$, M = term or a bit longer	→	→
	• VZP: wide Zr and very wide Ir	→	→
		*because r^2 increases	*because r^2 increases
Medium	• ZB/CM: Z% = 40 to 90; M = term	→	→
	• ZB/CD: Z% = 40 to 90 and low D ($\propto$ r2)	→	→
	• ZB/CD: Z% = 20 to 60 and high D ($\propto$ r2)	→	→
	• VZP: Zr = 20–80, M = term	→	→
	• VZP: Zr = 0–100, D = low (3–8 yrs)	→	→
	• VZP: Zr = 0–40, D = high (15–30 yrs), Ir wide ($\approx$ 6 pts)	→	→
	• VZD: $D_{max} \propto r^2$, Z% = 40 to 60, Ir wide	• VZD: $D_{max} \propto r^2$, Z% = 40 to 60, Ir wide	• VZD: $D_{max} \propto r^2$, Z% = 50 to 80, Ir wide
	• VZ^2 (VZP and VZD as above)		
High (aggressive)	• VZP: Zr = 0–100, Ir = low, narrow (1–2 pts)	→	→
	• VZD: Dr = 0 to whatever is OK ($\propto$ r2), Ir = anything but narrow, Z% = 50 to 90	→	→
	• VZ^2 (VZP and VZD as above)	→	→

Key: r^1 = interim risk; r^2 = close-out risk; CM = constant maturity; CD = constant duration; D = duration; M = maturity; Zr = Z Range; Dr = D Range; Ir = I Range; $\propto$ = varies with.
Note: low D = term plus whatever D you are willing to close out with; high D = term plus 15 years (up to max of 30).

Table 10.3 Average Results for Various Plans when "Ineffective" Parameter Combinations Are Removed—25-year Investment Term

	ZB	VZP	VZD	VZ^2
Interest rate scenario	7 "gentle" and 3 "real"	7 "gentle" and 3 "real"	7 "gentle" and 3 "real"	7 "gentle" and 3 "real"
Investment	$25K deposit	$25K deposit	$25K deposit	$25K deposit
Z	Z% = 50	Z Range = 0–100	Z% = 80	Z Range = 0–100
D	D = 30	D = 30	D Range = 0–30	D Range = 0–30
I	—	Low or wide	Low or wide	Low-low, low-wide, or wide-low*
Cash	$128,527	$128,527	$128,527	$128,527
Bonds	$145,719	$145,719	$145,719	$145,719
Plan Z	$231,035	$634,612	$393,962	$702,464
Plan vs. cash	80%	394%	207%	447%
Plan vs. bonds	59%	336%	170%	382%
Cash CRR	6.77%	6.77%	6.77%	6.77%
Bonds CRR	7.31%	7.31%	7.31%	7.31%
Plan Z CRR	9.30%	13.81%	11.66%	14.27%

*The wide-low and low-wide interest rate guesses were averaged to give them a 50 percent weighting, comparable to the other versions of Plan Z.

Note: CRR = equivalent annual compound rate of return.

your needs at the intersection of your term and risk level as you define them.

The Case for VZ^2

The choice of a suitable type of Plan Z can be much simplified once you recognize that VZ^2 is capable of mimicking any other form you might prefer.* But it is the primary candidate for other reasons, primarily because it works better than anything else, providing higher average returns than the other forms of Plan Z at little or no extra—and perhaps even less—risk.

* Its VZD component can be shut down to act like a constant-duration zero and its VZP component suppressed to emulate VZD. It can function like ZB but it cannot be programmed to follow the simple "buy and hold" of constant maturities. However, the wisdom of aspiring to this last is questionable. Problems with closeout risk can be handled in other ways (mentioned earlier in this chapter) without sacrificing the potential for high returns.

Table 10.4 Average Results for Various Plans when "Ineffective" Parameter Combinations Are Removed—15-Year Investment Term

	ZB	VZP	VZD	VZ²
Interest rate scenario	7 "gentle" and 3 "real"	7 "gentle" and 3 "real"	7 "gentle" and 3 "real"	7 "gentle" and 3 "real"
Investment	$25K deposit	$25K deposit	$25K deposit	$25K deposit
Z	Z% = 50	Z Range = 0–100	Z% = 80	Z Range = 0–100
D	D = 30	D = 30	D Range = 0–30	D Range = 0–30
I	—	Low or wide	Low or wide	Low-low, low-wide, or wide-low*
Cash	$67,625	$67,625	$67,625	$67,625
Bonds	$74,482	$74,482	$74,482	$74,482
Plan Z	$95,987	$132,640	$116,695	$136,919
Plan vs. cash	42%	96%	73%	102%
Plan vs. bonds	29%	78%	57%	84%
Cash CRR	6.86%	6.86%	6.86%	6.86%
Bonds CRR	7.55%	7.55%	7.55%	7.55%
Plan Z CRR	9.38%	11.77%	10.82%	12.00%

*The wide-low and low-wide interest rate guesses were averaged to give them a 50 percent weighting, comparable to the other versions of Plan Z.

Note: CRR = equivalent annual compound rate of return.

Why do we claim VZ² is the only reasonable choice, preferable to all others? Let's compare the varieties of Plan Z, observing each at the height of its powers. In Tables 10.3 and 10.4 we have selectively extended and reproduced results from previous tables, carefully excising those strategies identified in Table 10.1 as ineffective. Since these are elements of Plan Z in every investor's control, we are well within our rights to eliminate them. In contrast, the simulations presented in Chapters 5 through 8 were scattershot efforts that did not focus on workable strategies but that strove instead to test a variety of all approaches in an assortment of scenarios. We have not altered the interest rate scenarios, which function here just as they did in previous chapters. We have taken Plan Z's performances across all scenarios and averaged the results.

The first thing to notice is how far Plan Z, finally allowed to perform at its best, outdistances cash and bonds. By any measure—absolute dollars, percentages, or compound rates of return, whether at 15 years or 25—neither comes close to Plan Z, even in its less powerful forms. Indeed, in all our simulations thus far, no cash or

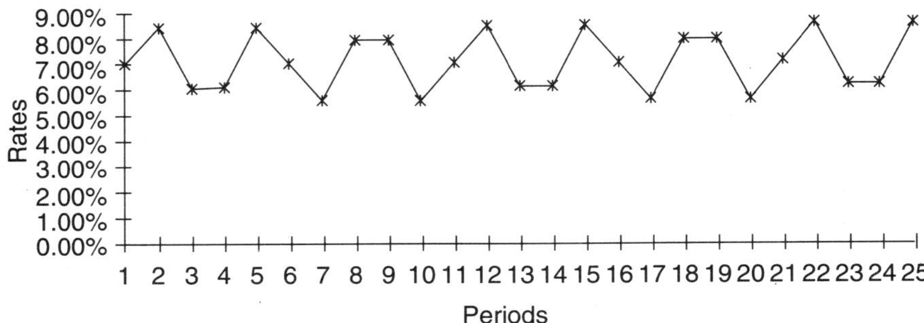

Figure 10.2 Special interest rate scenario.

bond investment has approached the heights that Plan Z has *at times* attained.* But here cash and bonds fail to measure up even to Plan Z's *average* performance across various scenarios once certain misguided tactics were abandoned.

We are forced to conclude that Plan Z is far superior to its fixed brethren and that VZ^2 is the best Plan Z has to offer.

An important confirmation of VZ^2's abilities is its tendency to smooth fluctuations in the equity stream—something it does better than any other type of Plan Z. What do we mean by this? Take the line that represents the value of your Plan Z holdings. As we have seen, it can be a bumpy ride. What VZ^2 does is iron out the kinks, smooth out the dips. The net effect can be a relatively uninterrupted ascent as though VZ^2 had straightened your equity string by tugging on it from both ends. Instead of a series of self-canceling ups and downs (such as those depicted in Figure 4.4), VZ^2 more often produces a succession of inclines and plateaus that minimize periods of loss and therefore make more money.

To show how Plan Z accomplishes this, we have constructed a special series of simulations. Figure 10.2 illustrates the interest rate scenario—especially configured to highlight an important characteristic of Plan Z present at all times but not always apparent—on which the succeeding charts are based. As you can see, rates

* Our conjecture is that for any plausible interest rate scenario that would provide the nearly 16 percent compound rate of return necessary to transform a $25,000 investment in cash or bonds into $1,000,000 after 25 years, there is no thoughtful application of Plan Z that would not return far more.

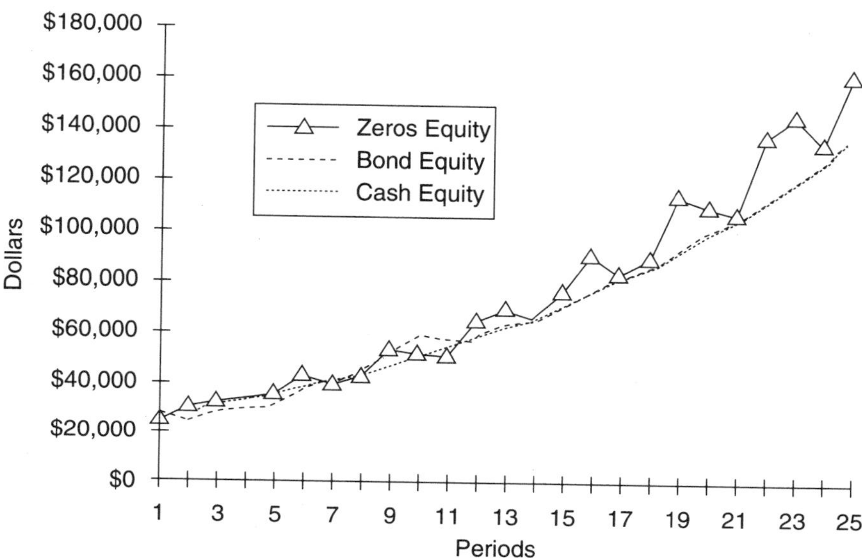

Figure 10.3 ZB50 with D = 15 produces $160,158.

oscillate in a narrow band between roughly 5.5 and 8.5 percent. Figures 10.3 through 10.12 will compare how the various forms of Plan Z—from primitive ZB to ultimate VZ²—are able to manage the task of converting these zigzag interest rate oscillations to dollars in your Plan Z account.

Figure 10.3 shows ZB at work with a Z percentage of 50 and constant-duration zeros of 15 years. The result after 25 years: $160,158. But the important point for our purposes is the way ZB's equity stream undulates and rises, each cycle getting larger and more exaggerated as the years wear on. Although it gets bigger, the pattern is the same: roughly three steps forward and two steps back.

The next graph (Figure 10.4) shows the first of three VZP efforts. All preserve the same average Z percent, equal to the 50 percent that ZB used in Figure 10.3. They achieve this same average, however, through three progressively wider Z Ranges: 35 to 65 percent, 20 to 80 percent, and 0 to 100 percent, while VZP's constant-duration zeros remain fixed at 15. You can see over the course of Figures 10.4, 10.5, and 10.6 that Plan Z's equity line

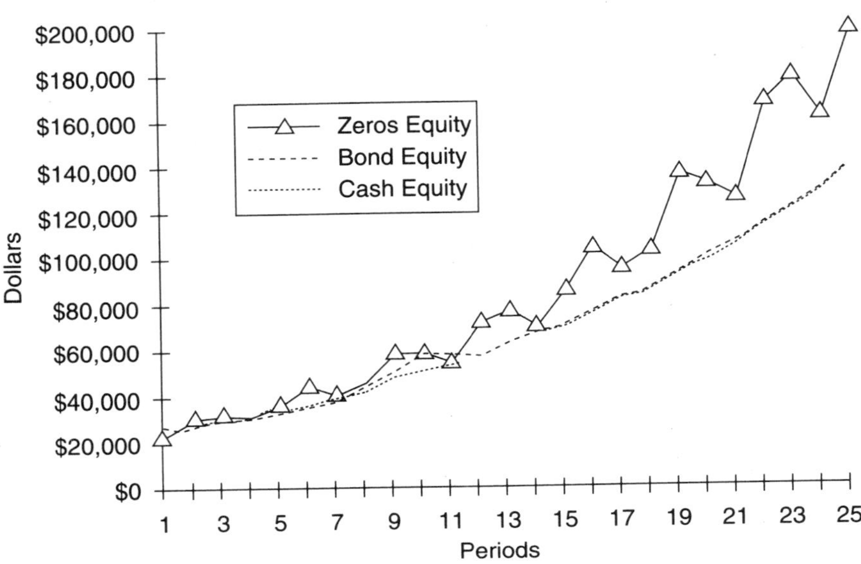

Figure 10.4 VZP with D = 15, Z% = 35 to 65 produces $197,538.

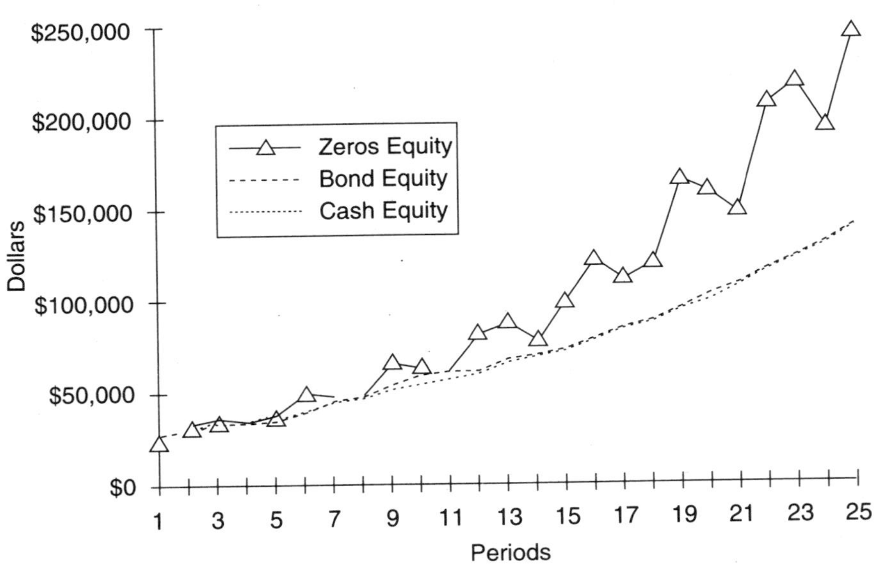

Figure 10.5 VZP with D = 15, Z% = 20 to 80 produces $239,666.

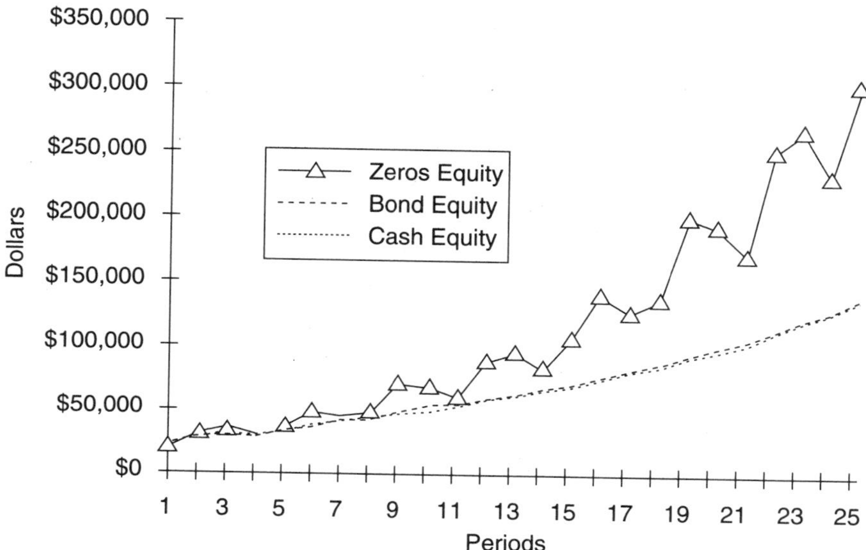

Figure 10.6 VZP with D = 15, Z% = 0 to 100 produces $302,681.

gradually pulls further away from cash as its Z Range widens. By rising above cash sooner, it reaches a higher level and a greater final yield. VZP, however, still continues to observe the same old two-step. The forward strides may be more assertive, but the backward drift is still there.

VZD is depicted in Figures 10.7, 10.8, and 10.9. Here we use a sequence of D Ranges, all centered around 15 years but with different widths: 10 to 20 years, 5 to 25 years, and 0 to 30 years. For VZD the Z percentage stays fixed—at 50 again. This time, the equity line gradually lengthens as the kinks are smoothed out. Fewer and fewer dips are evident until finally (Figure 10.9) there are none at all!

VZ² takes its turn in Figures 10.10 through 10.12. It pairs the same narrow, medium, and wide Z and D Ranges used separately by VZP and VZD above. As a result, the declines we saw in earlier graphs are not only flattened but are converted into positive gains. Thus, what once caused a loss now serves merely to slow down Plan Z's rate of gain.

Table 10.5 summarizes this exercise.

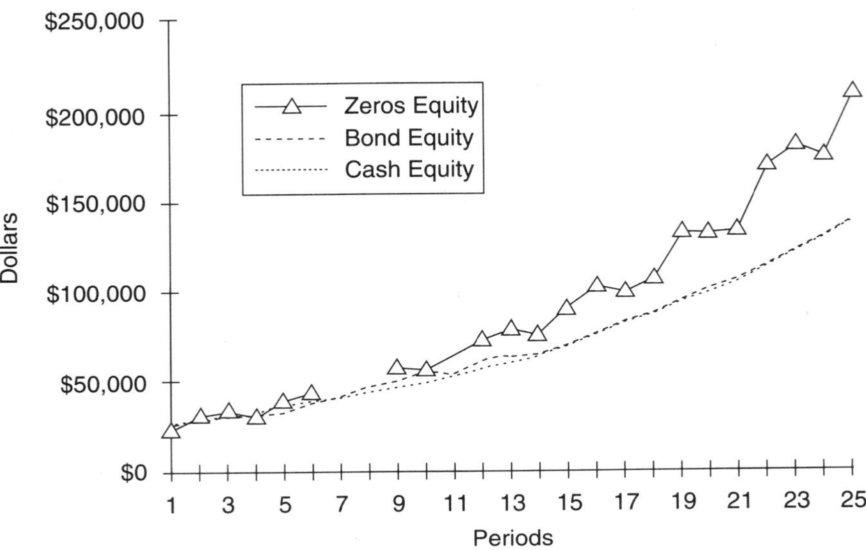

Figure 10.7 VZD with Z% = 50, D Range = 10 to 20 produces $206,177.

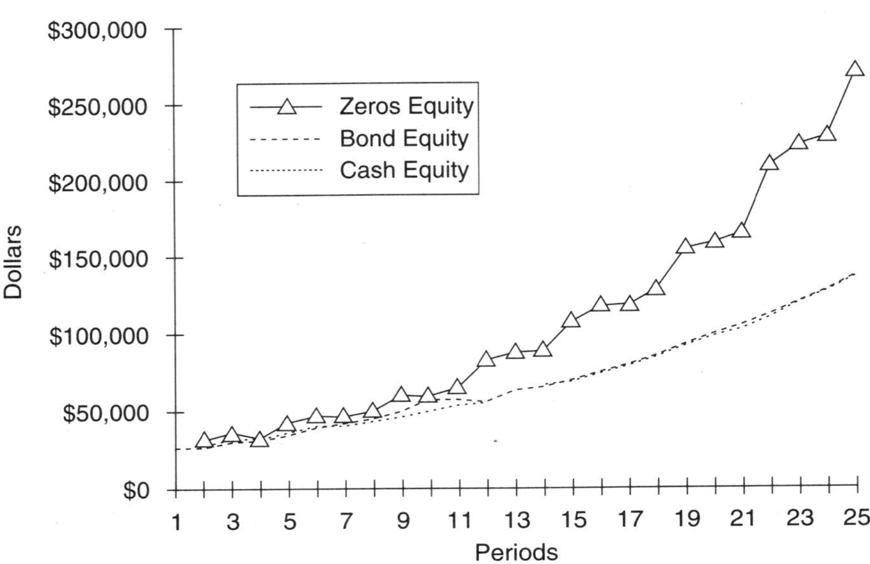

Figure 10.8 VZD with Z% = 50, D Range = 5 to 25 produces $271,635.

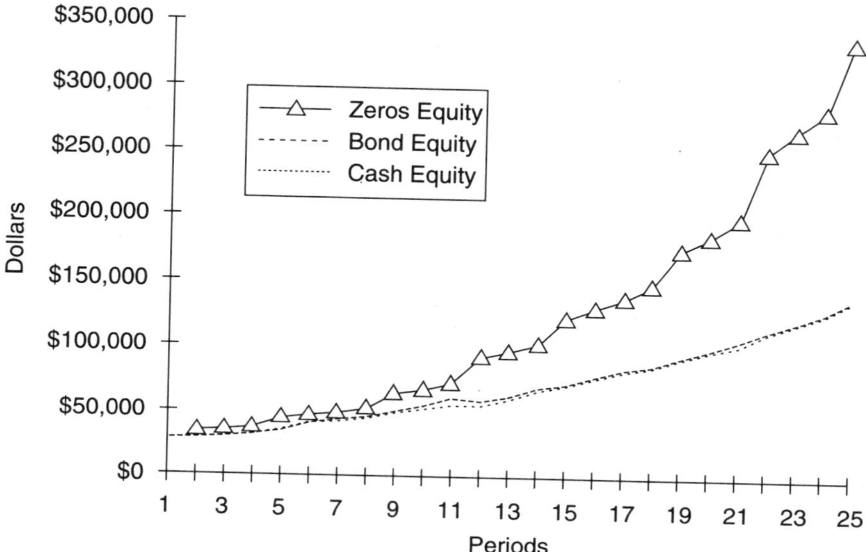

Figure 10.9 VZD with Z% = 50, D Range = 0 to 30 produces $335,588.

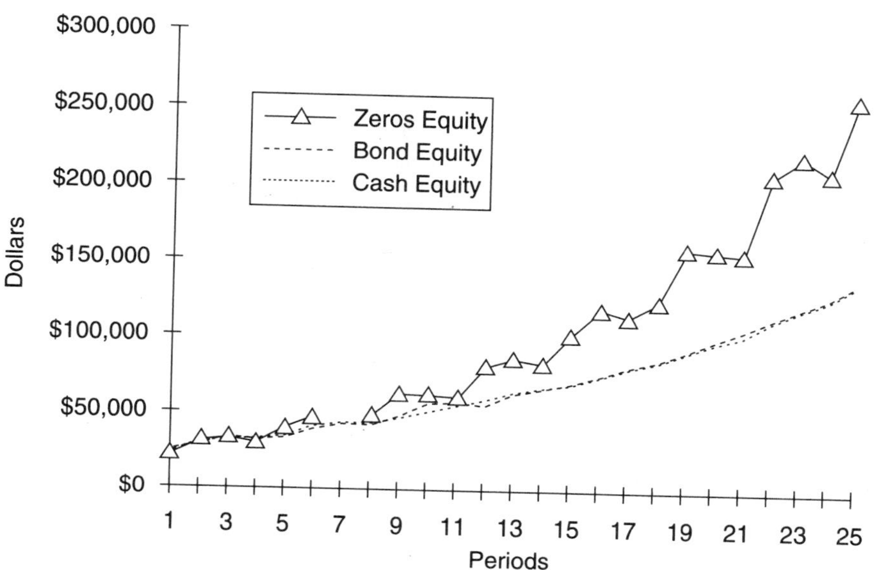

Figure 10.10 VZ^2 with narrow Z and D Ranges produces $258,669.

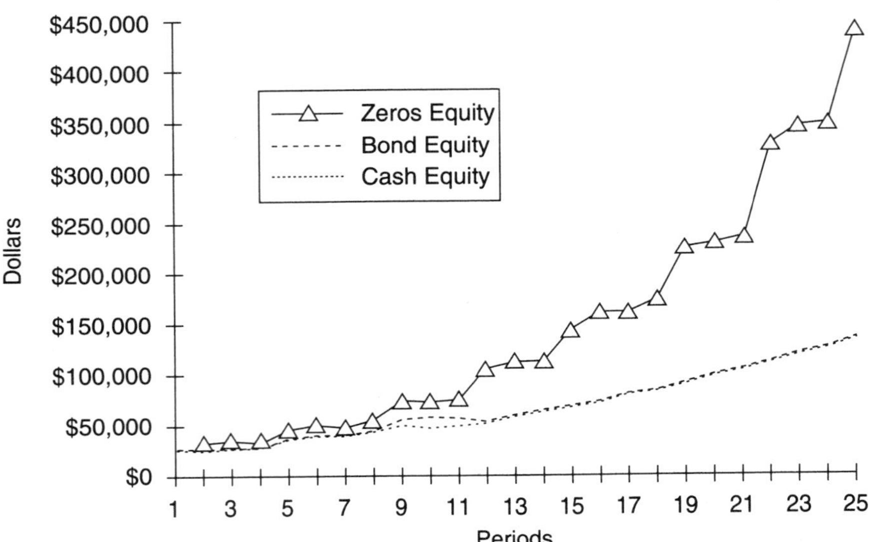

Figure 10.11 VZ² with medium Z and D Ranges produces $437,728.

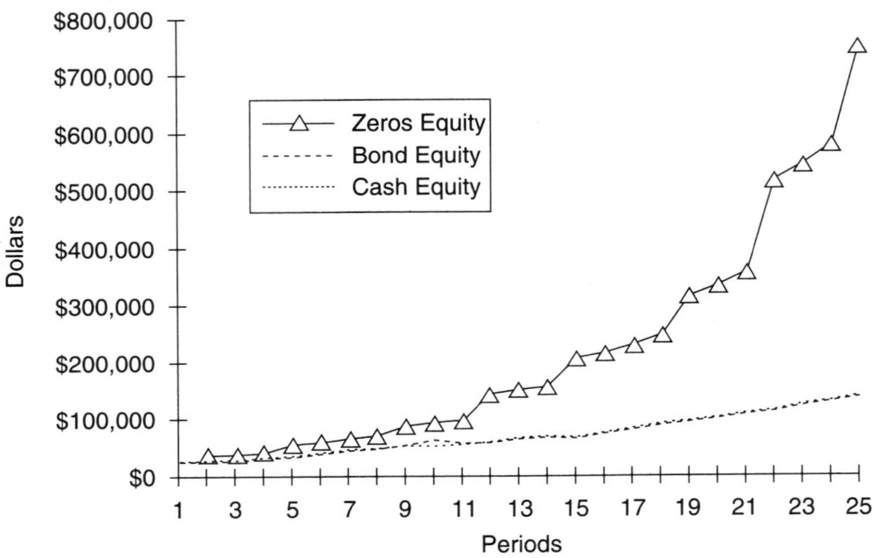

Figure 10.12 VZ² with wide Z and D Ranges produces $745,511.

Table 10.5 Parameters and Results of Special Simulation Runs

		VZP			VZD			VZ^2		
	ZB	**a**	**b**	**c**	**a**	**b**	**c**	**a**	**b**	**c**
Z	50	35–65	20–80	0–100	50	50	50	35–65	20–80	0–100
D	15	15	15	15	10–20	5–25	0–30	10–20	5–25	0–30
Iz Range	–	4–7	4–7	4–7	–	–	–	4–7	4–7	4–7
Id Range	–	–	–	–	7–10	7–10	7–10	7–10	7–10	7–10
Return	$160,158	$197,538	$239,666	$302,681	$206,177	$271,635	$335,588	$258,669	$437,728	$745,511
Detail in Figure	10–3	10–4	10–5	10–6	10–7	10–8	10–9	10–10	10–11	10–12

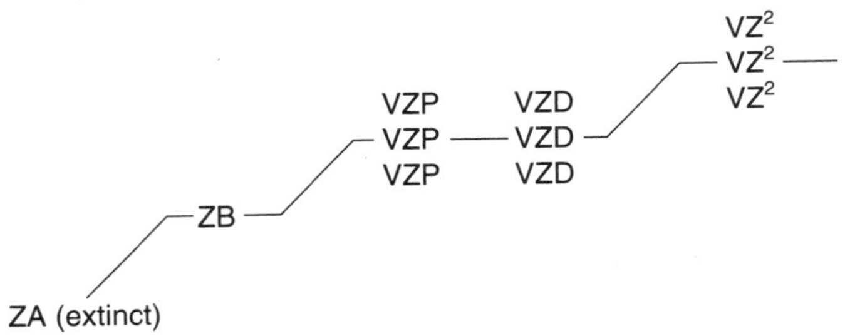

Figure 10.13 Plan Z evolutionary scale.

What we've done in this series of simulations is, essentially, to observe primitive ZB giving birth to VZ^2, by moving up the evolutionary ladder a step at a time, making only the minimum changes necessary to permit each advance to the next level (see Figure 10.13). First, we took ZB's *fixed Z percentage* and stretched it to create a small range, thereby giving birth to VZP. (We then widened that range about its center to let VZP flower fully.) Next, we went back to ZB and started over, doing the same, but this time for ZB's *fixed duration,* and thereby giving birth to VZD—again using the identical parameters as far as possible. Finally, we combined the budding, maturing, and fully blossomed versions of VZP with those of VZD to create VZ^2.

Look at Figure 10.3 (ZB) and then glance at Figures 10.4, 10.5, and 10.6. The only differences are that we have moved our Z_{min}/Z_{max} from 50/50 (ZB) to 35/65 to 20/80 to 0/100. (Plan ZB is really no more than a special case of VZP, the case when Z_{min} and Z_{max} are equal and the Z Range has no width.) As the Z Range is widened, ZB becomes VZP, and the equity line seems to float higher and higher; it seems to rise *vertically* ever more quickly away from the competition as the variable part of "variable Z percent" is increased. Now compare Figure 10.3 with Figures 10.7, 10.8, and 10.9. In this case the differences are that we have moved from a D_{min}/D_{max} of 15/15 to 10/20 to 5/25 to 0/30 (so Plan ZB is also a special case of VZD, the case when D_{min} and D_{max} are equal, and the D Range has no width). Glancing quickly at Figures 10.7, 10.8, and 10.9, we see that the Plan Z equity line gives the impression of being pulled successively further to the right, as if someone were tugging at its end, stretching the equity line *horizontally.* Finally, Figures 10.10, 10.11, and 10.12 show VZ², a combination of VZP and VZD. If you look at these three figures along with Figure 10.3, the combined effects of VZP's and VZD's actions give the impression that Plan Z's equity line is being pulled upward *and* to the right at the same time. Upward means *higher profits.* To the right means a smoother curve with fewer dips—that is, *less adversity.* Upward *and* to the right means *both.*

The upshot? That VZ² will not only return more money more often, but it also has a marked propensity to reduce interim volatility, minimizing the significance of the situation at start-up and lessening the chance of a negative result should you be forced to close out early. What more could you ask for?

In the course of this book we have explored several kinds of Plan Z. We took the time to rule out ZA (dollar-cost averaging with zeros) to spare you the trouble of trying it for yourself. But why did we bother with the rest if VZ² is so far superior? Simple. We had to. Plan Z's several species developed progressively, each forming the basis for what followed. Moreover, the path of discovery turned out to be ideal for educational purposes. We could design no better preparation for grasping Plan Z than a thorough examination of its ancestors. For one thing, vestigial forms are evident even in the last generation—the original idea behind ZB, for example, underlies all subsequent versions. Finally, VZ²'s immediate constituents—VZP and VZD—are prerequisites for understanding it.

Picking an I, Z, and D Range: VZ² Redux

If you wish to try your hand at anything other than VZ², you are welcome to do so. The most effective (and ineffective) settings have already been discussed, both in the chapters in which those versions were introduced and at various points throughout Part III. These findings have also been summarized in Tables 10.1 and 10.2.

We still recommend VZ². Another point in its favor is that you can't easily ruin it. As long as you do two things, you should make out okay: (1) Be sure your Iz_{min} is set lower than your $Id_{min,}$ and (2) place your Iz_{min} low in the expected interest rate range. One of the virtues of VZ^2 is that it divides the burden of covering the range of actual rates between two I Ranges along two axes instead of one. Therefore, it is possible to tilt your D Range toward high-duration zeros in search of "performance" while setting your Iz Range low in a defensive stance. It is true for all forms of Plan Z that aggressive selling is also a protective action that may help you unload high-priced zeros that have become vulnerable to a loss in value. But VZ^2 is in a better position to perform this twin function because it has twice the firepower. VZ^2 can be highly aggressive (buy) at one end of the interest rate range (high) in one form (duration) and highly defensive (sell) at the other end (low) in another form (Z percentage). Unlike the single I Range plans, VZ^2 does not confront you with the unpleasant choice between earning more or preserving your profits. You can do both at the same time.

For the reader who wishes to explore the infinite variety of specific interest rate scenarios and tactics on his own personal computer, a Plan Z software package is available that will enable you to reproduce all the interest rate scenarios and simulations in this book, as well as any others you may wish to create, test, or compare. You can more thoroughly pursue many of the ideas, suggestions, tips, and techniques that we could only mention or hint at in this book because of space limitations. With this software, you can test, customize, and optimize your personal Plan Z parameters. For information about the Plan Z simulator, call (212) 785-3900 or mail the coupon near the end of this book.

11

Portfolio Management with Plan Z

Scores of tracts have been written on the whys and wherefores of portfolio management, covering topics such as diversification, risk management, asset allocation, and so on, and so on. For the average investor who does not have 389 stocks in his portfolio or the prospect of large sums regularly flowing in and out every month, portfolio management can be summed up in four principles:

1. Don't put all your eggs in one basket.
2. Have a plan.
3. Have a plan.
4. Have a plan.

As to the matter of eggs, this is what is meant by diversification. The idea is to disperse your holdings to limit the damage that might be caused by a single act (for example, dropping the basket). To diversify, it is enough to make sure the elements in your portfolio are unrelated. If their performance is somehow linked or correlated so that one event or trend can hurt all or many, then they're not really diversified. If you owned only GM and Ford stock, for instance, you are asking for trouble when tough times befall the auto industry.

What's the best way to diversify? Spread out the risks among several different kinds of investments, not a large number of similar ones. Ideally, your portfolio should be set up so its various parts not only function independently but also complement one another by achieving offsetting gains. An example might be to pair an investment that does well during inflation with one that does poorly, or to match a stock in a cyclical industry with one that is countercyclical.

The motive for spreading out in this way is that there are limits to how far you can diversify within a single investment type. Take stocks. Certain economic factors affect all businesses. So, from one perspective, all stocks are correlated. During the '87 crash, Ford and GM suffered, but so did Coca-Cola and IBM. The best course, therefore, is to extend your portfolio into a variety of investments: real estate, collectibles, bonds, and so on. Plan Z is a prominent option. What makes Plan Z a particularly good instrument for diversification is that its investment characteristics are indeterminate; they depend a great deal on parameters *you* select. It doesn't necessarily correlate with any other investment type. In fact, when defined by two different investors, their plans may not even correlate well with each other.

Dollar-cost averaging and dynamic balancing can also help you diversify. You can use them together or singly to attenuate your risk by allotting funds in certain proportions among your investment areas—stocks, bonds, real estate, and so on—and, within those categories, diversifying further as desired. For example, you might decide that your stock holdings should never exceed 60 percent of your entire portfolio and that no more than 25 percent of your stock investments should reside in one sector and no less than 25 percent in another. You may choose to make an even finer distinction and restrict yourself to putting no more than half the funds allocated to a given sector in any one stock. To give a specific example, let's say you want to place a quarter of your portfolio in stocks and have this sum split four ways among the mining, health care, retail, and biotech sectors. At the next level, within the retail sector, you may want to maintain a 50–50 balance between Sears and Wal-Mart.

You can accomplish all this apportioning through dynamic balancing. As we know, it is a method that will not only regulate the diversification appropriate for the purposes of risk management but will also automatically move funds into and out of your various accounts at presumably opportune times, helping you take profits along the way.*

You are free to combine and nest dollar-cost averaging and dynamic balancing in as many ways and on as many levels as you want to create a manageable, rational portfolio that suits your needs. In addition to achieving diversification and augmenting returns, though, dollar-cost averaging and dynamic balancing have the ancillary benefit of forcing you to think clearly and rigorously about your goals, priorities, and views of the market. Merely by requiring that these be made explicit, they can help you make reasonable decisions. A prerequisite and reinforcement of this kind of orderly allocation is a plan.

The importance of planning cannot be overestimated. Although the value of spontaneity and improvisation is not to be denied, we are not talking about an activity at which you are likely to prosper by making it up as you go along. First of all, it's a complicated world out there. Second, there are other people playing this game, and they're *not* making things up as they go. They've got plans and printouts and lots more money than you do. So *you* need a plan to stay on your track and out of their way. It's simply useful to know where you are at all times and what you are doing.

Even if your plan is founded on nothing more than a feeling of discomfort when you have less than 20 percent of your savings in a money market fund, that's something. It gives you a guideline for

* This can help you achieve what is perhaps the most easily overlooked object of investing: to take money *out* of the market.

handling the unexpected, whether a change in fortune or a new investment opportunity, and provides the basis for a decision rule that reflects your actual interests and values. Even modest precepts will help insulate you from whim, impulse, the pressure of friends' advice, and the pull of the market.

It's important, though, not to force rules on yourself just for the sake of having them. Examine your own thoughts to discover what makes sense *to* you and *for* you, and then write it down, make it clear, and see how it fits with your other principles and commitments. In short, rules are not alien disciplinarians that you must obey out of duty or fear. They are a way of putting down in black and white the truths you know to be helpful for achieving investment success and attuning them to your goals. Your roster of personal rules may be as complex as a wiring diagram or simpler than a grocery list. To the extent that they accurately reflect your needs, opinions, and temperament, they can do nothing but help.

Epilogue

Answering the Skeptics

Those familiar with market theory will initially regard the claims of Plan Z skeptically because it professes to outperform the market average and—even more outrageous—do so automatically. In their view, no strategy, even an intelligent one, should be capable of consistently outperforming a broad, efficient market. How then is Plan Z possible?

Beating "the Street"

Thousands of professionals on "the Street" (that is, Wall Street) earn substantial salaries managing fixed-income investment portfolios. But the pressures for short-term results prevent many of them from adopting a Plan Z-like perspective (whether they recognize its virtues or not) because any plan that ran even a possibility of underperforming the competition in the near term would be proscribed. Most are not at liberty to be daring. They have too much at stake, personally and professionally, if they are wrong. This means there is little basis for choosing among various fixed-instrument funds of the same class. In fact, a recent study showed that the differentiating factor among bond fund returns was the fee they charged; their gross market performances were otherwise virtually identical.

As a class, the performance of these professionals cannot by definition be better than average. Were you to measure all the interest and capital gains earned by fixed instruments in a given year and divide it by the amount invested, that would be the average return. Every overperformance would be matched and canceled by some underperformance or other. Plan Z, however, claims consistent residence in the former camp.

To understand the Plan Z phenomenon, we must first address a fundamental question: What is the source of market returns in general? The answer (mentioned cursorily in Chapter 2) is twofold: investment and speculation. It is an element of Plan Z's strength that it seeks both types of returns as a matter of explicit design.

Investment returns are a payment for the use of capital, an inducement to postpone consumption or a reward for doing so. The mere fact that you use Plan Z entitles you to interest—just like anyone who saves instead of spending—because it perpetually puts every dollar you invest out on loan, whether long- or short-term or a mixture of both. Economic theory must grant Plan Z the investment return it is due.

But though Plan Z may keep your money loaned out at all times, continually absorbed in investment, it simultaneously engages in a regime of fairly aggressive speculation, through buying and selling zeros, moving from more to less volatile loans and back again. Successful speculation entails going against the crowd, exercising independent judgment, taking on all the risks of forecasting by betting that something is over- or undervalued, that it can be bought low or sold high—a fair synopsis of Plan Z's regular duties. When zero prices are falling and the crowd is selling, Plan Z steps up and buys. When they are buying and prices are rising, Plan Z stands ready to sell its supply. The higher zeros go and the more the market bids for them, the more aggressively Plan Z sells. The more dramatically zero prices fall and other market participants insistently discard them, the more willing Plan Z is to buy.

Thus, Plan Z earns a speculative profit as well as an investment return. Its speculative designation is bona fide. It takes real risks and it is not always right. Because of interim volatility, Plan Z at times exhibits losses of a size that most fixed-instrument investors couldn't or wouldn't tolerate. The foremost risk every Plan Z investor faces is the possibility of an unusual interest rate scenario that will produce a return lower than a safe investment in cash. Plan Z deserves every penny it makes from its speculative efforts.

It should satisfy any economist who questions Plan Z's prowess to learn that its claim to enhance the effective yield of fixed instruments is based on this double duty: Plan Z works both sides of the financial street. But this answer only raises another question from another quarter.

Plan Z apparently violates an important speculative dictum: Take care of your losses and your profits will take care of themselves. Plan Z doesn't dump its "losses" promptly, as this principle mandates, but *adds to them,* seemingly compounding any errors by pursuing zeros more aggressively when they fall in price. Moreover, it doesn't permit profits to "take care of themselves." Instead, it actively interferes, selling whenever profits materialize. Speculative ventures are not supposed to work this way. To a seasoned trader, Plan Z's methodology is a death sentence. Any market expert would tell you to abandon losing positions by selling out as quickly as you can and hold onto your winnings as long as possible. Yet Plan Z does not just ignore this strategy, it flagrantly contradicts it, doing just the opposite of what is advised. When the value of Plan Z's holdings decline, it buys more; when their value goes up, it sells. It is therefore understandable if doubts were heard from the direction of the Street. How can Plan Z possibly earn an extra speculative return when it violates the most basic rule of successful speculating?

The answer is that, unlike with most speculative vehicles, the price of a zero is *bounded,* existing entirely between the absolute limits of 0 and 100. Although other speculative vehicles share the same lower limit, zeros are exceptional in that their price can never exceed 100. In fact, they can't attain the level of 100 until maturity. (All of this is true of T-bills as well, but their absent volatility makes them unsuitable for speculative gain.) So, while selling a stock at 90 might be a serious mistake—it could be headed for 900—when a zero is sold at that price, we know it can be, at worst, a minor error. Likewise, if you cling to a declining stock you may lose your entire investment if it goes bankrupt. Zeros, however, *must* recoup their declines.

Speculators generally have a sound reason to cut their losses: Falling prices—for all the "bargains" they create—increase the chances that your investment is headed toward a lengthy stay in a price range lower than usual or perhaps a permanent resting place at a price of zilch. In short, they may portend an extended downtrend. The conventional wisdom says: get out while you can. Similarly, rising prices may indicate a sustained upward trend. So why not let your investments ride as high as they can?

The reason Plan Z can prosper by flouting orthodox thinking is that its absolute price boundaries obviate these rationales. Its conditions are different, so the same rules don't apply. Rising prices, rather than indicating the potential for a continuing upward trend, bring zeros closer to their absolute upper bound. With prices closer to the ceiling and farther from the floor, the potential for reward is lower because there is less room for growth, and the risk of a loss is greater because prices have farther to fall. The reverse would hold when prices have dropped.

A rate increase from 3 to 4 percent will cause zero prices to fall, and this may foretell a trend that will see rates go up as high as 6, 7, or 8 percent or more. But interest rate moves are not measured on the same scale as stock prices. The price of a share of common can go from 3 to 4 to 100—there's no telling. But interest rates just don't jump around to the same degree. This observation is even more compelling if you take the long view, as Plan Z does.

From that perspective, an exceedingly high interest rate, as high as 20 percent, can be more confidently regarded as aberrant. The likelihood is that rates will, for the most part, dwell in a narrower span where Plan Z can do its stuff.

Two other considerations exempt Plan Z from the usual trend-related admonitions.

1. Because investors should try to "aim low" with at least one of their two I Ranges, Plan Z's biggest worry is whether rates will move to an extremely high level and stay there for a while. This would surely short-circuit its motive power. But we are somewhat reassured by the idea that this kind of rate rise would almost certainly be due, in part, to high inflation, a good indicator of general economic volatility—precisely the circumstance that Plan Z thrives on. This difficulty may well then contain the seeds of its own solution.

2. If Plan Z sells into a price rise or buys into a decline, and the trend continues without coming back, then Plan Z will indeed have bought or sold too soon. But this will not necessarily be fatal. As long as rates fluctuate once they reach this new upper or lower range, Plan Z will still have an opportunity to engage in its trademark buy low, sell high activity. It will simply be displaced to a new register, if not between Z-40 and Z-90 (or D5 and D25) then between Z-70 and Z-100 (or D25 and D30). In the absolute worst case, a trend with *no* volatility, Plan Z will make no speculative profits, but it will earn an investment return. Thus, an interest rate trend does not represent the same kind of threat to Plan Z that it might to other speculative vehicles. The worst "threat" to Plan Z is merely the *denial* of an *opportunity* (to add speculative profits to its investment gains).

Because of its investment characteristics, this is the *only* loss Plan Z can incur: a loss of opportunity. It may well end with a return inferior to that of alternative investments, but never with a loss in nominal terms (if you stick with Treasury-backed zero coupon bonds). Pair this with the possibility of extraordinary returns and the strong plausibility of superior ones, and the case for Plan Z is compelling.

Appendix A

Calculating Your Variable Z Percentage and Variable Zero Duration Formulas

To determine your variable Z percentage (VZP) or variable zero duration (VZD), pick (1) the highest and lowest Z percentages you can imagine you'd want at any time (or the highest and lowest zero duration) and (2) the interest rates you expect will activate changes in either or both.* You should have four numbers: a maximum Z percentage (Z_{max}), a minimum Z percentage (Z_{min}), a maximum interest rate (I_{max}), and a minimum interest rate (I_{min}) (or a D_{max}, a D_{min}, an I_{max}, and an I_{min}).

There are two methods you can use to combine the figures you have chosen to arrive at the standard VZP or VZD formula: the long way and the short way.

* See Chapter 6 for a more complete discussion on picking the most beneficial interest rates for VZP and Chapter 7 on the optimal I Range for VZD.

The Long Way

The first step is to combine the four numbers you have chosen to form two equations by substituting for variables in the standard VZP formula (Z% = Ki + B) or VZD formula (D = Ki + B). This should read, "The Z percentage (or zero duration) is equal to K (a constant) multiplied by i (the interest rate) plus B (another constant)."

Example 1: VZP

Let's say you selected a Z percentage that ranges between 25 and 100—that is, you never want to have less than 25 percent of your funds in zeros and would not mind being 100 percent in them when rates are high (and when zero prices are very low). Let's also say you felt 6 percent will be a relatively low interest rate and 10 percent a high one over the forthcoming investment period. So when rates are at 10 percent or above, you want to be 100 percent invested in zeros, and when they are at 6 percent or less (when zero prices are high), you want to sell enough zeros to reduce your holdings to 25 percent.

Because you'll have a Z percentage of 25 when rates are at 6 percent, we can substitute 25 for the Z% and 6 for i in the standard VZP formula, giving us the following equation: $25 = 6K + B$. We also know you'll have a Z percentage of 100 when rates hit 10 percent. Using substitution again, we get a second equation: $100 = 10K + B$.

At this point a little algebra is required to solve for the constants that remain unknown. We take the first equation and subtract B from both sides, then divide both sides by 6. The result is the following new equation, isolating K on one side: $(25 - B)/6 = K$. We now have a way of defining K in terms other than itself. Let's take this new equivalent of K and plug it into the other equation to get $100 = 10\,(25 - B)/6 + B$. We solve B in a couple of steps:

$$100 = 10\,(25 - B)/6 + B$$
$$100 = (250 - 10B)/6 + B$$
$$600 = 250 - 10B + 6B$$
$$350 = -4B$$
$$B = -87.5$$

Now we can take this new bit of knowledge and substitute for B in the equation we derived earlier: K = [(25 − (−87.5))]/6. Thus we learn that K = 18.75. This gives us all the information we need to formulate your VZP. We replace K and B to get Z% = 18.75i − 87.5.

Example 2: VZD

Zelda in Chapter 10 selected a D_{max} of 30, a D_{min} of 5, and an Id Range of 3 to 13. Knowing this much alone, we can use the standard formula to generate two equations by pairing her D_{max} with her I_{max} and her D_{min} with her I_{min}. The first is

$$30 = K(13) + B$$

and the second is

$$5 = K(3) + B$$

Next we take one of the equations and solve for one of the variables. Let's try B this time. Drawing on our high school algebra, we subtract K(13) from both sides to isolate B. We know now that 30 − K(13) = B. We can take the lefthand side and plug it into the second equation in place of B so we have a new equation expressed entirely in terms of K:

$$5 = 3K + 30 - 13K$$

And we solve for K by subtracting 30 from both sides to isolate K:

$$5 - 30 = 3K - 13K$$
$$-25 = -10K$$

Dividing both sides by −10 gives you the solution 2.5 = K. We can now substitute this value for the earlier expression of B in terms of K, in the following steps:

$$B = 30 - 13K \qquad B = 30 - 32.5$$
$$B = 30 - 13\,(2.5) \qquad B = -2.5$$

When we put both constants in place we get the final formula: D = 2.5i − 2.5.

The Short Way

Solve for $K = (Z_{max} - Z_{min})/(I_{max} - I_{min})$ or $K = (D_{max} - D_{min})/(I_{max} - I_{min})$. When i is equal to your I_{min}, then the Z% (or D) should equal your Z_{min} (or D_{min}). (By the same token, when $i = I_{max}$, then your $Z\% = Z_{max}$ or your $D = D_{max}$.) Plug in either of these pairs and solve for B.

Armed with this equation, you can plot a line on a chart to graphically represent your variable Z percentage or variable zero duration.* An easy way to plot the line is to draw a straight line between the two points determined by your selection of rates and Z percentages or zero durations. In the example we have been using, the two points are (6, 25) and (10, 100).** This means that the x-coordinate for the first point is 6 and the y-coordinate is 25, whereas the x-coordinate for the other point is 10 and the y-coordinate is 100.

Easier yet is direct substitution of values in your VZP or VZD formula, replacing i as interest rates change to see what your chosen Z percentage or zero duration should be (given all your other choices). If you know that your $Z\% = 18.75i - 87.5$, then when rates are 8 percent you replace i with 8 and use multiplication and subtraction as indicated. Therefore, at 8 percent your Z percentage should be 62.5 percent.

You can perform this calculation as often as your program or curiosity requires.

* There is no law requiring a straight line between the two limiting assumptions on which your formula is based. They can be connected by a curve that is sinusoidal, exponential, or something else again. In fact, you can have discontinuous or discrete curves that connect multiple I Ranges. You can construct an interest rate map as difficult or complicated as you are willing to track.

** It turns out that the standard VZP formula is the equation for a straight line where the Z% is y, i is x, B is the y-intercept, and K is the slope (the change in y divided by the change in x).

Appendix B

Zero Coupon Bond Tables

The following three tables are a reference guide to zero prices and yields. All tables cover zeros of up to 30 years' duration. Table B.1 is a quick reference covering a yield range of 1 to 30 percent at intervals of 1 percent. Tables B.2 and B.3 provide a bit more precision: exact zero prices at yield intervals of only 1/4 percent. The range of yields runs from 3 to 23 percent. Tables B.4, B.5, B.6, B.7, and B.8 present zero prices for yields between 2 and 22 percent at 0.1 percent intervals.

All serve the same purpose and are used in identical fashion. The only difference among them is the level of precision they display. Duration (years to maturity) is ranged along the top, yields (interest rates) along the lefthand side. The remainder of each table contains zero coupon bond prices. If you know the duration and the yield, you can readily find the price wherever the selected column and row intersect. If you know the price and the duration, you can find the yield. And if you know the yield and the price, you can easily determine the duration.

Table B.1 Zero Prices and Yields between 1 and 30 Percent at 1 Percent Intervals

Interest rate	Years to maturity										
	30	**29**	**28**	**27**	**26**	**25**	**24**	**23**	**22**	**21**	**20**
1.00%	74.19	74.93	75.68	76.44	77.20	77.98	78.76	79.54	80.34	81.14	81.95
2.00%	55.21	56.31	57.44	58.59	59.76	60.95	62.17	63.42	64.68	65.98	67.30
3.00%	41.20	42.43	43.71	45.02	46.37	47.76	49.19	50.67	52.19	53.75	55.37
4.00%	30.83	32.07	33.35	34.68	36.07	37.51	39.01	40.57	42.20	43.88	45.64
5.00%	23.14	24.29	25.51	26.78	28.12	29.53	31.01	32.56	34.18	35.89	37.69
6.00%	17.41	18.46	19.56	20.74	21.98	23.30	24.70	26.18	27.75	29.42	31.18
7.00%	13.14	14.06	15.04	16.09	17.22	18.42	19.71	21.09	22.57	24.15	25.84
8.00%	9.94	10.73	11.59	12.52	13.52	14.60	15.77	17.03	18.39	19.87	21.45
9.00%	7.54	8.22	8.95	9.76	10.64	11.60	12.64	13.78	15.02	16.37	17.84
10.00%	5.73	6.30	6.93	7.63	8.39	9.23	10.15	11.17	12.28	13.51	14.86
11.00%	4.37	4.85	5.38	5.97	6.63	7.36	8.17	9.07	10.07	11.17	12.40
12.00%	3.34	3.74	4.19	4.69	5.25	5.88	6.59	7.38	8.26	9.26	10.37
13.00%	2.56	2.89	3.26	3.69	4.17	4.71	5.32	6.01	6.80	7.68	8.68
14.00%	1.96	2.24	2.55	2.91	3.31	3.78	4.31	4.91	5.60	6.38	7.28
15.00%	1.51	1.74	2.00	2.30	2.64	3.04	3.49	4.02	4.62	5.31	6.11
16.00%	1.16	1.35	1.57	1.82	2.11	2.45	2.84	3.29	3.82	4.43	5.14
17.00%	0.90	1.05	1.23	1.44	1.69	1.97	2.31	2.70	3.16	3.70	4.33
18.00%	0.70	0.82	0.97	1.15	1.35	1.60	1.88	2.22	2.62	3.09	3.65
19.00%	0.54	0.64	0.77	0.91	1.09	1.29	1.54	1.83	2.18	2.59	3.08
20.00%	0.42	0.51	0.61	0.73	0.87	1.05	1.26	1.51	1.81	2.17	2.61
21.00%	0.33	0.40	0.48	0.58	0.70	0.85	1.03	1.25	1.51	1.83	2.21
22.00%	0.26	0.31	0.38	0.47	0.57	0.69	0.85	1.03	1.26	1.54	1.87
23.00%	0.20	0.25	0.30	0.37	0.46	0.57	0.70	0.86	1.05	1.29	1.59
24.00%	0.16	0.20	0.24	0.30	0.37	0.46	0.57	0.71	0.88	1.09	1.35
25.00%	0.12	0.15	0.19	0.24	0.30	0.38	0.47	0.59	0.74	0.92	1.15
26.00%	0.10	0.12	0.15	0.19	0.25	0.31	0.39	0.49	0.62	0.78	0.98
27.00%	0.08	0.10	0.12	0.16	0.20	0.25	0.32	0.41	0.52	0.66	0.84
28.00%	0.06	0.08	0.10	0.13	0.16	0.21	0.27	0.34	0.44	0.56	0.72
29.00%	0.05	0.06	0.08	0.10	0.13	0.17	0.22	0.29	0.37	0.48	0.61
30.00%	0.04	0.05	0.06	0.08	0.11	0.14	0.18	0.24	0.31	0.40	0.53

(continued)

Table B.1 Continued

Interest rate	Years to maturity										
	20	19	18	17	16	15	14	13	12	11	10
1.00%	81.95	82.77	83.60	84.44	85.28	86.13	87.00	87.87	88.74	89.63	90.53
2.00%	67.30	68.64	70.02	71.42	72.84	74.30	75.79	77.30	78.85	80.43	82.03
3.00%	55.37	57.03	58.74	60.50	62.32	64.19	66.11	68.10	70.14	72.24	74.41
4.00%	45.64	47.46	49.36	51.34	53.39	55.53	57.75	60.06	62.46	64.96	67.56
5.00%	37.69	39.57	41.55	43.63	45.81	48.10	50.51	53.03	55.68	58.47	61.39
6.00%	31.18	33.05	35.03	37.14	39.36	41.73	44.23	46.88	49.70	52.68	55.84
7.00%	25.84	27.65	29.59	31.66	33.87	36.24	38.78	41.50	44.40	47.51	50.83
8.00%	21.45	23.17	25.02	27.03	29.19	31.52	34.05	36.77	39.71	42.89	46.32
9.00%	17.84	19.45	21.20	23.11	25.19	27.45	29.92	32.62	35.55	38.75	42.24
10.00%	14.86	16.35	17.99	19.78	21.76	23.94	26.33	28.97	31.86	35.05	38.55
11.00%	12.40	13.77	15.28	16.96	18.83	20.90	23.20	25.75	28.58	31.73	35.22
12.00%	10.37	11.61	13.00	14.56	16.31	18.27	20.46	22.92	25.67	28.75	32.20
13.00%	8.68	9.81	11.08	12.52	14.15	15.99	18.07	20.42	23.07	26.07	29.46
14.00%	7.28	8.29	9.46	10.78	12.29	14.01	15.97	18.21	20.76	23.66	26.97
15.00%	6.11	7.03	8.08	9.29	10.69	12.29	14.13	16.25	18.69	21.49	24.72
16.00%	5.14	5.96	6.91	8.02	9.30	10.79	12.52	14.52	16.85	19.54	22.67
17.00%	4.33	5.06	5.92	6.93	8.11	9.49	11.10	12.99	15.20	17.78	20.80
18.00%	3.65	4.31	5.08	6.00	7.08	8.35	9.85	11.63	13.72	16.19	19.11
19.00%	3.08	3.67	4.37	5.20	6.18	7.36	8.76	10.42	12.40	14.76	17.56
20.00%	2.61	3.13	3.76	4.51	5.41	6.49	7.79	9.35	11.22	13.46	16.15
21.00%	2.21	2.67	3.23	3.91	4.74	5.73	6.93	8.39	10.15	12.28	14.86
22.00%	1.87	2.29	2.79	3.40	4.15	5.07	6.18	7.54	9.20	11.22	13.69
23.00%	1.59	1.96	2.41	2.96	3.64	4.48	5.51	6.78	8.34	10.26	12.62
24.00%	1.35	1.68	2.08	2.58	3.20	3.97	4.92	6.10	7.57	9.38	11.64
25.00%	1.15	1.44	1.80	2.25	2.81	3.52	4.40	5.50	6.87	8.59	10.74
26.00%	0.98	1.24	1.56	1.97	2.48	3.12	3.93	4.96	6.25	7.87	9.92
27.00%	0.84	1.07	1.35	1.72	2.18	2.77	3.52	4.47	5.68	7.21	9.16
28.00%	0.72	0.92	1.18	1.50	1.93	2.47	3.16	4.04	5.17	6.62	8.47
29.00%	0.61	0.79	1.02	1.32	1.70	2.19	2.83	3.65	4.71	6.07	7.84
30.00%	0.53	0.68	0.89	1.16	1.50	1.95	2.54	3.30	4.29	5.58	7.25

Table B.1 Continued

Interest rate	Years to maturity										
	10	9	8	7	6	5	4	3	2	1	0
1.00%	90.53	91.43	92.35	93.27	94.20	95.15	96.10	97.06	98.03	99.01	100.00
2.00%	82.03	83.68	85.35	87.06	88.80	90.57	92.38	94.23	96.12	98.04	100.00
3.00%	74.41	76.64	78.94	81.31	83.75	86.26	88.85	91.51	94.26	97.09	100.00
4.00%	67.56	70.26	73.07	75.99	79.03	82.19	85.48	88.90	92.46	96.15	100.00
5.00%	61.39	64.46	67.68	71.07	74.62	78.35	82.27	86.38	90.70	95.24	100.00
6.00%	55.84	59.19	62.74	66.51	70.50	74.73	79.21	83.96	89.00	94.34	100.00
7.00%	50.83	54.39	58.20	62.27	66.63	71.30	76.29	81.63	87.34	93.46	100.00
8.00%	46.32	50.02	54.03	58.35	63.02	68.06	73.50	79.38	85.73	92.59	100.00
9.00%	42.24	46.04	50.19	54.70	59.63	64.99	70.84	77.22	84.17	91.74	100.00
10.00%	38.55	42.41	46.65	51.32	56.45	62.09	68.30	75.13	82.64	90.91	100.00
11.00%	35.22	39.09	43.39	48.17	53.46	59.35	65.87	73.12	81.16	90.09	100.00
12.00%	32.20	36.06	40.39	45.23	50.66	56.74	63.55	71.18	79.72	89.29	100.00
13.00%	29.46	33.29	37.62	42.51	48.03	54.28	61.33	69.31	78.31	88.50	100.00
14.00%	26.97	30.75	35.06	39.96	45.56	51.94	59.21	67.50	76.95	87.72	100.00
15.00%	24.72	28.43	32.69	37.59	43.23	49.72	57.18	65.75	75.61	86.96	100.00
16.00%	22.67	26.30	30.50	35.38	41.04	47.61	55.23	64.07	74.32	86.21	100.00
17.00%	20.80	24.34	28.48	33.32	38.98	45.61	53.37	62.44	73.05	85.47	100.00
18.00%	19.11	22.55	26.60	31.39	37.04	43.71	51.58	60.86	71.82	84.75	100.00
19.00%	17.56	20.90	24.87	29.59	35.21	41.90	49.87	59.34	70.62	84.03	100.00
20.00%	16.15	19.38	23.26	27.91	33.49	40.19	48.23	57.87	69.44	83.33	100.00
21.00%	14.86	17.99	21.76	26.33	31.86	38.55	46.65	56.45	68.30	82.64	100.00
22.00%	13.69	16.70	20.38	24.86	30.33	37.00	45.14	55.07	67.19	81.97	100.00
23.00%	12.62	15.52	19.09	23.48	28.88	35.52	43.69	53.74	66.10	81.30	100.00
24.00%	11.64	14.43	17.89	22.18	27.51	34.11	42.30	52.45	65.04	80.65	100.00
25.00%	10.74	13.42	16.78	20.97	26.21	32.77	40.96	51.20	64.00	80.00	100.00
26.00%	9.92	12.49	15.74	19.83	24.99	31.49	39.68	49.99	62.99	79.37	100.00
27.00%	9.16	11.64	14.78	18.77	23.83	30.27	38.44	48.82	62.00	78.74	100.00
28.00%	8.47	10.84	13.88	17.76	22.74	29.10	37.25	47.68	61.04	78.13	100.00
29.00%	7.84	10.11	13.04	16.82	21.70	27.99	36.11	46.58	60.09	77.52	100.00
30.00%	7.25	9.43	12.26	15.94	20.72	26.93	35.01	45.52	59.17	76.92	100.00

Table B.2 Zero Prices and Yields between 3 and 13 Percent at 0.25 Percent Intervals

Interest rate	Years to maturity										
	30	29	28	27	26	25	24	23	22	21	20
3.00%	41.20	42.43	43.71	45.02	46.37	47.76	49.19	50.67	52.19	53.75	55.37
3.25%	38.31	39.55	40.84	42.17	43.54	44.95	46.41	47.92	49.48	51.09	52.75
3.50%	35.63	36.87	38.17	39.50	40.88	42.31	43.80	45.33	46.92	48.56	50.26
3.75%	33.14	34.38	35.67	37.01	38.40	39.84	41.33	42.88	44.49	46.16	47.89
4.00%	30.83	32.07	33.35	34.68	36.07	37.51	39.01	40.57	42.20	43.88	45.64
4.25%	28.69	29.91	31.18	32.50	33.89	35.33	36.83	38.39	40.02	41.73	43.50
4.50%	26.70	27.90	29.16	30.47	31.84	33.27	34.77	36.34	37.97	39.68	41.46
4.75%	24.85	26.03	27.27	28.57	29.92	31.34	32.83	34.39	36.03	37.74	39.53
5.00%	23.14	24.29	25.51	26.78	28.12	29.53	31.01	32.56	34.18	35.89	37.69
5.25%	21.54	22.68	23.87	25.12	26.44	27.83	29.29	30.82	32.44	34.15	35.94
5.50%	20.06	21.17	22.33	23.56	24.86	26.22	27.67	29.19	30.79	32.49	34.27
5.75%	18.69	19.76	20.90	22.10	23.37	24.72	26.14	27.64	29.23	30.91	32.69
6.00%	17.41	18.46	19.56	20.74	21.98	23.30	24.70	26.18	27.75	29.42	31.18
6.25%	16.22	17.24	18.31	19.46	20.68	21.97	23.34	24.80	26.35	28.00	29.75
6.50%	15.12	16.10	17.15	18.26	19.45	20.71	22.06	23.49	25.02	26.65	28.38
6.75%	14.09	15.04	16.06	17.14	18.30	19.53	20.85	22.26	23.76	25.37	27.08
7.00%	13.14	14.06	15.04	16.09	17.22	18.42	19.71	21.09	22.57	24.15	25.84
7.25%	12.25	13.14	14.09	15.11	16.21	17.38	18.64	19.99	21.44	23.00	24.66
7.50%	11.42	12.28	13.20	14.19	15.25	16.40	17.63	18.95	20.37	21.90	23.54
7.75%	10.65	11.48	12.37	13.33	14.36	15.47	16.67	17.96	19.36	20.86	22.47
8.00%	9.94	10.73	11.59	12.52	13.52	14.60	15.77	17.03	18.39	19.87	21.45
8.25%	9.27	10.04	10.86	11.76	12.73	13.78	14.92	16.15	17.48	18.92	20.49
8.50%	8.65	9.39	10.19	11.05	11.99	13.01	14.12	15.31	16.62	18.03	19.56
8.75%	8.07	8.78	9.55	10.39	11.29	12.28	13.36	14.53	15.80	17.18	18.68
9.00%	7.54	8.22	8.95	9.76	10.64	11.60	12.64	13.78	15.02	16.37	17.84
9.25%	7.04	7.69	8.40	9.18	10.02	10.95	11.96	13.07	14.28	15.60	17.04
9.50%	6.57	7.19	7.88	8.63	9.45	10.34	11.33	12.40	13.58	14.87	16.28
9.75%	6.14	6.73	7.39	8.11	8.90	9.77	10.72	11.77	12.92	14.17	15.56
10.00%	5.73	6.30	6.93	7.63	8.39	9.23	10.15	11.17	12.28	13.51	14.86
10.25%	5.35	5.90	6.51	7.17	7.91	8.72	9.61	10.60	11.69	12.88	14.20
10.50%	5.00	5.53	6.11	6.75	7.46	8.24	9.11	10.06	11.12	12.29	13.58
10.75%	4.67	5.18	5.73	6.35	7.03	7.79	8.62	9.55	10.58	11.72	12.98
11.00%	4.37	4.85	5.38	5.97	6.63	7.36	8.17	9.07	10.07	11.17	12.40
11.25%	4.08	4.54	5.05	5.62	6.25	6.96	7.74	8.61	9.58	10.66	11.86
11.50%	3.82	4.26	4.75	5.29	5.90	6.58	7.34	8.18	9.12	10.17	11.34
11.75%	3.57	3.99	4.46	4.98	5.57	6.22	6.95	7.77	8.68	9.70	10.84
12.00%	3.34	3.74	4.19	4.69	5.25	5.88	6.59	7.38	8.26	9.26	10.37
12.25%	3.12	3.50	3.93	4.42	4.96	5.56	6.24	7.01	7.87	8.83	9.91
12.50%	2.92	3.29	3.70	4.16	4.68	5.26	5.92	6.66	7.49	8.43	9.48
12.75%	2.73	3.08	3.47	3.92	4.42	4.98	5.61	6.33	7.14	8.05	9.07
13.00%	2.56	2.89	3.26	3.69	4.17	4.71	5.32	6.01	6.80	7.68	8.68

Table B.2 Continued

Interest rate	Years to maturity										
	20	**19**	**18**	**17**	**16**	**15**	**14**	**13**	**12**	**11**	**10**
3.00%	55.37	57.03	58.74	60.50	62.32	64.19	66.11	68.10	70.14	72.24	74.41
3.25%	52.75	54.46	56.23	58.06	59.95	61.89	63.91	65.98	68.13	70.34	72.63
3.50%	50.26	52.02	53.84	55.72	57.67	59.69	61.78	63.94	66.18	68.49	70.89
3.75%	47.89	49.69	51.55	53.48	55.49	57.57	59.73	61.97	64.29	66.70	69.20
4.00%	45.64	47.46	49.36	51.34	53.39	55.53	57.75	60.06	62.46	64.96	67.56
4.25%	43.50	45.35	47.27	49.28	51.38	53.56	55.84	58.21	60.69	63.26	65.95
4.50%	41.46	43.33	45.28	47.32	49.45	51.67	54.00	56.43	58.97	61.62	64.39
4.75%	39.53	41.41	43.37	45.43	47.59	49.85	52.22	54.70	57.30	60.02	62.87
5.00%	37.69	39.57	41.55	43.63	45.81	48.10	50.51	53.03	55.68	58.47	61.39
5.25%	35.94	37.83	39.81	41.90	44.10	46.42	48.85	51.42	54.12	56.96	59.95
5.50%	34.27	36.16	38.15	40.24	42.46	44.79	47.26	49.86	52.60	55.49	58.54
5.75%	32.69	34.57	36.56	38.66	40.88	43.23	45.72	48.35	51.13	54.06	57.17
6.00%	31.18	33.05	35.03	37.14	39.36	41.73	44.23	46.88	49.70	52.68	55.84
6.25%	29.75	31.60	33.58	35.68	37.91	40.28	42.80	45.47	48.31	51.33	54.54
6.50%	28.38	30.22	32.19	34.28	36.51	38.88	41.41	44.10	46.97	50.02	53.27
6.75%	27.08	28.91	30.86	32.94	35.17	37.54	40.07	42.78	45.67	48.75	52.04
7.00%	25.84	27.65	29.59	31.66	33.87	36.24	38.78	41.50	44.40	47.51	50.83
7.25%	24.66	26.45	28.37	30.43	32.63	35.00	37.54	40.26	43.18	46.31	49.66
7.50%	23.54	25.31	27.20	29.25	31.44	33.80	36.33	39.06	41.99	45.13	48.52
7.75%	22.47	24.21	26.09	28.11	30.29	32.64	35.17	37.89	40.83	44.00	47.41
8.00%	21.45	23.17	25.02	27.03	29.19	31.52	34.05	36.77	39.71	42.89	46.32
8.25%	20.49	22.18	24.00	25.99	28.13	30.45	32.96	35.68	38.62	41.81	45.26
8.50%	19.56	21.22	23.03	24.99	27.11	29.41	31.91	34.63	37.57	40.76	44.23
8.75%	18.68	20.32	22.09	24.03	26.13	28.42	30.90	33.61	36.55	39.74	43.22
9.00%	17.84	19.45	21.20	23.11	25.19	27.45	29.92	32.62	35.55	38.75	42.24
9.25%	17.04	18.62	20.34	22.22	24.28	26.53	28.98	31.66	34.59	37.79	41.28
9.50%	16.28	17.83	19.52	21.38	23.41	25.63	28.07	30.73	33.65	36.85	40.35
9.75%	15.56	17.07	18.74	20.56	22.57	24.77	27.19	29.84	32.75	35.94	39.44
10.00%	14.86	16.35	17.99	19.78	21.76	23.94	26.33	28.97	31.86	35.05	38.55
10.25%	14.20	15.66	17.27	19.04	20.99	23.14	25.51	28.12	31.01	34.18	37.69
10.50%	13.58	15.00	16.58	18.32	20.24	22.36	24.71	27.31	30.18	33.34	36.84
10.75%	12.98	14.37	15.92	17.63	19.52	21.62	23.94	26.52	29.37	32.53	36.02
11.00%	12.40	13.77	15.28	16.96	18.83	20.90	23.20	25.75	28.58	31.73	35.22
11.25%	11.86	13.19	14.68	16.33	18.16	20.21	22.48	25.01	27.82	30.95	34.43
11.50%	11.34	12.64	14.09	15.72	17.52	19.54	21.78	24.29	27.08	30.20	33.67
11.75%	10.84	12.11	13.54	15.13	16.91	18.89	21.11	23.59	26.37	29.46	32.92
12.00%	10.37	11.61	13.00	14.56	16.31	18.27	20.46	22.92	25.67	28.75	32.20
12.25%	9.91	11.13	12.49	14.02	15.74	17.67	19.83	22.26	24.99	28.05	31.49
12.50%	9.48	10.67	12.00	13.50	15.19	17.09	19.22	21.63	24.33	27.37	30.79
12.75%	9.07	10.23	11.53	13.00	14.66	16.53	18.64	21.01	23.69	26.71	30.12
13.00%	8.68	9.81	11.08	12.52	14.15	15.99	18.07	20.42	23.07	26.07	29.46

(continued)

Table B.2 Continued

Interest rate	Years to maturity										
	10	**9**	**8**	**7**	**6**	**5**	**4**	**3**	**2**	**1**	**0**
3.00%	74.41	76.64	78.94	81.31	83.75	86.26	88.85	91.51	94.26	97.09	100.00
3.25%	72.63	74.99	77.42	79.94	82.54	85.22	87.99	90.85	93.80	96.85	100.00
3.50%	70.89	73.37	75.94	78.60	81.35	84.20	87.14	90.19	93.35	96.62	100.00
3.75%	69.20	71.80	74.49	77.28	80.18	83.19	86.31	89.54	92.90	96.39	100.00
4.00%	67.56	70.26	73.07	75.99	79.03	82.19	85.48	88.90	92.46	96.15	100.00
4.25%	65.95	68.76	71.68	74.73	77.90	81.21	84.66	88.26	92.01	95.92	100.00
4.50%	64.39	67.29	70.32	73.48	76.79	80.25	83.86	87.63	91.57	95.69	100.00
4.75%	62.87	65.86	68.99	72.26	75.70	79.29	83.06	87.00	91.14	95.47	100.00
5.00%	61.39	64.46	67.68	71.07	74.62	78.35	82.27	86.38	90.70	95.24	100.00
5.25%	59.95	63.10	66.41	69.89	73.56	77.43	81.49	85.77	90.27	95.01	100.00
5.50%	58.54	61.76	65.16	68.74	72.52	76.51	80.72	85.16	89.85	94.79	100.00
5.75%	57.17	60.46	63.94	67.61	71.50	75.61	79.96	84.56	89.42	94.56	100.00
6.00%	55.84	59.19	62.74	66.51	70.50	74.73	79.21	83.96	89.00	94.34	100.00
6.25%	54.54	57.95	61.57	65.42	69.51	73.85	78.47	83.37	88.58	94.12	100.00
6.50%	53.27	56.74	60.42	64.35	68.53	72.99	77.73	82.78	88.17	93.90	100.00
6.75%	52.04	55.55	59.30	63.30	67.58	72.14	77.01	82.20	87.75	93.68	100.00
7.00%	50.83	54.39	58.20	62.27	66.63	71.30	76.29	81.63	87.34	93.46	100.00
7.25%	49.66	53.26	57.12	61.27	65.71	70.47	75.58	81.06	86.94	93.24	100.00
7.50%	48.52	52.16	56.07	60.28	64.80	69.66	74.88	80.50	86.53	93.02	100.00
7.75%	47.41	51.08	55.04	59.30	63.90	68.85	74.19	79.94	86.13	92.81	100.00
8.00%	46.32	50.02	54.03	58.35	63.02	68.06	73.50	79.38	85.73	92.59	100.00
8.25%	45.26	48.99	53.04	57.41	62.15	67.28	72.83	78.83	85.34	92.38	100.00
8.50%	44.23	47.99	52.07	56.49	61.29	66.50	72.16	78.29	84.95	92.17	100.00
8.75%	43.22	47.00	51.12	55.59	60.45	65.74	71.50	77.75	84.56	91.95	100.00
9.00%	42.24	46.04	50.19	54.70	59.63	64.99	70.84	77.22	84.17	91.74	100.00
9.25%	41.28	45.10	49.28	53.83	58.81	64.25	70.20	76.69	83.78	91.53	100.00
9.50%	40.35	44.18	48.38	52.98	58.01	63.52	69.56	76.17	83.40	91.32	100.00
9.75%	39.44	43.29	47.51	52.14	57.22	62.80	68.93	75.65	83.02	91.12	100.00
10.00%	38.55	42.41	46.65	51.32	56.45	62.09	68.30	75.13	82.64	90.91	100.00
10.25%	37.69	41.55	45.81	50.51	55.68	61.39	67.68	74.62	82.27	90.70	100.00
10.50%	36.84	40.71	44.99	49.71	54.93	60.70	67.07	74.12	81.90	90.50	100.00
10.75%	36.02	39.89	44.18	48.93	54.19	60.02	66.47	73.62	81.53	90.29	100.00
11.00%	35.22	39.09	43.39	48.17	53.46	59.35	65.87	73.12	81.16	90.09	100.00
11.25%	34.43	38.31	42.62	47.41	52.75	58.68	65.28	72.63	80.80	89.89	100.00
11.50%	33.67	37.54	41.86	46.67	52.04	58.03	64.70	72.14	80.44	89.69	100.00
11.75%	32.92	36.79	41.12	45.95	51.35	57.38	64.12	71.66	80.08	89.49	100.00
12.00%	32.20	36.06	40.39	45.23	50.66	56.74	63.55	71.18	79.72	89.29	100.00
12.25%	31.49	35.34	39.67	44.53	49.99	56.11	62.99	70.70	79.36	89.09	100.00
12.50%	30.79	34.64	38.97	43.85	49.33	55.49	62.43	70.23	79.01	88.89	100.00
12.75%	30.12	33.96	38.29	43.17	48.67	54.88	61.88	69.77	78.66	88.69	100.00
13.00%	29.46	33.29	37.62	42.51	48.03	54.28	61.33	69.31	78.31	88.50	100.00

Table B.3 Zero Prices and Yields between 13 and 23 Percent at 0.25 Percent Intervals

Interest rate	Years to maturity										
	30	**29**	**28**	**27**	**26**	**25**	**24**	**23**	**22**	**21**	**20**
13.00%	2.56	2.89	3.26	3.17	4.71	4.32	5.32	6.01	6.80	7.68	8.68
13.25%	2.39	2.71	3.07	3.48	3.94	4.46	5.05	5.72	6.47	7.33	8.30
13.50%	2.24	2.54	2.88	3.27	3.72	4.22	4.79	5.43	6.17	7.00	7.94
13.75%	2.10	2.38	2.71	3.09	3.51	3.99	4.54	5.17	5.88	6.68	7.60
14.00%	1.96	2.24	2.55	2.91	3.31	3.78	4.31	4.91	5.60	6.38	7.28
14.25%	1.84	2.10	2.40	2.74	3.13	3.58	4.09	4.67	5.34	6.10	6.96
14.50%	1.72	1.97	2.26	2.58	2.96	3.39	3.88	4.44	5.08	5.82	6.67
14.75%	1.61	1.85	2.12	2.44	2.80	3.21	3.68	4.22	4.85	5.56	6.38
15.00%	1.51	1.74	2.00	2.30	2.64	3.04	3.49	4.02	4.62	5.31	6.11
15.25%	1.42	1.63	1.88	2.17	2.50	2.88	3.32	3.82	4.40	5.08	5.85
15.50%	1.33	1.53	1.77	2.04	2.36	2.73	3.15	3.64	4.20	4.85	5.60
15.75%	1.24	1.44	1.66	1.93	2.23	2.58	2.99	3.46	4.00	4.64	5.37
16.00%	1.16	1.35	1.57	1.82	2.11	2.45	2.84	3.29	3.82	4.43	5.14
16.25%	1.09	1.27	1.48	1.72	1.99	2.32	2.70	3.13	3.64	4.23	4.92
16.50%	1.02	1.19	1.39	1.62	1.89	2.20	2.56	2.98	3.47	4.05	4.71
16.75%	0.96	1.12	1.31	1.53	1.78	2.08	2.43	2.84	3.31	3.87	4.52
17.00%	0.90	1.05	1.23	1.44	1.69	1.97	2.31	2.70	3.16	3.70	4.33
17.25%	0.84	0.99	1.16	1.36	1.60	1.87	2.19	2.57	3.02	3.54	4.15
17.50%	0.79	0.93	1.09	1.29	1.51	1.77	2.08	2.45	2.88	3.38	3.97
17.75%	0.74	0.88	1.03	1.21	1.43	1.68	1.98	2.33	2.75	3.23	3.81
18.00%	0.70	0.82	0.97	1.15	1.35	1.60	1.88	2.22	2.62	3.09	3.65
18.25%	0.65	0.77	0.92	1.08	1.28	1.51	1.79	2.12	2.50	2.96	3.50
18.50%	0.61	0.73	0.86	1.02	1.21	1.44	1.70	2.02	2.39	2.83	3.35
18.75%	0.58	0.68	0.81	0.97	1.15	1.36	1.62	1.92	2.28	2.71	3.22
19.00%	0.54	0.64	0.77	0.91	1.09	1.29	1.54	1.83	2.18	2.59	3.08
19.25%	0.51	0.61	0.72	0.86	1.03	1.23	1.46	1.74	2.08	2.48	2.96
19.50%	0.48	0.57	0.68	0.81	0.97	1.16	1.39	1.66	1.99	2.37	2.84
19.75%	0.45	0.54	0.64	0.77	0.92	1.10	1.32	1.58	1.90	2.27	2.72
20.00%	0.42	0.51	0.61	0.73	0.87	1.05	1.26	1.51	1.81	2.17	2.61
20.25%	0.40	0.48	0.57	0.69	0.83	1.00	1.20	1.44	1.73	2.08	2.50
20.50%	0.37	0.45	0.54	0.65	0.78	0.94	1.14	1.37	1.65	1.99	2.40
20.75%	0.35	0.42	0.51	0.62	0.74	0.90	1.08	1.31	1.58	1.91	2.30
21.00%	0.33	0.40	0.48	0.58	0.70	0.85	1.03	1.25	1.51	1.83	2.21
21.25%	0.31	0.37	0.45	0.55	0.67	0.81	0.98	1.19	1.44	1.75	2.12
21.50%	0.29	0.35	0.43	0.52	0.63	0.77	0.93	1.13	1.38	1.67	2.03
21.75%	0.27	0.33	0.40	0.49	0.60	0.73	0.89	1.08	1.32	1.60	1.95
22.00%	0.26	0.31	0.38	0.47	0.57	0.69	0.85	1.03	1.26	1.54	1.87
22.25%	0.24	0.29	0.36	0.44	0.54	0.66	0.81	0.98	1.20	1.47	1.80
22.50%	0.23	0.28	0.34	0.42	0.51	0.63	0.77	0.94	1.15	1.41	1.73
22.75%	0.21	0.26	0.32	0.39	0.48	0.59	0.73	0.90	1.10	1.35	1.66
23.00%	0.20	0.25	0.30	0.37	0.46	0.57	0.70	0.86	1.05	1.29	1.59

(continued)

Table B.3 Continued

Interest rate	Years to maturity										
	20	**19**	**18**	**17**	**16**	**15**	**14**	**13**	**12**	**11**	**10**
12.00%	8.86	9.81	11.08	12.52	14.15	15.99	18.07	20.42	23.07	26.07	29.46
13.25%	8.30	9.40	10.65	12.06	13.66	15.47	17.52	19.84	22.47	25.44	28.81
13.50%	7.94	9.02	10.23	11.62	13.18	14.96	16.98	19.28	21.88	24.83	28.19
13.75%	7.60	8.65	9.84	11.19	12.73	14.48	16.47	18.73	21.31	24.24	27.57
14.00%	7.28	8.29	9.46	10.78	12.29	14.01	15.97	18.21	20.76	23.66	26.97
14.25%	6.96	7.97	9.09	10.39	11.87	13.56	15.49	17.70	20.22	23.10	26.39
14.50%	6.67	7.63	8.74	10.01	11.46	13.12	15.02	17.20	19.69	22.55	25.82
14.75%	6.38	7.32	8.40	9.64	11.07	12.70	14.57	16.72	19.19	22.02	25.26
15.00%	6.11	7.03	8.08	9.29	10.69	12.29	14.13	16.25	18.69	21.49	24.72
15.25%	5.85	6.74	7.77	8.96	10.32	11.90	13.71	15.80	18.21	20.99	24.19
15.50%	5.60	6.47	7.47	8.63	9.97	11.52	13.30	15.36	17.74	20.49	23.67
15.75%	5.37	6.21	7.19	8.32	9.63	11.15	12.90	14.94	17.29	20.01	23.16
16.00%	5.14	5.96	6.91	8.02	9.30	10.79	12.52	14.52	16.85	19.54	22.67
16.25%	4.92	5.72	6.65	7.73	8.99	10.45	12.15	14.12	16.42	19.08	22.19
16.50%	4.71	5.49	6.40	7.46	8.69	10.12	11.79	13.73	16.00	18.64	21.71
16.75%	4.52	5.27	6.16	7.19	8.39	9.80	11.44	13.36	15.59	18.20	21.25
17.00%	4.33	5.06	5.92	6.93	8.11	9.49	11.10	12.99	15.20	17.78	20.80
17.25%	4.15	4.86	5.70	6.68	7.84	9.19	10.78	12.63	14.81	17.37	20.36
17.50%	3.97	4.67	5.49	6.45	7.58	8.90	10.46	12.29	14.44	16.97	19.94
17.75%	3.81	4.48	5.28	6.22	7.32	8.62	10.15	11.95	14.08	16.57	19.52
18.00%	3.65	4.31	5.08	6.00	7.08	8.35	9.85	11.63	13.72	16.19	19.11
18.25%	3.50	4.14	4.89	5.79	6.84	8.09	9.57	11.31	13.38	15.82	18.71
18.50%	3.35	3.98	4.71	5.58	6.61	7.84	9.29	11.01	13.04	15.46	18.32
18.75%	3.22	3.82	4.54	5.39	6.40	7.59	9.02	10.71	12.72	15.10	17.93
19.00%	3.08	3.67	4.37	5.20	6.18	7.36	8.76	10.42	12.40	14.76	17.56
19.25%	2.96	3.53	4.20	5.01	5.98	7.13	8.50	10.14	12.09	14.42	17.20
19.50%	2.84	3.39	4.05	4.84	5.78	6.91	8.26	9.87	11.79	14.09	16.84
19.75%	2.72	3.26	3.90	4.67	5.59	6.70	8.02	9.60	11.50	13.77	16.49
20.00%	2.61	3.13	3.76	4.51	5.41	6.49	7.79	9.35	11.22	13.46	16.15
20.25%	2.50	3.01	3.62	4.35	5.23	6.29	7.56	9.10	10.94	13.15	15.82
20.50%	2.40	2.89	3.49	4.20	5.06	6.10	7.35	8.85	10.67	12.86	15.49
20.75%	2.30	2.78	3.36	4.05	4.90	5.91	7.14	8.62	10.41	12.57	15.17
21.00%	2.21	2.67	3.23	3.91	4.74	5.73	6.93	8.39	10.15	12.28	14.86
21.25%	2.12	2.57	3.12	3.78	4.58	5.56	6.74	8.17	9.90	12.01	14.56
21.50%	2.03	2.47	3.00	3.65	4.43	5.39	6.55	7.95	9.66	11.74	14.26
21.75%	1.95	2.38	2.89	3.52	4.29	5.22	6.36	7.74	9.43	11.48	13.97
22.00%	1.87	2.29	2.79	3.40	4.15	5.07	6.18	7.54	9.20	11.22	13.69
22.25%	1.80	2.20	2.69	3.29	4.02	4.91	6.01	7.34	8.97	10.97	13.41
22.50%	1.73	2.12	2.59	3.17	3.89	4.76	5.84	7.15	8.76	10.73	13.14
22.75%	1.66	2.04	2.50	3.07	3.76	4.62	5.67	6.96	8.55	10.49	12.88
23.00%	1.59	1.96	2.41	2.96	3.64	4.48	5.51	6.78	8.34	10.26	12.62

Table B.3 Continued

Interest rate	Years to maturity										
	10	**9**	**8**	**7**	**6**	**5**	**4**	**3**	**2**	**1**	**0**
13.00%	29.46	33.29	37.62	42.51	48.03	54.28	61.33	69.31	78.31	88.50	100.00
13.25%	28.81	32.63	36.96	41.85	47.40	53.68	60.79	68.85	77.97	88.30	100.00
13.50%	28.19	31.99	36.31	41.21	46.78	53.09	60.26	68.39	77.63	88.11	100.00
13.75%	27.57	31.36	35.68	40.58	46.16	52.51	59.73	67.94	77.29	87.91	100.00
14.00%	26.97	30.75	35.06	39.96	45.56	51.94	59.21	67.50	76.95	87.72	100.00
14.25%	26.39	30.15	34.45	39.36	44.96	51.37	58.69	67.06	76.61	87.53	100.00
14.50%	25.82	29.56	33.85	38.76	44.38	50.81	58.18	66.62	76.28	87.34	100.00
14.75%	25.26	28.99	33.26	38.17	43.80	50.26	57.68	66.18	75.94	87.15	100.00
15.00%	24.72	28.43	32.69	37.59	43.23	49.72	57.18	65.75	75.61	86.96	100.00
15.25%	24.19	27.88	32.13	37.03	42.67	49.18	56.68	65.32	75.29	86.77	100.00
15.50%	23.67	27.34	31.58	36.47	42.12	48.65	56.19	64.90	74.96	86.58	100.00
15.75%	23.16	26.81	31.03	35.92	41.58	48.13	55.71	64.48	74.64	86.39	100.00
16.00%	22.67	26.30	30.50	35.38	41.04	47.61	55.23	64.07	74.32	86.21	100.00
16.25%	22.19	25.79	29.98	34.85	40.52	47.10	54.76	63.65	74.00	86.02	100.00
16.50%	21.71	25.30	29.47	34.33	40.00	46.60	54.29	63.24	73.68	85.84	100.00
16.75%	21.25	24.81	28.97	33.82	39.49	46.10	53.82	62.84	73.36	85.65	100.00
17.00%	20.80	24.34	28.48	33.32	38.98	45.61	53.37	62.44	73.05	85.47	100.00
17.25%	20.36	23.88	28.00	32.83	38.49	45.13	52.91	62.04	72.74	85.29	100.00
17.50%	19.94	23.42	27.52	32.34	38.00	44.65	52.46	61.64	72.43	85.11	100.00
17.75%	19.52	22.98	27.06	31.86	37.52	44.18	52.02	61.25	72.12	84.93	100.00
18.00%	19.11	22.55	26.60	31.39	37.04	43.71	51.58	60.86	71.82	84.75	100.00
18.25%	18.71	22.12	26.16	30.93	36.58	43.25	51.14	60.48	71.52	84.57	100.00
18.50%	18.32	21.70	25.72	30.48	36.12	42.80	50.71	60.10	71.21	84.39	100.00
18.75%	17.93	21.30	25.29	30.03	35.66	42.35	50.29	59.72	70.91	84.21	100.00
19.00%	17.56	20.90	24.87	29.59	35.21	41.90	49.87	59.34	70.62	84.03	100.00
19.25%	17.20	20.51	24.45	29.16	34.77	41.47	49.45	58.97	70.32	83.36	100.00
19.50%	16.84	20.12	24.05	28.74	34.34	41.04	49.04	58.60	70.03	83.68	100.00
19.75%	16.49	19.75	23.65	28.32	33.91	40.61	48.63	58.23	69.73	83.51	100.00
20.00%	16.15	19.38	23.26	27.91	33.49	40.19	48.23	57.87	69.44	83.33	100.00
20.25%	15.82	19.02	22.87	27.50	33.07	39.77	47.83	57.51	69.16	83.16	100.00
20.50%	15.49	18.67	22.50	27.11	32.66	39.36	47.43	57.15	68.87	82.99	100.00
20.75%	15.17	18.32	22.13	26.72	32.26	38.96	47.04	56.80	68.58	82.82	100.00
21.00%	14.86	17.99	21.76	26.33	31.86	38.55	46.65	56.45	68.30	82.64	100.00
21.25%	14.56	17.65	21.41	25.96	31.47	38.16	46.27	56.10	68.02	82.47	100.00
21.50%	14.26	17.33	21.06	25.58	31.08	37.77	45.89	55.75	67.74	82.30	100.00
21.75%	13.97	17.01	20.71	25.22	30.70	37.38	45.51	55.41	67.46	82.14	100.00
22.00%	13.69	16.70	20.38	24.86	30.33	37.00	45.14	55.07	67.19	81.97	100.00
22.25%	13.41	16.40	20.05	24.51	29.96	36.62	44.77	54.73	66.91	81.80	100.00
22.50%	13.14	16.10	19.72	24.16	29.59	36.25	44.41	54.40	66.64	81.63	100.00
22.75%	12.88	15.81	19.40	23.81	29.23	35.88	44.05	54.07	66.37	81.47	100.00
23.00%	12.62	15.52	19.09	23.48	28.88	35.52	43.69	53.74	66.10	81.30	100.00

Table B.4 Zero Prices and Yields between 2 and 6 Percent at 0.1 Percent Intervals

Interest rate	Years to maturity										
	30	29	28	27	26	25	24	23	22	21	20
2.00%	55.21	56.31	57.44	58.59	59.76	60.95	62.17	63.42	64.68	65.98	67.30
2.10%	53.61	54.73	55.88	57.06	58.25	59.48	60.73	62.00	63.30	64.63	65.99
2.20%	52.06	53.20	54.37	55.57	56.79	58.04	59.32	60.62	61.96	63.32	64.71
2.30%	50.55	51.71	52.90	54.12	55.36	56.64	57.94	59.27	60.64	62.03	63.46
2.40%	49.09	50.27	51.48	52.71	53.98	55.27	56.60	57.96	59.35	60.77	62.23
2.50%	47.67	48.87	50.09	51.34	52.62	53.94	55.29	56.67	58.09	59.54	61.03
2.60%	46.30	47.50	48.74	50.01	51.31	52.64	54.01	55.41	56.85	58.33	59.85
2.70%	44.97	46.18	47.43	48.71	50.02	51.37	52.76	54.19	55.65	57.15	58.69
2.80%	43.67	44.90	46.15	47.44	48.77	50.14	51.54	52.99	54.47	55.99	57.56
2.90%	42.42	43.65	44.91	46.22	47.56	48.93	50.35	51.81	53.32	54.86	56.45
3.00%	41.20	42.43	43.71	45.02	46.37	47.76	49.19	50.67	52.19	53.75	55.37
3.10%	40.02	41.26	42.54	43.85	45.21	46.62	48.06	49.55	51.09	52.67	54.30
3.20%	38.87	40.11	41.40	42.72	44.09	45.50	46.96	48.46	50.01	51.61	53.26
3.30%	37.76	39.00	40.29	41.62	42.99	44.41	45.88	47.39	48.95	50.57	52.24
3.40%	36.68	37.92	39.21	40.55	41.92	43.35	44.82	46.35	47.92	49.55	51.24
3.50%	35.63	36.87	38.17	39.50	40.88	42.31	43.80	45.33	46.92	48.56	50.26
3.60%	34.61	35.86	37.15	38.48	39.87	41.31	42.79	44.33	45.93	47.58	49.30
3.70%	33.62	34.87	36.16	37.50	38.88	40.32	41.81	43.36	44.96	46.63	48.35
3.80%	32.66	33.91	35.19	36.53	37.92	39.36	40.86	42.41	44.02	45.69	47.43
3.90%	31.73	32.97	34.26	35.59	36.98	38.42	39.92	41.48	43.10	44.78	46.53
4.00%	30.83	32.07	33.35	34.68	36.07	37.51	39.01	40.57	42.20	43.88	45.64
4.10%	29.96	31.18	32.46	33.79	35.18	36.62	38.12	39.69	41.31	43.01	44.77
4.20%	29.11	30.33	31.60	32.93	34.31	35.75	37.25	38.82	40.45	42.15	43.92
4.30%	28.28	29.50	30.76	32.09	33.47	34.91	36.41	37.97	39.60	41.31	43.08
4.40%	27.48	28.69	29.95	31.27	32.64	34.08	35.58	37.14	38.78	40.48	42.27
4.50%	26.70	27.90	29.16	30.47	31.84	33.27	34.77	36.34	37.97	39.68	41.46
4.60%	25.94	27.14	28.39	29.69	31.06	32.49	33.98	35.54	37.18	38.89	40.68
4.70%	25.21	26.40	27.64	28.94	30.30	31.72	33.21	34.77	36.41	38.12	39.91
4.80%	24.50	25.68	26.91	28.20	29.55	30.97	32.46	34.02	35.65	37.36	39.15
4.90%	23.81	24.98	26.20	27.48	28.83	30.24	31.72	33.28	34.91	36.62	38.41
5.00%	23.14	24.29	25.51	26.78	28.12	29.53	31.01	32.56	34.18	35.89	37.69
5.10%	22.49	23.63	24.84	26.11	27.44	28.84	30.31	31.85	33.48	35.18	36.98
5.20%	21.85	22.99	24.19	25.44	26.77	28.16	29.62	31.16	32.78	34.49	36.28
5.30%	21.24	22.37	23.55	24.80	26.11	27.50	28.95	30.49	32.11	33.81	35.60
5.40%	20.64	21.76	22.93	24.17	25.48	26.85	28.30	29.83	31.44	33.14	34.93
5.50%	20.06	21.17	22.33	23.56	24.86	26.22	27.67	29.19	30.79	32.49	34.27
5.60%	19.50	20.59	21.75	22.97	24.25	25.61	27.04	28.56	30.16	31.85	33.63
5.70%	18.96	20.04	21.18	22.39	23.66	25.01	26.44	27.94	29.54	31.22	33.00
5.80%	18.43	19.49	20.63	21.82	23.09	24.43	25.84	27.34	28.93	30.61	32.38
5.90%	17.91	18.97	20.09	21.27	22.53	23.86	25.26	26.75	28.33	30.00	31.77
6.00%	17.41	18.46	19.56	20.74	21.98	23.30	24.70	26.18	27.75	29.42	31.18

Table B.4 Continued

Interest rate	Years to maturity										
	20	**19**	**18**	**17**	**16**	**15**	**14**	**13**	**12**	**11**	**10**
2.00%	67.30	68.64	70.02	71.42	72.84	74.30	75.79	77.30	78.85	80.43	82.03
2.10%	65.99	67.38	68.79	70.24	71.71	73.22	74.75	76.32	77.93	79.56	81.23
2.20%	64.71	66.14	67.59	69.08	70.60	72.15	73.74	75.36	77.02	78.71	80.44
2.30%	63.46	64.92	66.41	67.94	69.50	71.10	72.73	74.41	76.12	77.87	79.66
2.40%	62.23	63.72	65.25	66.82	68.42	70.06	71.75	73.47	75.23	77.04	78.89
2.50%	61.03	62.55	64.12	65.72	67.36	69.05	70.77	72.54	74.36	76.21	78.12
2.60%	59.85	61.40	63.00	64.64	66.32	68.04	69.81	71.63	73.49	75.40	77.36
2.70%	58.69	60.28	61.91	63.58	65.29	67.06	68.87	70.73	72.64	74.60	76.61
2.80%	57.56	59.17	60.83	62.53	64.29	66.09	67.94	69.84	71.79	73.80	75.87
2.90%	56.45	58.09	59.78	61.51	63.29	65.13	67.02	68.96	70.96	73.02	75.14
3.00%	55.37	57.03	58.74	60.50	62.32	64.19	66.11	68.10	70.14	72.24	74.41
3.10%	54.30	55.99	57.72	59.51	61.36	63.26	65.22	67.24	69.33	71.48	73.69
3.20%	53.26	54.96	56.72	58.54	60.41	62.35	64.34	66.40	68.52	70.72	72.98
3.30%	52.24	53.96	55.74	57.58	59.48	61.45	63.47	65.57	67.73	69.97	72.28
3.40%	51.24	52.98	54.78	56.64	58.57	60.56	62.62	64.75	66.95	69.23	71.58
3.50%	50.26	52.02	53.84	55.72	57.67	59.69	61.78	63.94	66.18	68.49	70.89
3.60%	49.30	51.07	52.91	54.81	56.79	58.83	60.95	63.14	65.42	67.77	70.21
3.70%	48.35	50.14	52.00	53.92	55.92	57.99	60.13	62.36	64.66	67.06	69.54
3.80%	47.43	49.23	51.10	53.05	55.06	57.15	59.32	61.58	63.92	66.35	68.87
3.90%	46.53	48.34	50.23	52.18	54.22	56.33	58.53	60.81	63.18	65.65	68.21
4.00%	45.64	47.46	49.36	51.34	53.39	55.53	57.75	60.06	62.46	64.96	67.56
4.10%	44.77	46.61	48.52	50.51	52.58	54.73	56.98	59.31	61.74	64.27	66.91
4.20%	43.92	45.76	47.68	49.69	51.77	53.95	56.21	58.58	61.04	63.60	66.27
4.30%	43.08	44.94	46.87	48.88	50.99	53.18	55.47	57.85	60.34	62.93	65.64
4.40%	42.27	44.13	46.07	48.09	50.21	52.42	54.73	57.13	59.65	62.27	65.01
4.50%	41.46	43.33	45.28	47.32	49.45	51.67	54.00	56.43	58.97	61.62	64.39
4.60%	40.68	42.55	44.51	46.55	48.70	50.94	53.28	55.73	58.29	60.97	63.78
4.70%	39.91	41.78	43.75	45.80	47.96	50.21	52.57	55.04	57.63	60.34	63.17
4.80%	39.15	41.03	43.00	45.07	47.23	49.50	51.87	54.36	56.97	59.71	62.57
4.90%	38.41	40.30	42.27	44.34	46.51	48.79	51.19	53.69	56.32	59.08	61.98
5.00%	37.69	39.57	41.55	43.63	45.81	48.10	50.51	53.03	55.68	58.47	61.39
5.10%	36.98	38.86	40.85	42.93	45.12	47.42	49.84	52.38	55.05	57.86	60.81
5.20%	36.28	38.17	40.15	42.24	44.44	46.75	49.18	51.74	54.43	57.26	60.23
5.30%	35.60	37.49	39.47	41.56	43.77	46.09	48.53	51.10	53.81	56.66	59.66
5.40%	34.93	36.82	38.80	40.90	43.11	45.44	47.89	50.47	53.20	56.07	59.10
5.50%	34.27	36.16	38.15	40.24	42.46	44.79	47.26	49.86	52.60	55.49	58.54
5.60%	33.63	35.51	37.50	39.60	41.82	44.16	46.63	49.25	52.00	54.92	57.99
5.70%	33.00	34.88	36.87	38.97	41.19	43.54	46.02	48.64	51.42	54.35	57.44
5.80%	32.38	34.26	36.25	38.35	40.57	42.93	45.42	48.05	50.84	53.78	56.90
5.90%	31.77	33.65	35.63	37.74	39.96	42.32	44.82	47.46	50.26	53.23	56.37
6.00%	31.18	33.05	35.03	37.14	39.36	41.73	44.23	46.88	49.70	52.68	55.84

(continued)

Table B.4 Continued

Interest rate	Years to maturity										
	10	9	8	7	6	5	4	3	2	1	0
2.00%	82.03	83.68	85.35	87.06	88.80	90.57	92.38	94.23	96.12	98.04	100.00
2.10%	81.23	82.94	84.68	86.46	88.28	90.13	92.02	93.96	95.93	97.94	100.00
2.20%	80.44	82.21	84.02	85.87	87.76	89.69	91.66	93.68	95.74	97.85	100.00
2.30%	79.66	81.49	83.37	85.28	87.25	89.25	91.31	93.41	95.55	97.75	100.00
2.40%	78.89	80.78	82.72	84.70	86.74	88.82	90.95	93.13	95.37	97.66	100.00
2.50%	78.12	80.07	82.07	84.13	86.23	88.39	90.60	92.86	95.18	97.56	100.00
2.60%	77.36	79.37	81.44	83.55	85.73	87.96	90.24	92.59	95.00	97.47	100.00
2.70%	76.61	78.68	80.80	82.99	85.23	87.53	89.89	92.32	94.81	97.37	100.00
2.80%	75.87	77.99	80.18	82.42	84.73	87.10	89.54	92.05	94.63	97.28	100.00
2.90%	75.14	77.31	79.56	81.86	84.24	86.68	89.19	91.78	94.44	97.18	100.00
3.00%	74.41	76.64	78.94	81.31	83.75	86.26	88.85	91.51	94.26	97.09	100.00
3.10%	73.69	75.98	78.33	80.76	83.26	85.84	88.50	91.25	94.08	96.99	100.00
3.20%	72.98	75.32	77.73	80.21	82.78	85.43	88.16	90.98	93.89	96.90	100.00
3.30%	72.28	74.66	77.13	79.67	82.30	85.02	87.82	90.72	93.71	96.81	100.00
3.40%	71.58	74.01	76.53	79.13	81.82	84.61	87.48	90.46	93.53	96.71	100.00
3.50%	70.89	73.37	75.94	78.60	81.35	84.20	87.14	90.19	93.35	96.62	100.00
3.60%	70.21	72.74	75.36	78.07	80.88	83.79	86.81	89.93	93.17	96.53	100.00
3.70%	69.54	72.11	74.78	77.54	80.41	83.39	86.47	89.67	92.99	96.43	100.00
3.80%	68.87	71.49	74.20	77.02	79.95	82.99	86.14	89.41	92.81	96.34	100.00
3.90%	68.21	70.87	73.63	76.51	79.49	82.59	85.81	89.16	92.63	96.25	100.00
4.00%	67.56	70.26	73.07	75.99	79.03	82.19	85.48	88.90	92.46	96.15	100.00
4.10%	66.91	69.65	72.51	75.48	78.58	81.80	85.15	88.64	92.28	96.06	100.00
4.20%	66.27	69.05	71.95	74.98	78.13	81.41	84.83	88.39	92.10	95.97	100.00
4.30%	65.64	68.46	71.40	74.47	77.68	81.02	84.50	88.13	91.92	95.88	100.00
4.40%	65.01	67.87	70.86	73.98	77.23	80.63	84.18	87.88	91.75	95.79	100.00
4.50%	64.39	67.29	70.32	73.48	76.79	80.25	83.86	87.63	91.57	95.69	100.00
4.60%	63.78	66.71	69.78	72.99	76.35	79.86	83.54	87.38	91.40	95.60	100.00
4.70%	63.17	66.14	69.25	72.51	75.91	79.48	83.22	87.13	91.22	95.51	100.00
4.80%	62.57	65.58	68.72	72.02	75.48	79.10	82.90	86.88	91.05	95.42	100.00
4.90%	61.98	65.02	68.20	71.54	75.05	78.73	82.58	86.63	90.88	95.33	100.00
5.00%	61.39	64.46	67.68	71.07	74.62	78.35	82.27	86.38	90.70	95.24	100.00
5.10%	60.81	63.91	67.17	70.60	74.20	77.98	81.96	86.14	90.53	95.15	100.00
5.20%	60.23	63.37	66.66	70.13	73.77	77.61	81.65	85.89	90.36	95.06	100.00
5.30%	59.66	62.83	66.16	69.66	73.36	77.24	81.34	85.65	90.19	94.97	100.00
5.40%	59.10	62.29	65.66	69.20	72.94	76.88	81.03	85.40	90.02	94.88	100.00
5.50%	58.54	61.76	65.16	68.74	72.52	76.51	80.72	85.16	89.85	94.79	100.00
5.60%	57.99	61.24	64.67	68.29	72.11	76.15	80.42	84.92	89.68	94.70	100.00
5.70%	57.44	60.72	64.18	67.84	71.71	75.79	80.11	84.68	89.51	94.61	100.00
5.80%	56.90	60.20	63.70	67.39	71.30	75.43	79.81	84.44	89.34	94.52	100.00
5.90%	56.37	59.69	63.22	66.95	70.90	75.08	79.51	84.20	89.17	94.43	100.00
6.00%	55.84	59.19	62.74	66.51	70.50	74.73	79.21	83.96	89.00	94.34	100.00

Table B.5 Zero Prices and Yields between 6 and 10 Percent at 0.1 Percent Intervals

Interest rate	Years to maturity										
	30	**29**	**28**	**27**	**26**	**25**	**24**	**23**	**22**	**21**	**20**
6.00%	17.41	18.46	19.56	20.74	21.98	23.30	24.70	26.18	27.75	29.42	31.18
6.10%	16.93	17.96	19.05	20.22	21.45	22.76	24.15	25.62	27.18	28.84	30.60
6.20%	16.45	17.47	18.56	19.71	20.93	22.23	23.61	25.07	26.62	28.27	30.03
6.30%	16.00	17.00	18.07	19.21	20.42	21.71	23.08	24.53	26.08	27.72	29.47
6.40%	15.55	16.55	17.60	18.73	19.93	21.21	22.56	24.01	25.54	27.18	28.92
6.50%	15.12	16.10	17.15	18.26	19.45	20.71	22.06	23.49	25.02	26.65	28.38
6.60%	14.70	15.67	16.70	17.81	18.98	20.23	21.57	22.99	24.51	26.13	27.85
6.70%	14.29	15.25	16.27	17.36	18.52	19.76	21.09	22.50	24.01	25.62	27.33
6.80%	13.90	14.84	15.85	16.93	18.08	19.31	20.62	22.02	23.52	25.12	26.83
6.90%	13.51	14.44	15.44	16.50	17.64	18.86	20.16	21.55	23.04	24.63	26.33
7.00%	13.14	14.06	15.04	16.09	17.22	18.42	19.71	21.09	22.57	24.15	25.84
7.10%	12.77	13.68	14.65	15.69	16.81	18.00	19.28	20.65	22.11	23.68	25.36
7.20%	12.42	13.32	14.27	15.30	16.40	17.58	18.85	20.21	21.66	23.22	24.89
7.30%	12.08	12.96	13.91	14.92	16.01	17.18	18.43	19.78	21.22	22.77	24.43
7.40%	11.75	12.61	13.55	14.55	15.63	16.78	18.03	19.36	20.79	22.33	23.98
7.50%	11.42	12.28	13.20	14.19	15.25	16.40	17.63	18.95	20.37	21.90	23.54
7.60%	11.11	11.95	12.86	13.84	14.89	16.02	17.24	18.55	19.96	21.48	23.11
7.70%	10.80	11.63	12.53	13.50	14.53	15.65	16.86	18.16	19.55	21.06	22.68
7.80%	10.51	11.33	12.21	13.16	14.19	15.29	16.49	17.77	19.16	20.65	22.27
7.90%	10.22	11.02	11.90	12.84	13.85	14.94	16.12	17.40	18.77	20.26	21.86
8.00%	9.94	10.73	11.59	12.52	13.52	14.60	15.77	17.03	18.39	19.87	21.45
8.10%	9.67	10.45	11.29	12.21	13.20	14.27	15.42	16.67	18.02	19.48	21.06
8.20%	9.40	10.17	11.01	11.91	12.89	13.94	15.09	16.32	17.66	19.11	20.68
8.30%	9.14	9.90	10.73	11.62	12.58	13.62	14.75	15.98	17.31	18.74	20.30
8.40%	8.89	9.64	10.45	11.33	12.28	13.31	14.43	15.64	16.96	18.38	19.93
8.50%	8.65	9.39	10.19	11.05	11.99	13.01	14.12	15.31	16.62	18.03	19.56
8.60%	8.42	9.14	9.93	10.78	11.71	12.71	13.81	14.99	16.28	17.68	19.20
8.70%	8.19	8.90	9.67	10.51	11.43	12.42	13.50	14.68	15.96	17.35	18.85
8.80%	7.96	8.66	9.43	10.26	11.16	12.14	13.21	14.37	15.64	17.01	18.51
8.90%	7.75	8.44	9.19	10.01	10.90	11.87	12.92	14.07	15.32	16.69	18.17
9.00%	7.54	8.22	8.95	9.76	10.64	11.60	12.64	13.78	15.02	16.37	17.84
9.10%	7.33	8.00	8.73	9.52	10.39	11.33	12.37	13.49	14.72	16.06	17.52
9.20%	7.13	7.79	8.51	9.29	10.14	11.08	12.10	13.21	14.42	15.75	17.20
9.30%	6.94	7.59	8.29	9.06	9.91	10.83	11.83	12.93	14.14	15.45	16.89
9.40%	6.75	7.39	8.08	8.84	9.67	10.58	11.58	12.66	13.86	15.16	16.58
9.50%	6.57	7.19	7.88	8.63	9.45	10.34	11.33	12.40	13.58	14.87	16.28
9.60%	6.39	7.01	7.68	8.42	9.22	10.11	11.08	12.14	13.31	14.59	15.99
9.70%	6.22	6.82	7.49	8.21	9.01	9.88	10.84	11.89	13.05	14.31	15.70
9.80%	6.05	6.65	7.30	8.01	8.80	9.66	10.61	11.65	12.79	14.04	15.42
9.90%	5.89	6.47	7.11	7.82	8.59	9.44	10.38	11.40	12.53	13.77	15.14
10.00%	5.73	6.30	6.93	7.63	8.39	9.23	10.15	11.17	12.28	13.51	14.86

(continued)

Table B.5 Continued

Interest rate	Years to maturity										
	20	**19**	**18**	**17**	**16**	**15**	**14**	**13**	**12**	**11**	**10**
6.00%	31.18	33.05	35.03	37.14	39.36	41.73	44.23	46.88	49.70	52.68	55.84
6.10%	30.60	32.46	34.44	36.55	38.78	41.14	43.65	46.31	49.14	52.14	55.32
6.20%	30.03	31.89	33.87	35.97	38.20	40.56	43.08	45.75	48.59	51.60	54.80
6.30%	29.47	31.32	33.30	35.39	37.62	39.99	42.51	45.19	48.04	51.07	54.28
6.40%	28.92	30.77	32.74	34.83	37.06	39.43	41.96	44.64	47.50	50.54	53.78
6.50%	28.38	30.22	32.19	34.28	36.51	38.88	41.41	44.10	46.97	50.02	53.27
6.60%	27.85	29.69	31.65	33.74	35.97	38.34	40.87	43.57	46.44	49.51	52.77
6.70%	27.33	29.17	31.12	33.21	35.43	37.80	40.34	43.04	45.92	49.00	52.28
6.80%	26.83	28.65	30.60	32.68	34.90	37.28	39.81	42.52	45.41	48.50	51.79
6.90%	26.33	28.15	30.09	32.16	34.38	36.76	39.29	42.00	44.90	48.00	51.31
7.00%	25.84	27.65	29.59	31.66	33.87	36.24	38.78	41.50	44.40	47.51	50.83
7.10%	25.36	27.16	29.09	31.16	33.37	35.74	38.28	41.00	43.91	47.02	50.36
7.20%	24.89	26.69	28.61	30.67	32.88	35.24	37.78	40.50	43.42	46.54	49.89
7.30%	24.43	26.22	28.13	30.19	32.39	34.75	37.29	40.01	42.93	46.07	49.43
7.40%	23.98	25.76	27.66	29.71	31.91	34.27	36.81	39.53	42.46	45.60	48.97
7.50%	23.54	25.31	27.20	29.25	31.44	33.80	36.33	39.06	41.99	45.13	48.52
7.60%	23.11	24.86	26.75	28.79	30.97	33.33	35.86	38.59	41.52	44.68	48.07
7.70%	22.68	24.43	26.31	28.34	30.52	32.87	35.40	38.12	41.06	44.22	47.63
7.80%	22.27	24.00	25.87	27.89	30.07	32.41	34.94	37.67	40.60	43.77	47.19
7.90%	21.86	23.58	25.45	27.46	29.62	31.97	34.49	37.22	40.16	43.33	46.75
8.00%	21.45	23.17	25.02	27.03	29.19	31.52	34.05	36.77	39.71	42.89	46.32
8.10%	21.06	22.77	24.61	26.60	28.76	31.09	33.61	36.33	39.27	42.45	45.89
8.20%	20.68	22.37	24.21	26.19	28.34	30.66	33.18	35.90	38.84	42.02	45.47
8.30%	20.30	21.98	23.81	25.78	27.92	30.24	32.75	35.47	38.41	41.60	45.05
8.40%	19.93	21.60	23.41	25.38	27.51	29.82	32.33	35.04	37.99	41.18	44.64
8.50%	19.56	21.22	23.03	24.99	27.11	29.41	31.91	34.63	37.57	40.76	44.23
8.60%	19.20	20.86	22.65	24.60	26.71	29.01	31.51	34.21	37.16	40.35	43.82
8.70%	18.85	20.49	22.28	24.22	26.32	28.61	31.10	33.81	36.75	39.95	43.42
8.80%	18.51	20.14	21.91	23.84	25.94	28.22	30.70	33.41	36.35	39.54	43.02
8.90%	18.17	19.79	21.55	23.47	25.56	27.83	30.31	33.01	35.95	39.15	42.63
9.00%	17.84	19.45	21.20	23.11	25.19	27.45	29.92	32.62	35.55	38.75	42.24
9.10%	17.52	19.11	20.85	22.75	24.82	27.08	29.54	32.23	35.16	38.36	41.86
9.20%	17.20	18.78	20.51	22.40	24.46	26.71	29.17	31.85	34.78	37.98	41.47
9.30%	16.89	18.46	20.18	22.05	24.10	26.34	28.80	31.47	34.40	37.60	41.10
9.40%	16.58	18.14	19.85	21.71	23.75	25.99	28.43	31.10	34.02	37.22	40.72
9.50%	16.28	17.83	19.52	21.38	23.41	25.63	28.07	30.73	33.65	36.85	40.35
9.60%	15.99	17.52	19.20	21.05	23.07	25.28	27.71	30.37	33.29	36.48	39.98
9.70%	15.70	17.22	18.89	20.72	22.73	24.94	27.36	30.01	32.92	36.12	39.62
9.80%	15.42	16.93	18.58	20.41	22.41	24.60	27.01	29.66	32.57	35.76	39.26
9.90%	15.14	16.64	18.28	20.09	22.08	24.27	26.67	29.31	32.21	35.40	38.91
10.00%	14.86	16.35	17.99	19.78	21.76	23.94	26.33	28.97	31.86	35.05	38.55

Table B.5 Continued

Interest rate	Years to maturity										
	10	**9**	**8**	**7**	**6**	**5**	**4**	**3**	**2**	**1**	**0**
6.00%	55.84	59.19	62.74	66.51	70.50	74.73	79.21	83.96	89.00	94.34	100.00
6.10%	55.32	58.69	62.27	66.07	70.10	74.37	78.91	83.72	88.83	94.25	100.00
6.20%	54.80	58.19	61.80	65.63	69.70	74.02	78.61	83.49	88.66	94.16	100.00
6.30%	54.28	57.70	61.34	65.20	69.31	73.68	78.32	83.25	88.50	94.07	100.00
6.40%	53.78	57.22	60.88	64.78	68.92	73.33	78.02	83.02	88.33	93.98	100.00
6.50%	53.27	56.74	60.42	64.35	68.53	72.99	77.73	82.78	88.17	93.90	100.00
6.60%	52.77	56.26	59.97	63.93	68.15	72.65	77.44	82.55	88.00	93.81	100.00
6.70%	52.28	55.79	59.52	63.51	67.77	72.31	77.15	82.32	87.84	93.72	100.00
6.80%	51.79	55.32	59.08	63.10	67.39	71.97	76.86	82.09	87.67	93.63	100.00
6.90%	51.31	54.85	58.64	62.68	67.01	71.63	76.58	81.86	87.51	93.55	100.00
7.00%	50.83	54.39	58.20	62.27	66.63	71.30	76.29	81.63	87.34	93.46	100.00
7.10%	50.36	53.94	57.77	61.87	66.26	70.97	76.00	81.40	87.18	93.37	100.00
7.20%	49.89	53.49	57.34	61.47	65.89	70.64	75.72	81.17	87.02	93.28	100.00
7.30%	49.43	53.04	56.91	61.07	65.52	70.31	75.44	80.95	86.86	93.20	100.00
7.40%	48.97	52.60	56.49	60.67	65.16	69.98	75.16	80.72	86.69	93.11	100.00
7.50%	48.52	52.16	56.07	60.28	64.80	69.66	74.88	80.50	86.53	93.02	100.00
7.60%	48.07	51.72	55.65	59.88	64.44	69.33	74.60	80.27	86.37	92.94	100.00
7.70%	47.63	51.29	55.24	59.50	64.08	69.01	74.33	80.05	86.21	92.85	100.00
7.80%	47.19	50.87	54.83	59.11	63.72	68.69	74.05	79.83	86.05	92.76	100.00
7.90%	46.75	50.44	54.43	58.73	63.37	68.37	73.78	79.60	85.89	92.68	100.00
8.00%	46.32	50.02	54.03	58.35	63.02	68.06	73.50	79.38	85.73	92.59	100.00
8.10%	45.89	49.61	53.63	57.97	62.67	67.74	73.23	79.16	85.58	92.51	100.00
8.20%	45.47	49.20	53.23	57.60	62.32	67.43	72.96	78.94	85.42	92.42	100.00
8.30%	45.05	48.79	52.84	57.23	61.98	67.12	72.69	78.73	85.26	92.34	100.00
8.40%	44.64	48.39	52.45	56.86	61.63	66.81	72.42	78.51	85.10	92.25	100.00
8.50%	44.23	47.99	52.07	56.49	61.29	66.50	72.16	78.29	84.95	92.17	100.00
8.60%	43.82	47.59	51.68	56.13	60.96	66.20	71.89	78.07	84.79	92.08	100.00
8.70%	43.42	47.20	51.31	55.77	60.62	65.89	71.63	77.86	84.63	92.00	100.00
8.80%	43.02	46.81	50.93	55.41	60.29	65.59	71.36	77.64	84.48	91.91	100.00
8.90%	42.63	46.42	50.56	55.06	59.96	65.29	71.10	77.43	84.32	91.83	100.00
9.00%	42.24	46.04	50.19	54.70	59.63	64.99	70.84	77.22	84.17	91.74	100.00
9.10%	41.86	45.66	49.82	54.35	59.30	64.70	70.58	77.01	84.01	91.66	100.00
9.20%	41.47	45.29	49.46	54.01	58.97	64.40	70.32	76.79	83.86	91.58	100.00
9.30%	41.10	44.92	49.10	53.66	58.65	64.11	70.07	76.58	83.71	91.49	100.00
9.40%	40.72	44.55	48.74	53.32	58.33	63.81	69.81	76.37	83.55	91.41	100.00
9.50%	40.35	44.18	48.38	52.98	58.01	63.52	69.56	76.17	83.40	91.32	100.00
9.60%	39.98	43.82	48.03	52.64	57.69	63.23	69.30	75.96	83.25	91.24	100.00
9.70%	39.62	43.47	47.68	52.31	57.38	62.95	69.05	75.75	83.10	91.16	100.00
9.80%	39.26	43.11	47.33	51.97	57.07	62.66	68.80	75.54	82.95	91.07	100.00
9.90%	38.91	42.76	46.99	51.64	56.76	62.38	68.55	75.34	82.80	90.99	100.00
10.00%	38.55	42.41	46.65	51.32	56.45	62.09	68.30	75.13	82.64	90.91	100.00

Table B.6 Zero Prices and Yields between 10 and 14 Percent at 0.1 Percent Intervals

Interest rate	Years to maturity 30	29	28	27	26	25	24	23	22	21	20
10.00%	5.73	6.30	6.93	7.63	8.39	9.23	10.15	11.17	12.28	13.51	14.86
10.10%	5.58	6.14	6.76	7.44	8.19	9.02	9.93	10.94	12.04	13.26	14.60
10.20%	5.43	5.98	6.59	7.26	8.00	8.82	9.72	10.71	11.80	13.01	14.33
10.30%	5.28	5.83	6.43	7.09	7.82	8.62	9.51	10.49	11.57	12.76	14.08
10.40%	5.14	5.67	6.26	6.92	7.63	8.43	9.31	10.27	11.34	12.52	13.82
10.50%	5.00	5.53	6.11	6.75	7.46	8.24	9.11	10.06	11.12	12.29	13.58
10.60%	4.87	5.38	5.95	6.59	7.28	8.06	8.91	9.85	10.90	12.05	13.33
10.70%	4.74	5.24	5.81	6.43	7.11	7.88	8.72	9.65	10.68	11.83	13.09
10.80%	4.61	5.11	5.66	6.27	6.95	7.70	8.53	9.45	10.47	11.61	12.86
10.90%	4.49	4.98	5.52	6.12	6.79	7.53	8.35	9.26	10.27	11.39	12.63
11.00%	4.37	4.85	5.38	5.97	6.63	7.36	8.17	9.07	10.07	11.17	12.40
11.10%	4.25	4.72	5.25	5.83	6.48	7.20	8.00	8.88	9.87	10.96	12.18
11.20%	4.14	4.60	5.12	5.69	6.33	7.04	7.83	8.70	9.68	10.76	11.96
11.30%	4.03	4.48	4.99	5.55	6.18	6.88	7.66	8.52	9.49	10.56	11.75
11.40%	3.92	4.37	4.87	5.42	6.04	6.73	7.49	8.35	9.30	10.36	11.54
11.50%	3.82	4.26	4.75	5.29	5.90	6.58	7.34	8.18	9.12	10.17	11.34
11.60%	3.72	4.15	4.63	5.16	5.76	6.43	7.18	8.01	8.94	9.98	11.14
11.70%	3.62	4.04	4.51	5.04	5.63	6.29	7.03	7.85	8.77	9.79	10.94
11.80%	3.52	3.94	4.40	4.92	5.50	6.15	6.88	7.69	8.60	9.61	10.74
11.90%	3.43	3.84	4.29	4.80	5.38	6.02	6.73	7.53	8.43	9.43	10.55
12.00%	3.34	3.74	4.19	4.69	5.25	5.88	6.59	7.38	8.26	9.26	10.37
12.10%	3.25	3.64	4.08	4.58	5.13	5.75	6.45	7.23	8.10	9.08	10.18
12.20%	3.16	3.55	3.98	4.47	5.01	5.63	6.31	7.08	7.95	8.92	10.00
12.30%	3.08	3.46	3.88	4.36	4.90	5.50	6.18	6.94	7.79	8.75	9.83
12.40%	3.00	3.37	3.79	4.26	4.79	5.38	6.05	6.80	7.64	8.59	9.65
12.50%	2.92	3.29	3.70	4.16	4.68	5.26	5.92	6.66	7.49	8.43	9.48
12.60%	2.84	3.20	3.61	4.06	4.57	5.15	5.80	6.53	7.35	8.27	9.32
12.70%	2.77	3.12	3.52	3.96	4.47	5.03	5.67	6.39	7.21	8.12	9.15
12.80%	2.70	3.04	3.43	3.87	4.36	4.92	5.55	6.26	7.07	7.97	8.99
12.90%	2.63	2.96	3.35	3.78	4.27	4.82	5.44	6.14	6.93	7.82	8.83
13.00%	2.56	2.89	3.26	3.69	4.17	4.71	5.32	6.01	6.80	7.68	8.68
13.10%	2.49	2.82	3.18	3.60	4.07	4.61	5.21	5.89	6.67	7.54	8.53
13.20%	2.42	2.74	3.11	3.52	3.98	4.51	5.10	5.77	6.54	7.40	8.38
13.30%	2.36	2.68	3.03	3.43	3.89	4.41	4.99	5.66	6.41	7.26	8.23
13.40%	2.30	2.61	2.96	3.35	3.80	4.31	4.89	5.54	6.29	7.13	8.09
13.50%	2.24	2.54	2.88	3.27	3.72	4.22	4.79	5.43	6.17	7.00	7.94
13.60%	2.18	2.48	2.81	3.20	3.63	4.13	4.69	5.32	6.05	6.87	7.81
13.70%	2.12	2.42	2.75	3.12	3.55	4.04	4.59	5.22	5.93	6.75	7.67
13.80%	2.07	2.35	2.68	3.05	3.47	3.95	4.49	5.11	5.82	6.62	7.54
13.90%	2.02	2.30	2.61	2.98	3.39	3.86	4.40	5.01	5.71	6.50	7.41
14.00%	1.96	2.24	2.55	2.91	3.31	3.78	4.31	4.91	5.60	6.38	7.28

Table B.6 Continued

Interest rate	Years to maturity										
	20	19	18	17	16	15	14	13	12	11	10
10.00%	14.86	16.35	17.99	19.78	21.76	23.94	26.33	28.97	31.86	35.05	38.55
10.10%	14.60	16.07	17.69	19.48	21.45	23.62	26.00	28.63	31.52	34.70	38.21
10.20%	14.33	15.80	17.41	19.18	21.14	23.30	25.67	28.29	31.18	34.36	37.86
10.30%	14.08	15.53	17.13	18.89	20.83	22.98	25.35	27.96	30.84	34.01	37.52
10.40%	13.82	15.26	16.85	18.60	20.54	22.67	25.03	27.63	30.51	33.68	37.18
10.50%	13.58	15.00	16.58	18.32	20.24	22.36	24.71	27.31	30.18	33.34	36.84
10.60%	13.33	14.75	16.31	18.04	19.95	22.06	24.40	26.99	29.85	33.01	36.51
10.70%	13.09	14.49	16.05	17.76	19.66	21.77	24.10	26.67	29.53	32.69	36.18
10.80%	12.86	14.25	15.79	17.49	19.38	21.47	23.79	26.36	29.21	32.36	35.86
10.90%	12.63	14.01	15.53	17.23	19.10	21.18	23.49	26.05	28.89	32.04	35.54
11.00%	12.40	13.77	15.28	16.96	18.83	20.90	23.20	25.75	28.58	31.73	35.22
11.10%	12.18	13.53	15.04	16.71	18.56	20.62	22.91	25.45	28.28	31.42	34.90
11.20%	11.96	13.30	14.79	16.45	18.29	20.34	22.62	25.16	27.97	31.11	34.59
11.30%	11.75	13.08	14.56	16.20	18.03	20.07	22.34	24.86	27.67	30.80	34.28
11.40%	11.54	12.86	14.32	15.96	17.78	19.80	22.06	24.57	27.38	30.50	33.97
11.50%	11.34	12.64	14.09	15.72	17.52	19.54	21.78	24.29	27.08	30.20	33.67
11.60%	11.14	12.43	13.87	15.48	17.27	19.28	21.51	24.01	26.79	29.90	33.37
11.70%	10.94	12.22	13.65	15.24	17.03	19.02	21.24	23.73	26.51	29.61	33.07
11.80%	10.74	12.01	13.43	15.01	16.79	18.77	20.98	23.46	26.22	29.32	32.78
11.90%	10.55	11.81	13.21	14.79	16.55	18.52	20.72	23.19	25.94	29.03	32.49
12.00%	10.37	11.61	13.00	14.56	16.31	18.27	20.46	22.92	25.67	28.75	32.20
12.10%	10.18	11.42	12.80	14.35	16.08	18.03	20.21	22.65	25.39	28.47	31.91
12.20%	10.00	11.22	12.59	14.13	15.85	17.79	19.96	22.39	25.12	28.19	31.63
12.30%	9.83	11.04	12.39	13.92	15.63	17.55	19.71	22.13	24.86	27.91	31.35
12.40%	9.65	10.85	12.20	13.71	15.41	17.32	19.47	21.88	24.59	27.64	31.07
12.50%	9.48	10.67	12.00	13.50	15.19	17.09	19.22	21.63	24.33	27.37	30.79
12.60%	9.32	10.49	11.81	13.30	14.98	16.86	18.99	21.38	24.07	27.11	30.52
12.70%	9.15	10.31	11.62	13.10	14.76	16.64	18.75	21.13	23.82	26.84	30.25
12.80%	8.99	10.14	11.44	12.90	14.56	16.42	18.52	20.89	23.57	26.58	29.99
12.90%	8.83	9.97	11.26	12.71	14.35	16.20	18.29	20.65	23.32	26.32	29.72
13.00%	8.68	9.81	11.08	12.52	14.15	15.99	18.07	20.42	23.07	26.07	29.46
13.10%	8.53	9.64	10.91	12.33	13.95	15.78	17.85	20.18	22.83	25.82	29.20
13.20%	8.38	9.48	10.73	12.15	13.75	15.57	17.63	19.95	22.59	25.57	28.94
13.30%	8.23	9.32	10.56	11.97	13.56	15.37	17.41	19.72	22.35	25.32	28.69
13.40%	8.09	9.17	10.40	11.79	13.37	15.16	17.20	19.50	22.11	25.08	28.44
13.50%	7.94	9.02	10.23	11.62	13.18	14.96	16.98	19.28	21.88	24.83	28.19
13.60%	7.81	8.87	10.07	11.44	13.00	14.77	16.78	19.06	21.65	24.59	27.94
13.70%	7.67	8.72	9.92	11.27	12.82	14.57	16.57	18.84	21.42	24.36	27.69
13.80%	7.54	8.58	9.76	11.11	12.64	14.38	16.37	18.63	21.20	24.12	27.45
13.90%	7.41	8.43	9.61	10.94	12.46	14.20	16.17	18.42	20.98	23.89	27.21
14.00%	7.28	8.29	9.46	10.78	12.29	14.01	15.97	18.21	20.76	23.66	26.97

(continued)

Table B.6 Continued

Interest rate	Years to maturity										
	10	9	8	7	6	5	4	3	2	1	0
10.00%	38.55	42.41	46.65	51.32	56.45	62.09	68.30	75.13	82.64	90.91	100.00
10.10%	38.21	42.06	46.31	50.99	56.14	61.81	68.05	74.93	82.49	90.83	100.00
10.20%	37.86	41.72	45.98	50.67	55.84	61.53	67.81	74.72	82.34	90.74	100.00
10.30%	37.52	41.38	45.65	50.35	55.53	61.25	67.56	74.52	82.20	90.66	100.00
10.40%	37.18	41.05	45.32	50.03	55.23	60.98	67.32	74.32	82.05	90.58	100.00
10.50%	36.84	40.71	44.99	49.71	54.93	60.70	67.07	74.12	81.90	90.50	100.00
10.60%	36.51	40.38	44.66	49.40	54.63	60.43	66.83	73.92	81.75	90.42	100.00
10.70%	36.18	40.06	44.34	49.09	54.34	60.15	66.59	73.72	81.60	90.33	100.00
10.80%	35.86	39.73	44.02	48.78	54.05	59.88	66.35	73.52	81.46	90.25	100.00
10.90%	35.54	39.41	43.71	48.47	53.75	59.61	66.11	73.32	81.31	90.17	100.00
11.00%	35.22	39.09	43.39	48.17	53.46	59.35	65.87	73.12	81.16	90.09	100.00
11.10%	34.90	38.78	43.08	47.86	53.18	59.08	65.64	72.92	81.02	90.01	100.00
11.20%	34.59	38.46	42.77	47.56	52.89	58.81	65.40	72.73	80.87	89.93	100.00
11.30%	34.28	38.15	42.47	47.26	52.61	58.55	65.17	72.53	80.73	89.85	100.00
11.40%	33.97	37.85	42.16	46.97	52.32	58.29	64.93	72.33	80.58	89.77	100.00
11.50%	33.67	37.54	41.86	46.67	52.04	58.03	64.70	72.14	80.44	89.69	100.00
11.60%	33.37	37.24	41.56	46.38	51.76	57.77	64.47	71.95	80.29	89.61	100.00
11.70%	33.07	36.94	41.26	46.09	51.49	57.51	64.24	71.75	80.15	89.53	100.00
11.80%	32.78	36.65	40.97	45.80	51.21	57.25	64.01	71.56	80.00	89.45	100.00
11.90%	32.49	36.35	40.68	45.52	50.94	57.00	63.78	71.37	79.86	89.37	100.00
12.00%	32.20	36.06	40.39	45.23	50.66	56.74	63.55	71.18	79.72	89.29	100.00
12.10%	31.91	35.77	40.10	44.95	50.39	56.49	63.33	70.99	79.58	89.21	100.00
12.20%	31.63	35.49	39.82	44.67	50.12	56.24	63.10	70.80	79.44	89.13	100.00
12.30%	31.35	35.20	39.53	44.40	49.86	55.99	62.88	70.61	79.29	89.05	100.00
12.40%	31.07	34.92	39.25	44.12	49.59	55.74	62.65	70.42	79.15	88.97	100.00
12.50%	30.79	34.64	38.97	43.85	49.33	55.49	62.43	70.23	79.01	88.89	100.00
12.60%	30.52	34.37	38.70	43.57	49.06	55.25	62.21	70.05	78.87	88.81	100.00
12.70%	30.25	34.09	38.42	43.30	48.80	55.00	61.99	69.86	78.73	88.73	100.00
12.80%	29.99	33.82	38.15	43.04	48.55	54.76	61.77	69.67	78.59	88.65	100.00
12.90%	29.72	33.55	37.88	42.77	48.29	54.52	61.55	69.49	78.45	88.57	100.00
13.00%	29.46	33.29	37.62	42.51	48.03	54.28	61.33	69.31	78.31	88.50	100.00
13.10%	29.20	33.02	37.35	42.24	47.78	54.04	61.12	69.12	78.18	88.42	100.00
13.20%	28.94	32.76	37.09	41.98	47.52	53.80	60.90	68.94	78.04	88.34	100.00
13.30%	28.69	32.50	36.83	41.72	47.27	53.56	60.68	68.76	77.90	88.26	100.00
13.40%	28.44	32.25	36.57	41.47	47.02	53.33	60.47	68.57	77.76	88.18	100.00
13.50%	28.19	31.99	36.31	41.21	46.78	53.09	60.26	68.39	77.63	88.11	100.00
13.60%	27.94	31.74	36.06	40.96	46.53	52.86	60.05	68.21	77.49	88.03	100.00
13.70%	27.69	31.49	35.80	40.71	46.28	52.63	59.84	68.03	77.35	87.95	100.00
13.80%	27.45	31.24	35.55	40.46	46.04	52.39	59.63	67.85	77.22	87.87	100.00
13.90%	27.21	30.99	35.30	40.21	45.80	52.17	59.42	67.68	77.08	87.80	100.00
14.00%	26.97	30.75	35.06	39.96	45.56	51.94	59.21	67.50	76.95	87.72	100.00

Table B.7 Zero Prices and Yields between 14 and 18 Percent at 0.1 Percent Intervals

Interest rate	Years to maturity										
	30	**29**	**28**	**27**	**26**	**25**	**24**	**23**	**22**	**21**	**20**
14.00%	1.96	2.24	2.55	2.91	3.31	3.78	4.31	4.91	5.60	6.38	7.28
14.10%	1.91	2.18	2.49	2.84	3.24	3.70	4.22	4.81	5.49	6.27	7.15
14.20%	1.86	2.13	2.43	2.77	3.17	3.62	4.13	4.72	5.39	6.15	7.03
14.30%	1.81	2.07	2.37	2.71	3.10	3.54	4.04	4.62	5.28	6.04	6.90
14.40%	1.77	2.02	2.31	2.65	3.03	3.46	3.96	4.53	5.18	5.93	6.78
14.50%	1.72	1.97	2.26	2.58	2.96	3.39	3.88	4.44	5.08	5.82	6.67
14.60%	1.68	1.92	2.20	2.52	2.89	3.31	3.80	4.35	4.99	5.72	6.55
14.70%	1.63	1.87	2.15	2.46	2.83	3.24	3.72	4.27	4.89	5.61	6.44
14.80%	1.59	1.83	2.10	2.41	2.76	3.17	3.64	4.18	4.80	5.51	6.33
14.90%	1.55	1.78	2.05	2.35	2.70	3.10	3.57	4.10	4.71	5.41	6.22
15.00%	1.51	1.74	2.00	2.30	2.64	3.04	3.49	4.02	4.62	5.31	6.11
15.10%	1.47	1.69	1.95	2.24	2.58	2.97	3.42	3.94	4.53	5.22	6.00
15.20%	1.43	1.65	1.90	2.19	2.52	2.91	3.35	3.86	4.45	5.12	5.90
15.30%	1.40	1.61	1.86	2.14	2.47	2.85	3.28	3.78	4.36	5.03	5.80
15.40%	1.36	1.57	1.81	2.09	2.41	2.79	3.21	3.71	4.28	4.94	5.70
15.50%	1.33	1.53	1.77	2.04	2.36	2.73	3.15	3.64	4.20	4.85	5.60
15.60%	1.29	1.49	1.73	2.00	2.31	2.67	3.08	3.56	4.12	4.76	5.51
15.70%	1.26	1.46	1.69	1.95	2.26	2.61	3.02	3.49	4.04	4.68	5.41
15.80%	1.23	1.42	1.64	1.90	2.21	2.55	2.96	3.43	3.97	4.59	5.32
15.90%	1.20	1.39	1.61	1.86	2.16	2.50	2.90	3.36	3.89	4.51	5.23
16.00%	1.16	1.35	1.57	1.82	2.11	2.45	2.84	3.29	3.82	4.43	5.14
16.10%	1.14	1.32	1.53	1.78	2.06	2.39	2.78	3.23	3.75	4.35	5.05
16.20%	1.11	1.29	1.49	1.74	2.02	2.34	2.72	3.16	3.68	4.27	4.96
16.30%	1.08	1.25	1.46	1.70	1.97	2.29	2.67	3.10	3.61	4.20	4.88
16.40%	1.05	1.22	1.42	1.66	1.93	2.24	2.61	3.04	3.54	4.12	4.80
16.50%	1.02	1.19	1.39	1.62	1.89	2.20	2.56	2.98	3.47	4.05	4.71
16.60%	1.00	1.16	1.36	1.58	1.84	2.15	2.51	2.92	3.41	3.97	4.63
16.70%	0.97	1.13	1.32	1.55	1.80	2.10	2.46	2.87	3.35	3.90	4.56
16.80%	0.95	1.11	1.29	1.51	1.76	2.06	2.41	2.81	3.28	3.83	4.48
16.90%	0.92	1.08	1.26	1.48	1.73	2.02	2.36	2.76	3.22	3.77	4.40
17.00%	0.90	1.05	1.23	1.44	1.69	1.97	2.31	2.70	3.16	3.70	4.33
17.10%	0.88	1.03	1.20	1.41	1.65	1.93	2.26	2.65	3.10	3.63	4.25
17.20%	0.86	1.00	1.17	1.38	1.61	1.89	2.22	2.60	3.05	3.57	4.18
17.30%	0.83	0.98	1.15	1.35	1.58	1.85	2.17	2.55	2.99	3.51	4.11
17.40%	0.81	0.95	1.12	1.32	1.54	1.81	2.13	2.50	2.93	3.44	4.04
17.50%	0.79	0.93	1.09	1.29	1.51	1.77	2.08	2.45	2.88	3.38	3.97
17.60%	0.77	0.91	1.07	1.26	1.48	1.74	2.04	2.40	2.83	3.32	3.91
17.70%	0.75	0.89	1.04	1.23	1.44	1.70	2.00	2.36	2.77	3.26	3.84
17.80%	0.73	0.86	1.02	1.20	1.41	1.66	1.96	2.31	2.72	3.21	3.78
17.90%	0.72	0.84	0.99	1.17	1.38	1.63	1.92	2.27	2.67	3.15	3.71
18.00%	0.70	0.82	0.97	1.15	1.35	1.60	1.88	2.22	2.62	3.09	3.65

(continued)

Table B.7 Continued

Interest rate	Years to maturity										
	20	**19**	**18**	**17**	**16**	**15**	**14**	**13**	**12**	**11**	**10**
14.00%	7.28	8.29	9.46	10.78	12.29	14.01	15.97	18.21	20.76	23.66	26.97
14.10%	7.15	8.16	9.31	10.62	12.12	13.83	15.78	18.00	20.54	23.43	26.74
14.20%	7.03	8.02	9.16	10.46	11.95	13.65	15.58	17.80	20.32	23.21	26.51
14.30%	6.90	7.89	9.02	10.31	11.78	13.47	15.39	17.60	20.11	22.99	26.27
14.40%	6.78	7.76	8.88	10.16	11.62	13.29	15.21	17.40	19.90	22.77	26.05
14.50%	6.67	7.63	8.74	10.01	11.46	13.12	15.02	17.20	19.69	22.55	25.82
14.60%	6.55	7.51	8.60	9.86	11.30	12.95	14.84	17.01	19.49	22.33	25.59
14.70%	6.44	7.38	8.47	9.71	11.14	12.78	14.66	16.81	19.29	22.12	25.37
14.80%	6.33	7.26	8.34	9.57	10.99	12.61	14.48	16.62	19.09	21.91	25.15
14.90%	6.22	7.14	8.21	9.43	10.84	12.45	14.31	16.44	18.89	21.70	24.93
15.00%	6.11	7.03	8.08	9.29	10.69	12.29	14.13	16.25	18.69	21.49	24.72
15.10%	6.00	6.91	7.96	9.16	10.54	12.13	13.96	16.07	18.50	21.29	24.50
15.20%	5.90	6.80	7.83	9.02	10.39	11.97	13.79	15.89	18.31	21.09	24.29
15.30%	5.80	6.69	7.71	8.89	10.25	11.82	13.63	15.71	18.12	20.89	24.08
15.40%	5.70	6.58	7.59	8.76	10.11	11.67	13.46	15.54	17.93	20.69	23.87
15.50%	5.60	6.47	7.47	8.63	9.97	11.52	13.30	15.36	17.74	20.49	23.67
15.60%	5.51	6.37	7.36	8.51	9.83	11.37	13.14	15.19	17.56	20.30	23.47
15.70%	5.41	6.26	7.24	8.38	9.70	11.22	12.98	15.02	17.38	20.11	23.26
15.80%	5.32	6.16	7.13	8.26	9.56	11.08	12.83	14.85	17.20	19.92	23.06
15.90%	5.23	6.06	7.02	8.14	9.43	10.93	12.67	14.69	17.02	19.73	22.86
16.00%	5.14	5.96	6.91	8.02	9.30	10.79	12.52	14.52	16.85	19.54	22.67
16.10%	5.05	5.86	6.81	7.90	9.18	10.65	12.37	14.36	16.67	19.36	22.47
16.20%	4.96	5.77	6.70	7.79	9.05	10.52	12.22	14.20	16.50	19.17	22.28
16.30%	4.88	5.68	6.60	7.68	8.93	10.38	12.07	14.04	16.33	18.99	22.09
16.40%	4.80	5.58	6.50	7.56	8.81	10.25	11.93	13.89	16.16	18.82	21.90
16.50%	4.71	5.49	6.40	7.46	8.69	10.12	11.79	13.73	16.00	18.64	21.71
16.60%	4.63	5.40	6.30	7.35	8.57	9.99	11.65	13.58	15.83	18.46	21.53
16.70%	4.56	5.32	6.20	7.24	8.45	9.86	11.51	13.43	15.67	18.29	21.34
16.80%	4.48	5.23	6.11	7.14	8.34	9.74	11.37	13.28	15.51	18.12	21.16
16.90%	4.40	5.15	6.02	7.03	8.22	9.61	11.24	13.13	15.35	17.95	20.98
17.00%	4.33	5.06	5.92	6.93	8.11	9.49	11.10	12.99	15.20	17.78	20.80
17.10%	4.25	4.98	5.83	6.83	8.00	9.37	10.97	12.85	15.04	17.61	20.63
17.20%	4.18	4.90	5.75	6.73	7.89	9.25	10.84	12.70	14.89	17.45	20.45
17.30%	4.11	4.82	5.66	6.64	7.78	9.13	10.71	12.56	14.74	17.29	20.28
17.40%	4.04	4.75	5.57	6.54	7.68	9.02	10.58	12.43	14.59	17.13	20.11
17.50%	3.97	4.67	5.49	6.45	7.58	8.90	10.46	12.29	14.44	16.97	19.94
17.60%	3.91	4.59	5.40	6.35	7.47	8.79	10.33	12.15	14.29	16.81	19.77
17.70%	3.84	4.52	5.32	6.26	7.37	8.68	10.21	12.02	14.15	16.65	19.60
17.80%	3.78	4.45	5.24	6.17	7.27	8.57	10.09	11.89	14.00	16.50	19.43
17.90%	3.71	4.38	5.16	6.09	7.17	8.46	9.97	11.76	13.86	16.34	19.27
18.00%	3.65	4.31	5.08	6.00	7.08	8.35	9.85	11.63	13.72	16.19	19.11

Table B.7 Continued

Interest rate	Years to maturity										
	10	**9**	**8**	**7**	**6**	**5**	**4**	**3**	**2**	**1**	**0**
14.00%	26.97	30.75	35.06	39.96	45.56	51.94	59.21	67.50	76.95	87.72	100.00
14.10%	26.74	30.51	34.81	39.72	45.32	51.71	59.00	67.32	76.81	87.64	100.00
14.20%	26.51	30.27	34.57	39.48	45.08	51.48	58.79	67.14	76.68	87.57	100.00
14.30%	26.27	30.03	34.33	39.24	44.85	51.26	58.59	66.97	76.54	87.49	100.00
14.40%	26.05	29.80	34.09	39.00	44.61	51.04	58.38	66.79	76.41	87.41	100.00
14.50%	25.82	29.56	33.85	38.76	44.38	50.81	58.18	66.62	76.28	87.34	100.00
14.60%	25.59	29.33	33.61	38.52	44.15	50.59	57.98	66.44	76.14	87.26	100.00
14.70%	25.37	29.10	33.38	38.29	43.92	50.37	57.78	66.27	76.01	87.18	100.00
14.80%	25.15	28.88	33.15	38.05	43.69	50.15	57.57	66.10	75.88	87.11	100.00
14.90%	24.93	28.65	32.92	37.82	43.46	49.93	57.37	65.92	75.75	87.03	100.00
15.00%	24.72	28.43	32.69	37.59	43.23	49.72	57.18	65.75	75.61	86.96	100.00
15.10%	24.50	28.20	32.46	37.37	43.01	49.50	56.98	65.58	75.48	86.88	100.00
15.20%	24.29	27.99	32.24	37.14	42.78	49.29	56.78	65.41	75.35	86.81	100.00
15.30%	24.08	27.77	32.02	36.91	42.56	49.07	56.58	65.24	75.22	86.73	100.00
15.40%	23.87	27.55	31.79	36.69	42.34	48.86	56.39	65.07	75.09	86.66	100.00
15.50%	23.67	27.34	31.58	36.47	42.12	48.65	56.19	64.90	74.96	86.58	100.00
15.60%	23.47	27.13	31.36	36.25	41.90	48.44	56.00	64.73	74.83	86.51	100.00
15.70%	23.26	26.92	31.14	36.03	41.69	48.23	55.80	64.57	74.70	86.43	100.00
15.80%	23.06	26.71	30.93	35.81	41.47	48.02	55.61	64.40	74.57	86.36	100.00
15.90%	22.86	26.50	30.71	35.60	41.26	47.82	55.42	64.23	74.44	86.28	100.00
16.00%	22.67	26.30	30.50	35.38	41.04	47.61	55.23	64.07	74.32	86.21	100.00
16.10%	22.47	26.09	30.29	35.17	40.83	47.41	55.04	63.90	74.19	86.13	100.00
16.20%	22.28	25.89	30.09	34.96	40.62	47.20	54.85	63.74	74.06	86.06	100.00
16.30%	22.09	25.69	29.88	34.75	40.41	47.00	54.66	63.57	73.93	85.98	100.00
16.40%	21.90	25.49	29.67	34.54	40.21	46.80	54.47	63.41	73.81	85.91	100.00
16.50%	21.71	25.30	29.47	34.33	40.00	46.60	54.29	63.24	73.68	85.84	100.00
16.60%	21.53	25.10	29.27	34.13	39.79	46.40	54.10	63.08	73.55	85.76	100.00
16.70%	21.34	24.91	29.07	33.92	39.59	46.20	53.92	62.92	73.43	85.69	100.00
16.80%	21.16	24.72	28.87	33.72	39.39	46.00	53.73	62.76	73.30	85.62	100.00
16.90%	20.98	24.53	28.67	33.52	39.18	45.81	53.55	62.60	73.18	85.54	100.00
17.00%	20.80	24.34	28.48	33.32	38.98	45.61	53.37	62.44	73.05	85.47	100.00
17.10%	20.63	24.15	28.28	33.12	38.78	45.42	53.18	62.28	72.93	85.40	100.00
17.20%	20.45	23.97	28.09	32.92	38.59	45.22	53.00	62.12	72.80	85.32	100.00
17.30%	20.28	23.79	27.90	32.73	38.39	45.03	52.82	61.96	72.68	85.25	100.00
17.40%	20.11	23.60	27.71	32.53	38.19	44.84	52.64	61.80	72.55	85.18	100.00
17.50%	19.94	23.42	27.52	32.34	38.00	44.65	52.46	61.64	72.43	85.11	100.00
17.60%	19.77	23.25	27.34	32.15	37.81	44.46	52.28	61.49	72.31	85.03	100.00
17.70%	19.60	23.07	27.15	31.96	37.61	44.27	52.11	61.33	72.19	84.96	100.00
17.80%	19.43	22.89	26.97	31.77	37.42	44.08	51.93	61.17	72.06	84.89	100.00
17.90%	19.27	22.72	26.78	31.58	37.23	43.90	51.75	61.02	71.94	84.82	100.00
18.00%	19.11	22.55	26.60	31.39	37.04	43.71	51.58	60.86	71.82	84.75	100.00

Table B.8 Zero Prices and Yields between 18 and 22 Percent at 0.1 Percent Intervals

Interest rate	Years to maturity										
	30	**29**	**28**	**27**	**26**	**25**	**24**	**23**	**22**	**21**	**20**
18.00%	0.70	0.82	0.97	1.15	1.35	1.60	1.88	2.22	2.62	3.09	3.65
18.10%	0.68	0.80	0.95	1.12	1.32	1.56	1.85	2.18	2.57	3.04	3.59
18.20%	0.66	0.78	0.93	1.09	1.29	1.53	1.81	2.14	2.53	2.99	3.53
18.30%	0.65	0.76	0.90	1.07	1.27	1.50	1.77	2.10	2.48	2.93	3.47
18.40%	0.63	0.75	0.88	1.05	1.24	1.47	1.74	2.06	2.43	2.88	3.41
18.50%	0.61	0.73	0.86	1.02	1.21	1.44	1.70	2.02	2.39	2.83	3.35
18.60%	0.60	0.71	0.84	1.00	1.19	1.41	1.67	1.98	2.34	2.78	3.30
18.70%	0.58	0.69	0.82	0.98	1.16	1.38	1.63	1.94	2.30	2.73	3.24
18.80%	0.57	0.68	0.80	0.95	1.13	1.35	1.60	1.90	2.26	2.68	3.19
18.90%	0.56	0.66	0.79	0.93	1.11	1.32	1.57	1.87	2.22	2.64	3.14
19.00%	0.54	0.64	0.77	0.91	1.09	1.29	1.54	1.83	2.18	2.59	3.08
19.10%	0.53	0.63	0.75	0.89	1.06	1.27	1.51	1.79	2.14	2.55	3.03
19.20%	0.51	0.61	0.73	0.87	1.04	1.24	1.48	1.76	2.10	2.50	2.98
19.30%	0.50	0.60	0.71	0.85	1.02	1.21	1.45	1.73	2.06	2.46	2.93
19.40%	0.49	0.58	0.70	0.83	1.00	1.19	1.42	1.69	2.02	2.41	2.88
19.50%	0.48	0.57	0.68	0.81	0.97	1.16	1.39	1.66	1.99	2.37	2.84
19.60%	0.47	0.56	0.67	0.80	0.95	1.14	1.36	1.63	1.95	2.33	2.79
19.70%	0.45	0.54	0.65	0.78	0.93	1.12	1.34	1.60	1.91	2.29	2.74
19.80%	0.44	0.53	0.64	0.76	0.91	1.09	1.31	1.57	1.88	2.25	2.70
19.90%	0.43	0.52	0.62	0.74	0.89	1.07	1.28	1.54	1.84	2.21	2.65
20.00%	0.42	0.51	0.61	0.73	0.87	1.05	1.26	1.51	1.81	2.17	2.61
20.10%	0.41	0.49	0.59	.0.71	0.85	1.03	1.23	1.48	1.78	2.14	2.57
20.20%	0.40	0.48	0.58	0.70	0.84	1.01	1.21	1.45	1.75	2.10	2.52
20.30%	0.39	0.47	0.57	0.68	0.82	0.98	1.18	1.43	1.71	2.06	2.48
20.40%	0.38	0.46	0.55	0.67	0.80	0.96	1.16	1.40	1.68	2.03	2.44
20.50%	0.37	0.45	0.54	0.65	0.78	0.94	1.14	1.37	1.65	1.99	2.40
20.60%	0.36	0.44	0.53	0.64	0.77	0.93	1.12	1.35	1.62	1.96	2.36
20.70%	0.35	0.43	0.52	0.62	0.75	0.91	1.09	1.32	1.59	1.92	2.32
20.80%	0.35	0.42	0.50	0.61	0.73	0.89	1.07	1.30	1.57	1.89	2.28
20.90%	0.34	0.41	0.49	0.59	0.72	0.87	1.05	1.27	1.54	1.86	2.25
21.00%	0.33	0.40	0.48	0.58	0.70	0.85	1.03	1.25	1.51	1.83	2.21
21.10%	0.32	0.39	0.47	0.57	0.69	0.83	1.01	1.22	1.48	1.79	2.17
21.20%	0.31	0.38	0.46	0.56	0.67	0.82	0.99	1.20	1.46	1.76	2.14
21.30%	0.30	0.37	0.45	0.54	0.66	0.80	0.97	1.18	1.43	1.73	2.10
21.40%	0.30	0.36	0.44	0.53	0.65	0.78	0.95	1.16	1.40	1.70	2.07
21.50%	0.29	0.35	0.43	0.52	0.63	0.77	0.93	1.13	1.38	1.67	2.03
21.60%	0.28	0.34	0.42	0.51	0.62	0.75	0.92	1.11	1.35	1.65	2.00
21.70%	0.28	0.34	0.41	0.50	0.61	0.74	0.90	1.09	1.33	1.62	1.97
21.80%	0.27	0.33	0.40	0.49	0.59	0.72	0.88	1.07	1.31	1.59	1.94
21.90%	0.26	0.32	0.39	0.48	0.58	0.71	0.86	1.05	1.28	1.56	1.91
22.00%	0.26	0.31	0.38	0.47	0.57	0.69	0.85	1.03	1.26	1.54	1.87

Table B.8 Continued

Interest rate	Years to maturity										
	20	19	18	17	16	15	14	13	12	11	10
18.00%	3.65	4.31	5.08	6.00	7.08	8.35	9.85	11.63	13.72	16.19	19.11
18.10%	3.59	4.24	5.01	5.91	6.98	8.25	9.74	11.50	13.58	16.04	18.95
18.20%	3.53	4.17	4.93	5.83	6.89	8.14	9.62	11.38	13.45	15.89	18.79
18.30%	3.47	4.10	4.86	5.74	6.80	8.04	9.51	11.25	13.31	15.75	18.63
18.40%	3.41	4.04	4.78	5.66	6.70	7.94	9.40	11.13	13.18	15.60	18.47
18.50%	3.35	3.98	4.71	5.58	6.61	7.84	9.29	11.01	13.04	15.46	18.32
18.60%	3.30	3.91	4.64	5.50	6.53	7.74	9.18	10.89	12.91	15.31	18.16
18.70%	3.24	3.85	4.57	5.42	6.44	7.64	9.07	10.77	12.78	15.17	18.01
18.80%	3.19	3.79	4.50	5.35	6.35	7.55	8.97	10.65	12.65	15.03	17.86
18.90%	3.14	3.73	4.43	5.27	6.27	7.45	8.86	10.54	12.53	14.89	17.71
19.00%	3.08	3.67	4.37	5.20	6.18	7.36	8.76	10.42	12.40	14.76	17.56
19.10%	3.03	3.61	4.30	5.12	6.10	7.27	8.65	10.31	12.28	14.62	17.41
19.20%	2.98	3.55	4.24	5.05	6.02	7.18	8.55	10.20	12.15	14.49	17.27
19.30%	2.93	3.50	4.17	4.98	5.94	7.09	8.45	10.08	12.03	14.35	17.12
19.40%	2.88	3.44	4.11	4.91	5.86	7.00	8.35	9.98	11.91	14.22	16.98
19.50%	2.84	3.39	4.05	4.84	5.78	6.91	8.26	9.87	11.79	14.09	16.84
19.60%	2.79	3.34	3.99	4.77	5.71	6.82	8.16	9.76	11.67	13.96	16.70
19.70%	2.74	3.28	3.93	4.70	5.63	6.74	8.07	9.66	11.56	13.83	16.56
19.80%	2.70	3.23	3.87	4.64	5.56	6.65	7.97	9.55	11.44	13.71	16.42
19.90%	2.65	3.18	3.81	4.57	5.48	6.57	7.88	9.45	11.33	13.58	16.29
20.00%	2.61	3.13	3.76	4.51	5.41	6.49	7.79	9.35	11.22	13.46	16.15
20.10%	2.57	3.08	3.70	4.44	5.34	6.41	7.70	9.25	11.10	13.34	16.02
20.20%	2.52	3.03	3.65	4.38	5.27	6.33	7.61	9.15	10.99	13.21	15.88
20.30%	2.48	2.99	3.59	4.32	5.20	6.25	7.52	9.05	10.88	13.09	15.75
20.40%	2.44	2.94	3.54	4.26	5.13	6.17	7.43	8.95	10.78	12.98	15.62
20.50%	2.40	2.89	3.49	4.20	5.06	6.10	7.35	8.85	10.67	12.86	15.49
20.60%	2.36	2.85	3.43	4.14	4.99	6.02	7.26	8.76	10.56	12.74	15.36
20.70%	2.32	2.80	3.38	4.08	4.93	5.95	7.18	8.67	10.46	12.62	15.24
20.80%	2.28	2.76	3.33	4.03	4.86	5.87	7.10	8.57	10.36	12.51	15.11
20.90%	2.25	2.72	3.28	3.97	4.80	5.80	7.02	8.48	10.25	12.40	14.99
21.00%	2.21	2.67	3.23	3.91	4.74	5.73	6.93	8.39	10.15	12.28	14.86
21.10%	2.17	2.63	3.19	3.86	4.67	5.66	6.85	8.30	10.05	12.17	14.74
21.20%	2.14	2.59	3.14	3.81	4.61	5.59	6.78	8.21	9.95	12.06	14.62
21.30%	2.10	2.55	3.09	3.75	4.55	5.52	6.70	8.12	9.86	11.95	14.50
21.40%	2.07	2.51	3.05	3.70	4.49	5.45	6.62	8.04	9.76	11.85	14.38
21.50%	2.03	2.47	3.00	3.65	4.43	5.39	6.55	7.95	9.66	11.74	14.26
21.60%	2.00	2.43	2.96	3.60	4.38	5.32	6.47	7.87	9.57	11.63	14.15
21.70%	1.97	2.40	2.92	3.55	4.32	5.26	6.40	7.78	9.47	11.53	14.03
21.80%	1.94	2.36	2.87	3.50	4.26	5.19	6.32	7.70	9.38	11.43	13.92
21.90%	1.91	2.32	2.83	3.45	4.21	5.13	6.25	7.62	9.29	11.32	13.80
22.00%	1.87	2.29	2.79	3.40	4.15	5.07	6.18	7.54	9.20	11.22	13.69

(continued)

Table B.8 Continued

Interest rate	Years to maturity										
	10	9	8	7	6	5	4	3	2	1	0
18.00%	19.11	22.55	26.60	31.39	37.04	43.71	51.58	60.86	71.82	84.75	100.00
18.10%	18.95	22.37	26.42	31.21	36.86	43.53	51.40	60.71	71.70	84.67	100.00
18.20%	18.79	22.20	26.25	31.02	36.67	43.34	51.23	60.55	71.58	84.60	100.00
18.30%	18.63	22.04	26.07	30.84	36.48	43.16	51.06	60.40	71.45	84.53	100.00
18.40%	18.47	21.87	25.89	30.66	36.30	42.98	50.89	60.25	71.33	84.46	100.00
18.50%	18.32	21.70	25.72	30.48	36.12	42.80	50.71	60.10	71.21	84.39	100.00
18.60%	18.16	21.54	25.55	30.30	35.93	42.62	50.54	59.94	71.09	84.32	100.00
18.70%	18.01	21.38	25.37	30.12	35.75	42.44	50.37	59.79	70.97	84.25	100.00
18.80%	17.86	21.22	25.20	29.94	35.57	42.26	50.20	59.64	70.85	84.18	100.00
18.90%	17.71	21.06	25.03	29.77	35.39	42.08	50.03	59.49	70.74	84.10	100.00
19.00%	17.56	20.90	24.87	29.59	35.21	41.90	49.87	59.34	70.62	84.03	100.00
19.10%	17.41	20.74	24.70	29.42	35.04	41.73	49.70	59.19	70.50	83.96	100.00
19.20%	17.27	20.58	24.54	29.25	34.86	41.55	49.53	59.04	70.38	83.89	100.00
19.30%	17.12	20.43	24.37	29.07	34.69	41.38	49.37	58.90	70.26	83.82	100.00
19.40%	16.98	20.28	24.21	28.90	34.51	41.21	49.20	58.75	70.14	83.75	100.00
19.50%	16.84	20.12	24.05	28.74	34.34	41.04	49.04	58.60	70.03	83.68	100.00
19.60%	16.70	19.97	23.89	28.57	34.17	40.86	48.87	58.45	69.91	83.61	100.00
19.70%	16.56	19.82	23.73	28.40	34.00	40.69	48.71	58.31	69.79	83.54	100.00
19.80%	16.42	19.67	23.57	28.24	33.83	40.52	48.55	58.16	69.68	83.47	100.00
19.90%	16.29	19.53	23.41	28.07	33.66	40.36	48.39	58.02	69.56	83.40	100.00
20.00%	16.15	19.38	23.26	27.91	33.49	40.19	48.23	57.87	69.44	83.33	100.00
20.10%	16.02	19.24	23.10	27.75	33.32	40.02	48.06	57.73	69.33	83.26	100.00
20.20%	15.88	19.09	22.95	27.58	33.16	39.85	47.91	57.58	69.21	83.19	100.00
20.30%	15.75	18.95	22.80	27.42	32.99	39.69	47.75	57.44	69.10	83.13	100.00
20.40%	15.62	18.81	22.65	27.27	32.83	39.52	47.59	57.30	68.98	83.06	100.00
20.50%	15.49	18.67	22.50	27.11	32.66	39.36	47.43	57.15	68.87	82.99	100.00
20.60%	15.36	18.53	22.35	26.95	32.50	39.20	47.27	57.01	68.76	82.92	100.00
20.70%	15.24	18.39	22.20	26.79	32.34	39.04	47.12	56.87	68.64	82.85	100.00
20.80%	15.11	18.26	22.05	26.64	32.18	38.87	46.96	56.73	68.53	82.78	100.00
20.90%	14.99	18.12	21.91	26.49	32.02	38.71	46.81	56.59	68.41	82.71	100.00
21.00%	14.86	17.99	21.76	26.33	31.86	38.55	46.65	56.45	68.30	82.64	100.00
21.10%	14.74	17.85	21.62	26.18	31.71	38.40	46.50	56.31	68.19	82.58	100.00
21.20%	14.62	17.72	21.48	26.03	31.55	38.24	46.34	56.17	68.08	82.51	100.00
21.30%	14.50	17.59	21.34	25.88	31.39	38.08	46.19	56.03	67.96	82.44	100.00
21.40%	14.38	17.46	21.20	25.73	31.24	37.92	46.04	55.89	67.85	82.37	100.00
21.50%	14.26	17.33	21.06	25.58	31.08	37.77	45.89	55.75	67.74	82.30	100.00
21.60%	14.15	17.20	20.92	25.44	30.93	37.61	45.74	55.62	67.63	82.24	100.00
21.70%	14.03	17.08	20.78	25.29	30.78	37.46	45.59	55.48	67.52	82.17	100.00
21.80%	13.92	16.95	20.65	25.15	30.63	37.30	45.44	55.34	67.41	82.10	100.00
21.90%	13.80	16.83	20.51	25.00	30.48	37.15	45.29	55.21	67.30	82.03	100.00
22.00%	13.69	16.70	20.38	24.86	30.33	37.00	45.14	55.07	67.19	81.97	100.00

Index

Customize Your Investment Strategy
and Save $25 with the

PLAN Z SIMULATOR SOFTWARE

If you wish to explore the infinite variety of scenarios and tactics discussed in this book, a software package designed specifically for Plan Z, is scheduled for release on **July 1, 1993**. PLAN Z SIMULATOR will run on IBM-PCs and compatibles under Microsoft Windows 3.0+ and will enable you to reproduce all the interest rate scenarios and simulations in the book, as well as any others you may wish to create, test, or compare. In addition, the program incorporates many of the ideas, suggestions, tips and techniques that are only mentioned or hinted at in the book. This software will help you customize your personal Plan Z parameters and optimize your investment strategy.

For detailed information about the
PLAN Z SIMULATOR SOFTWARE,
call 1-800-446-6779
(in New York State call 212-785-3900)

SAVE $25 ON THE PLAN Z SIMULATOR . . .
SEE THE SPECIAL DISCOUNT OFFER ON THE
REVERSE SIDE OF THIS PAGE

SAVE $25
ON PLAN Z SIMULATOR SOFTWARE!

Call 1-800-446-6779
(in New York State, call 212-785-3900)
to receive information and an order form for
the PLAN Z SIMULATOR.

Then enclose the coupon below (copies or facsimilies will not be accepted) with your order form to get a $25 discount off the regular price of $79!

Name ______________________________

Address ______________________________

____

____

I want to save $25 on the PLAN Z SIMULATOR (the regular price is $79). I have enclosed my order form with this original coupon.

Signature ______________________________

Allow 4–6 weeks for delivery. Price may be subject to change without notice.